No Make-U₁

NO MAKE-UP

·

Straight Tales from

a Queer Life

·

Jeremy Norman

Elliott & Thompson
London

CONTENTS

CONTENTS

For Derek

I did not set out to write an autobiography. The idea for this work developed from a series of memoirs of friends departed that I wrote largely for my own amusement and to share with those close to me. Once it became apparent that these pieces were of sufficient broader interest that they might be considered for publication, I realised that they needed to be cemented round the story of my life in order to give them context and meaning.

The stories, while principally about other people, subtly reveal much about me. As the stories are complete in themselves, it has inevitably entailed some repetition of incidents in my life that are germane to more than one tale. They also, of necessity, go back in time to sometimes pre-date their place in the broader tale. There does not seem to be an easy answer to these necessary repetitions that make the tales entire, but I have striven to keep them to the minimum.

This book is a series of jottings and reflections on people that I have known and events and businesses with which I have been associated. I have included gay social history from the 1960s, 1970s and 1980s – the period when I was learning to lead a gay life in London. Much has changed since those now far-off days. I have also touched on themes and questions where I feel that my experience has something to teach others, such as in the area of drugs and the law.

My business life has encompassed publishing *Burke's Peerage*, the studbook of the titled and landed classes, and creating Heaven, the world's most famous gay nightclub. My property businesses have centred round three large commercial buildings in London that my partners and I own freehold. The Furniture Cave in the King's Road, Chelsea, contains 45,000 square feet of space tenanted principally by antique dealers but also includes three nightclubs, Embargo (which I started but no longer own), Crazy Larry's and Rumi Bar together with some office spaces. My company owns a warehouse development in Macklin Street, Covent Garden, comprising the first branch of Soho Gyms; the offices of the model agency, Models 1, and J. Lindeberg, a Swedish fashion house. In addition, we developed 8 modernist apartments on three additional floors, now all sold. We built a mixed-use development in Clapham High Street housing another Soho Gym and a Revolution vodka bar. While not perhaps the most exciting side of my business career, these commercial property holdings have been the financial engine that has driven my more exotic business ventures. I have also been a Name at Lloyds and a vendor of fresh pasta.

On the personal side, I have enjoyed a lifetime (27 years to date) of requited love with my partner, Derek Frost, but I have also held the hands of close friends dying on the battlefield of AIDS. If suffering ennobles then I feel that I have earned my ducal strawberry leaves. I also felt I have something to say and some inaccuracies to correct concerning the development of AIDS awareness and the birth of the charitable response to the disease. It is important to remind those growing up gay today of the struggles we faced and the disbelief and horror that were the twin reactions to the mounting death toll in the USA.

Few are ready or willing to learn from the experiences of others, especially those older than themselves. Everyone seems to make the same mistakes afresh, but I do believe that all that one can hope to achieve in a book such as this is to prompt certain questions and suggest possible answers. Oh, and amuse a little on the way.

I am by nature a private and somewhat diffident person not given to self-promotion but there was a story to tell and I was clearly the person to tell it. I must own to the fact that I had long felt the need to correct the inaccuracies often reported concerning the origins of my nightclub Heaven and the genesis of dance music that became known as 'house' or 'rave'. I knew that I, and the team at Heaven, had made a significant contribution to the dance scene and to the genesis of gay liberation. I felt that this had never been properly acknowledged. Probably because I usually encouraged others to front my various businesses, no gay journalist has ever interviewed me nor thought to ask how Heaven came about or who conceived the vision. The connection has never been explored between Heaven, the charity Crusaid and Soho Gyms where so many gay men train; all three were wholly or mainly my creation.

I have lived through the formative years of gay liberation, from the days when such love was illegal – my friend, Lord Montagu of Beaulieu, was imprisoned for a year in Winchester gaol – to the day when two people of the same sex could be joined in civil partnership; a journey of about forty years. My life partner, Derek, and I were among the first to do so on December 21st 2005, the day the act became law. Discrimination in the workplace on account of sexuality has been made illegal. These changes have affected the way gay people lead their lives and have enabled men – especially –- to lead happy and emotionally fulfilled lives in contrast to the furtive, sublimated existence led by so many of those chronicled here. I felt I had played a small part in helping to shape the social changes that have brought this about.

If this book has a central theme, it is about the misery and subterfuge forced on previous generations of gay people and the unhappiness caused thereby not only to themselves but to their families. An extraordinary shift has occurred in public attitudes to homosexuality enabling hundreds of thousands of gay men to feel secure enough to come out. In ever increasing numbers, gay men are showing their heads above the parapet and are leading normal lives.

There have been three core liberation struggles within mature western democracies in the last hundred years: women's liberation; black liberation and gay liberation. They have many similarities but, as the old adage goes, 'If you're black, you don't have to tell your mother.' Gay people could choose to remain hidden, that is to 'pass'. The majority, in fear of both social ostracism and job security, chose to hide their sexuality often from even their close family. The liberation achieved in the last fifteen or so years has enabled gay men especially to come out. Our substantial numbers, about 8 to 10 per cent of the population, has both amazed law-makers and the public alike. The greater our numbers, the more gay people find the courage to come out. Somewhere about 1995, gay identity reached 'The Tipping Point' and the number of new out gay people became a flood. I think the forced outings brought about by AIDS had a great deal to do with this. When Rock Hudson died of AIDS, it became apparent that no man was above suspicion and that gay men could be normal in every other respect. The epidemic elicited sympathy from the liberal élite for the immense suffering of gay men at both personal and collective levels. Many young gay people today fail to appreciate just how much my generation suffered from AIDS and discrimination; they take their freedom for granted.

Since university, I have been 'out' and open about my sexuality. I am proud to have been involved in the struggle for equality during its critical years and I hope that my efforts have, in some small way, helped the cause of gay liberation. By treating my sexuality as a matter of no consequence to all I meet, whether influential or ordinary, I have sought to redefine sexuality as an aspect of a person no more worthy of consideration than the colour of one's skin. Generations of gay Englishmen retreated into the buttoned-up, tight-lipped pedantry of the academic world or the art establishment to end their days in dry seclusion from a loveless life. I was not about to become one of them.

The stories I tell are sometimes funny and sometimes poignant; I hope they amuse but their purpose is to illustrate the often extreme reactions of people faced with prejudice. It is important to remember the revulsion with which homosexuality, especially male homosexuality, was viewed until very recently. Until 1967, men with natures such as mine were harried by the law, blackmailed and imprisoned, so please forgive me if I fume with some righteous indignation along the way. I firmly believe that the percentage of men who are gay does not vary over time, only the number who feel confident enough to express their sexuality openly. It therefore follows, given the hundreds of thousands of 'out' gay men now living in Britain, that forty years ago there must have been very many closeted and unhappy men living lives in fear and denial.

My stories reflect the different strategies gay men developed for dealing with the prejudice; some such as 'Decibelle' (Tony Galliers-Pratt) and Kim Tickell became outrageous and play-acted a travesty to diffuse the hatred of the righteous masses; others determined to prove themselves to the world, either socially like the 'duchess chasers' or politically like Sir Edward Heath and other members of parliament; some hid behind a mask of respectability like Colonel Newty. As the play *Another Country* so eloquently expressed, Guy Burgess became a traitor, so alienated and rejected did he feel from the society in which he was brought up. I feel sure that the same factors motivated Anthony Blunt. A few, like Ferdinand Coudert, came out late in life often after a life-change such as the death of a wife. The majority of gays sublimated their sexuality and either made do with furtive anonymous couplings, thereby leading twisted and damaged lives, or decided to marry and raise a family, forget their early gay experiences and behave as though they never happened. I give examples of all these types and it is interesting to speculate how these men would have behaved and lived their lives had they been young today, now such subterfuge is no longer necessary.

I have confined most of my memoirs to friends no longer alive. I have no wish to alienate the living and any biographical piece must strive to achieve honesty. There are other stories I would like to tell, but they must wait until the main characters depart the scene – unless of course I predecease them.

'To thine own self be true' – that is my text and the subject of my sermon. What countless misery and opportunities for happiness were lost by those forced into celibacy by a heartless church or into an unhappy loveless marriage by parents or social pressures. Braver souls, as many of these tales illustrate, came to terms with their natures early in life and risked the consequences.

Even today, in rural areas, provincial towns and in many countries abroad, gay men are persecuted. In Egypt, the police raided a gay gathering on a Nile boat, arrested and imprisoned those on board. In India, all gay sex is illegal and men are forced both by family and religion into marriage; many seek sex with other men in parks or cars in constant fear of the police. Koti boys, those too obviously effeminate to take the road of subterfuge, are outcasts forced to become male prostitutes or take menial jobs to survive. In Iran recently, two teenage boys were given 200 lashes and then hanged publicly, ostensibly for raping a younger boy but more plausibly solely for their homosexuality. The battle is far from won.

In my experience, being gay is innate and not a matter of choice. It is not even about whom you have sex with. A celibate monk can be either gay or straight even if he never has sex with anyone. It therefore follows that such an in-built trait should have the protection of the law against persecution or prejudice, in the same way that blacks and women enjoy equality. You can justly criticise a man for what he believes but not for the way he was born.

Most gay men have a hard time growing-up and have little support or protection from bullying and incessant teasing. I dream of a time when schools and parents will learn to recognise and support the different natures of their children and teach them that what they feel is all right and their desires are as natural as any heterosexual.

There has always been a sharp contrast, in my life as much as in the lives of countless other gay men, between the social life of parties and work, and the nights spent on Hampstead Heath or in darkened clubs seeking sex with other men. For many gay men sexual encounters need to be rough, masochistic or dirty to be truly fulfilling. It could be argued that this represents an element of self-hatred or at least self-abuse. Finding love with an equal and love with a person and not a sexual object is something that few in previous generations were able to achieve; such was the negative indoctrination to which gay men were subjected in childhood and adolescence.

My parallel journey has been a generational one. I was born in 1947 but my father was born in 1895, so I was raised by older parents in an Edwardian patrician atmosphere and imbued with old-fashioned values. I have come on a long journey to emerge as a 21st-century citizen with many of the values that it implies. Having said that, I still cherish many of the, now much derided, values of an English gentleman. I believe in courtesy and the consideration to others, especially those less fortunate. I believe in politeness, honesty and civility. I mourn the loss of respect for others and the freedom to be different inherent in that belief.

The main events of my life have touched on many of the seminal themes of the latter part of the twentieth century: the student unrest of

1968; the emergence of individualism as opposed to national allegiance; the triumph of science over the superstition of religious dogmas, at least in the enlightened West; the victory of racial and sexual toleration; the complete defeat of economic socialism by capitalism; the new interest and appreciation of fine food; the 'body awareness' that has led to the gym culture and the accelerating pace of technical innovation, above all in the field of computer science and communication. I have, on the whole, embraced and welcomed these changes; I believe I have managed not only to keep pace but I have often been in the forefront of their implementation. I have welcomed change, particularly social change. I am completely at ease chatting in a coffee shop or working out in one of my Soho gyms alongside classless young Londoners; I look, think and feel at one with the present era I inhabit.

Music has played an important role in my life; sometimes classical, but mostly dance music and electronic sounds now classified as Ambient, Lounge or Chill. The heady repetitive beat of contemporary sounds echoes the fast pace of urban youth and has been the soundtrack to my life. It has a symmetry that is as pleasing to my ear as are classical forms of architecture to my eye. Heaven was a pioneer in the introduction of this genre of dance music to Londoners through the innovation of Hi-NRG music in the early 1980s: it now forms the bedrock of club culture. Even as I write, I still enjoy the latest in contemporary music and try to keep up with the trends in this field. Some of my most enjoyable moments are spent listening to my I-pod through Bose headphones.

Fashions in music, clothes and decorative styles have accelerated and merged to the point where it is hard to imagine anything wholly new or non-derivative. I have, in a small way, been at the forefront of a number of fashionable innovations. I believe I have some sense for spotting new trends: in nightclubs; property; music and the fashion for health clubs – I opened my first gym, Power Station, in 1983; I am currently the proprietor of Soho Gyms, a London gym chain with five health clubs. We are have just launched our fifth and largest Soho Gym in Brad Street, Waterloo. The club covers some 14,000 square feet of dramatic triple-height space within four railway arches.

Derek and I have a wide diversity of friends and acquaintances and are blind to social and racial distinctions. We are in tune with the contemporary London scene where people mix and are judged on their merits alone; our businesses reflect these beliefs. London gay society today is arguably the first truly mixed society devoid of national antagonisms and rivalry, where all may participate in true equality. Much of youthful straight society now follows the same norms. Gay society is however alarmingly ageist and subjected to demanding body fascism; those who are older, less than beautiful or out of condition are generally shunned. We have much to learn in tolerance here. A man over fifty who enters a room full of younger gay men might well think he has become invisible. Contemporary society generally is guilty of a wilful neglect of the aged and unlike traditional societies, shows them scant respect.

I am fortunate to be born into an era of peace and ever-growing prosperity in a country where, for the most part, personal freedom is enshrined in law. When I was young, we had penal personal taxation that encouraged emigration of the most able and repressed initiative in those that remained. Exchange control made it difficult for people to spend their own money abroad, so things were far from perfect. Conscription into the armed services ended while I was still a child leaving me free to determine my own start in life.

I have made and lost large sums of money in my various business ventures. My least successful business ventures seem often to have involved food. I invested in a restaurant, 33 St James's, started by my friend Derek Johns and lost my investment. The restaurant was launched on the back of Derek's achievement in winning *Master Chef* on television in 1993, the first man to do so.

I started a business called Pasta Pasta that sold delicious fresh pasta and sauces. After an initial flurry of press interest and commercial success, the business faltered and finally closed resulting in a total loss for all the investors. It would be easy to blame the supermarkets who adopted the idea and undercut our prices with an inferior product, but I should have foreseen this.

My participation in Mardi Gras, an annual London gay celebration and music festival, was another total write-off. Last but by no means least, I was a name at Lloyd's on the infamous Peter Cameron Webb syndicates, where the rot at Lloyds started. You can't get it right all the time. As my Yorkshire uncle Gordon was fond of saying, 'If my foresight was half as good as my hindsight, I'd be richer by a damn-sight.'

I have started two AIDS charities, Crusaid and AIDS Ark, and can humbly claim to have been partly responsible for keeping a few people alive. I have been blessed with a few close friends whom I cherish and an inordinately large acquaintance of the rich, famous, beautiful and bizarre. As a nightclub owner, I have first hand experience of drugs, the underworld and urban youth culture.

I have had a few close shaves: I was on a passenger train that crashed near Rugeley, Staffordshire in 1986, en route for Derbyshire; I've abandoned a sinking motorboat in rough seas off Portland Bill in 1986 and the fates decreed that I refused an invitation to the party on the *Marchioness*: a pleasure boat which sank on the Thames with the tragic loss of many young lives. I have dined with dukes in grand country houses and partied with rent boys. I have lived on the edge and savoured fully the flavours that life has to offer.

My life story has been a frenzied dance and a feast of pleasures. God, in whom I do not believe, will judge me kindly, I hope. I like to believe that I have shed a little love in the world and enhanced the lives of some of those I have touched along the way. Beyond all else, I have had and am still having, a huge amount of fun.

❧ Acknowledgements

My first attempt at writing was in 2001 inspired by Bruno Conde who suggested I set down the story of Alan Taulbee that I had told him. I received further encouragement from Prof. Del Kolve of (UCLA retired) and his partner Larry Luchtel. Del cast his expert eye over some of my chapters and made helpful suggestions. Other friends, especially in the publishing world, saw parts of the book and gave me advice including Gillon Aitken, Andrew and Fiona Duncan and my brother-in-law, Duncan Baird. I am grateful for their enthusiasm; it gave me the confidence to continue. Above all I am indebted to Michael Waterhouse, himself a published author, who not only encouraged me but introduced me to my publisher. Other friends have helped or encouraged me; in particular, Max Wakefield and Maurits Kalff. I had had long discussions with both about the form and content of the work.

I am indebted to Gerard Noel for alerting me to Leda Farrant's small book on Diana Delamere and the murder of Lord Erroll, that he discovered in the London Library. This book corroborated my assertion of Diana's lesbian affair with Lady Patricia Fairweather, the key plank in my theory concerning the solution to the murder.

Monica Gotz of Key West listened patiently to my readings from the book and clearly enjoyed them. Her encouragement was inspirational; sadly, she has since died young and I will miss her.

Alasdair Brown has helped me organize the launch for my book and his contacts and advice have been invaluable.

Derek Frost has been tireless in his love and support, having read and re-read the manuscript and he has been my severest critic. He has urged me on when I had doubts and kept my excesses in check.

There are many other friends who have provided information and helpful suggestions. I hope they will forgive me if I do not mention them all by name.

It is unusual for someone relatively unknown to secure a publishing deal for their autobiography, so my principal debt of gratitude is to my publisher, Elliott & Thompson, who have been prepared to back my book by publishing it; the greatest compliment that can be paid an author. I trust their faith in me will be rewarded.

This book is all my own work and I am entirely responsible for the views expressed herein.

The lost family fortune

Chapter One

❦ My Family: Childhood & Early Years – 1947–53

My grandfather drove a streetcar in Chicago; his son, my father married a god-daughter of Queen Victoria. My life is one of contrasts painted in chiaroscuro exemplified by these two extremes. I was born lucky and privileged but not particularly rich.

I am a baby-boomer, an immediate post-war child of older parents. Indeed my father had a son, Robert (Bob), from a previous marriage who was killed on active service in the Second World War. I was brought up with the mores and patrician ethos of a pre-war or even Edwardian child, ill equipped to deal with the rough and tumble of contemporary life.

My parents had two children; my brother Remington (Rem for short), born on 3 December 1945; and me. I was born on 18th May 1947. By the time I went to prep school, my father was too ill to work. He died of a thrombosis while under the knife in 1958. I was just eleven. Our household now comprised my mother, nanny, my brother Rem and I.

I remember my childhood as a period of unhappiness; I was, on the whole, lonely, shy and cautious. All the while, I sensed my difference from other boys and felt that the world I grew up in was hostile to my true nature.

Although I was born at The Baby Shop, a nursing home in Wigmore Street where the smartest little children were hatched, we lived for my first few years in a modest house with a large garden in the village of Tadley in Hampshire.

My earliest memories are of walks with Nanny to collect wild strawberries along the hedgerows. I held her hand as we walked along the green lanes to an old cottage where the two old women who lived alone drew their water from a well. I basked in her simple smile and warm embraces. The long hot summers of childhood memory were spent in our swimming pool being splashed by Daddy and pushed under the water by Rem.

We grew our own fruit and vegetables with the assistance of both a gardener and a garden boy. My earliest memories are of bottling fruit in the autumn in large Kilner jars and gorging myself until I was sick on ripe gooseberries and greengages. Rationing and the lack of refrigeration encouraged such home industry. The house was not connected to the mains electricity and I remember the thump as the generator kicked-in and the hum it made that helped to send me to sleep.

My brother Rem and I lived in the nursery and looked to Nanny for everything, especially emotional support. For me she was the principle fount of love, perhaps less so for Rem as he was already two and a half when Nanny was engaged to look after us. We loved our parents in a dutiful way and I was to grow close to my mother in adolescence. It could be said perhaps, too close. The opinions I was taught to respect were those of an older generation and totally out of keeping with the modern world. Having few friends of my own age amplified this sense of belonging to an earlier generation. We were taught to be overly polite and formal to adults and were never allowed to be wild or disrespectful, even had I wanted to be. I was shy with grown-ups and not at ease with other children who must have thought me prim – a right little mummy's boy.

I don't remember a television in those early years and comics were not permitted. The first time I saw television was on the day of The Queen's coronation in 1953. Although we had toys, we largely made our own fun and invented games and pastimes. The war being such a recent event, war games loomed large in our imaginations. I liked cowboys and especially Indians. I sided with the Indians who seemed so much more interesting and romantic.

Author (left) with brother Rem and Nanny

Girls made me nervous and so I was not, like many gay boys, able to find solace and companionship in their company; I think deep down I was afraid that spending time in the company of girls might draw attention to and encourage my feminine side. As a young boy, I loved soft things, silky materials and pretty clothes. I loved the thought of dressing-up but was far too shy and self-conscious to reveal this fascination. I was a solitary child who found refuge in my vivid imagination. My male fantasies were about guns and shooting, field-craft and stalking. I played solo games and explored the country-side collecting insects; all things I could indulge in alone.

My father instilled in me a rigid Edwardian vision of manliness. I knew he expected me to be rugged and brave and that as a man I was meant to conceal physical fear; I felt quite ill equipped to do so. I was a timid and gentle little boy. I hated the cold and suffered badly from chilblains and chapped hands. I liked warmth and comfort and soft clothes. I was scared of being hurt, bruised or even getting dirty and wet.

I can recall women neighbours commenting on my long curly blond locks. I was a pretty child and quite girlish to look at. How I resented the customary comment, 'What beautiful curly hair, you should have been girl!' Not quite what an insecure pretty-boy wants to hear.

From this distance, memories are patchy and consist of flashes rather than whole scenes. I recall vividly a maroon flannel blazer that I adored both for its colour and texture; it was probably my first grown-up but-toned jacket. I suppose clothes were still rationed. I hated to be parted from this adored garment, imbuing it with a magical, almost fetishistic quality and felt grown-up wearing it. I loved its scarlet colour and soft felt fabric.

My teddy bear was the most important person in my life after Nanny and Mummy. With my love of unusual sounding portentous names, I christened it Edward Albert Tremain, Teddy for short, and wove fanci-ful stories around it and its cast of imaginary friends including two gen-tlemen called Corley and Dudiment. I called myself Joff the engine driver and my brother was Chuff the fireman. Joff stuck and became my family nickname well into my teens. Even at this tender age, I lived largely in my imagination, which was both rich and inventive.

The world of the nursery must have been just as cosy and safe as I remember. Teas by the fireside with toast and dripping; stories read to me by Nanny in her flat characterless monotone. I did not mind; the soothing familiarity of her sweet voice was enough for me. In that magic world, I felt safe from the larger boys and girls who teased me.

I now know that my mother developed tuberculosis when I was three or four and that I also contracted it. I do not remember feeling ill, only the irksome restrictions of being forbidden to play or walk anywhere. I was taken around in a pushchair; I thought this a great indignity for someone no longer a baby. I was reminded of this illness when, on matriculating at Cambridge, I was X-rayed and a shadow from pul-monary TB was found on my lung.

I always wanted to be a grown-up and to be older than my years. My cognitive abilities were always far in advance of my chronological age.

The disparity seemed even greater as I looked so young. I don't believe in re-incarnation but in a strange way I felt I was old and wise and was frustrated by not being taken seriously: I hated to be thought a baby. Somewhere within me, even then, was a strong determination to succeed and prove myself worthy of my parents' love. I must have been intelligent but I think my diffidence stopped me from showing it.

Quite early on, I developed a good memory and an enquiring mind with a love of recondite facts, especially in the areas of names and geography; a facility that remains with me to this day. I can still recall the unusual names of people and places including long departed foreign leaders or obscure capital cities. I could sometimes astound adults by using long words or with my general knowledge. I was asked to define the word *botanical* at prep school and I replied, 'pertaining to the study of plants.' I did not seek to attract attention so I usually kept these abilities to myself. In the general run of schoolwork, no one thought me particularly bright and I was a slow developer, particularly physically.

Holidays were always a difficult time: I loved the company of Mummy and Nanny but my brother Rem and I were apart both in years and interests. Early on, I longed for a special friend of my own and had early romantic visions of a handsome older dark boy loving me and being my close companion. How I longed for that wonder boy to come into my life and make everything feel all right.

Mother, Peggy Harvard Johnson

My mother, Peggy, was born on 11 April 1909, the eldest child of Percy and Clarice Johnson. Percy had inherited the family firm, George Bassett & Co, jointly with his brother William. Together, they ran the firm successfully and oversaw its floatation on the London Stock Exchange in 1926.

A girl who had everything, my mother was beautiful, charming and the daughter of a rich doting father who spoilt her in every way. She never had to work and she never did. She danced so beautifully and naturally that, before the war, she won the bronze medal at the Empire Dancing championships at the Albert Hall. She had been persuaded to partner an experienced male dancer at the last moment, when his usual partner was suddenly indisposed. She had film-star good looks, as the Hollywood-style portrait of her shows. The sole trait that let her down was her tendency to slouch and appear round-shouldered. In her childhood, she had been taught to juggle in an effort to cure this postural inadequacy. The treatment didn't work, but she acquired a party trick for life.

Mother's portrait taken in Hollywood – early 1930s

She enjoyed a gilded youth full of fun and privilege. She wintered in St Moritz and spent her summers in the South of France. She had a succession of eligible and handsome suitors including Count Mogi Apponi, a Hungarian nobleman. He followed her across Europe from St Moritz to Biarritz and wrote her love letters, still in my possession, proposing marriage and promising a life of endless social glamour with invitations to stay at some of Europe's grandest palaces.

Peggy's doings were chronicled in the gossip columns of the day. She even had a poem to her favourite dachshund published in the *Sketch*. Her family must have been disappointed when she fell for a married man fourteen years older than her and still not yet divorced.

As luck would have it, good luck for me I suppose, my mother fell in love with an impecunious married man much older than her, my father, Roland Norman. She had to wait a few years for my father to get a divorce from his first wife, a woman some nine years his senior, Victoria Legge.

They first met before the war in the Casino at Biarritz. My mother was playing the gambling card game, chemin de fer, on the lowest stakes table, with her usual success. Always lucky at cards or games of chance, she was winning. She knew a friend of my father in the same gambling syndicate and was urged to play for them at the top table. That night she won them a small fortune and my mother treasured the diamond brooch she was given as a present for the large win she had that night. She also met her future husband and fell in love.

My mother was an heiress who was in the end, to her great surprise and sadness, largely cut out of her father's will. Mother was left with an adequate but by no means sensational income. What little she had was annually eroded by inflation. The capital value diminished steadily over the years because the money was held in tight trust. It was poorly invested, for the most part in gilt-edged government stock, which depreciated rapidly in the years of inflation after the war.

These fixed-interest government bonds were the means by which the government financed its annual budget deficits. The National Debt would have grown quickly to insolvent proportions had it not been for the effects of inflation in the 20th Century. The real value of the debt to be repaid fell so dramatically, as did the market value, reducing the debt to an ever more manageable size. In the end, it was the pensioners and small savers, the investors in War Loan and Consols 2.5%, those who could least afford to lose, who financed the profligacy of the post-war years. To add insult to injury, the minute income was savagely taxed as 'unearned income'. The rates rapidly rose to 98%, so that the effective robbery of the helpless was rendered entire.

I can still smell my mother's lingering perfume and hear the rustle of her silk evening dress as she bent over the bed to kiss me goodnight before going off to a dance or dinner. 'Be careful not to mess-up my hair,' she would say as her diamond earrings brushed my cheek. I thought she was beautiful but I was somehow envious of her attractiveness to men.

My mother admitted that eventually she broke with conventional morality by having an affair with my father before his divorce came through; they were finally able to marry in 1944.

Throughout my childhood and teens, I had a close and loving relationship with my mother but she was ultimately a selfish woman. She was snobbish and vain and never did anything for anyone outside her immediate family. She even managed to avoid war work. How she managed to do so remains a mystery. All women, even married women, were conscripted unless they had small children. Apart from a short spell in the government's censorship department, my mother spent most of the war living in the country with my grandmother.

She became adept at finding ways to avoid rationing. One gambit she discovered was to place orders with a department store in Gibraltar. It was still possible to send packages by post, even during wartime, and Gibraltar as a colony was in the Stirling area. Many goods and foodstuffs were available in Gibraltar, located as it was next to neutral Spain. My mother received parcels of nylon stockings, coffee and make-up, items generally unavailable in wartime Britain. Had she put her formidable intelligence and cunning to better use, who knows what she might have achieved?

It was ultimately her inability to truly accept my homosexuality that pushed us apart. When I told her, she was mostly concerned about how the news would affect her – what would her friends think? This is a by no means uncommon reaction as I was to discover from talking to friends. She never really accepted my nature; she felt I had told her a lie to hurt her for some unknown reason; I was her beautiful son and could not possibly be so flawed. It was ultimately her unwillingness to accept and embrace my boyfriend Derek that distanced me from her. She would never remember his birthday and would sometimes spell his name incorrectly, Derrick instead of Derek. This can only have been deliberate, or if not, at the very least it was wilfully careless and therefore wounding. These little things hurt, but her cold politeness to him hurt even more. She ultimately was the loser by her actions. She often made it clear to me by making deeply anti-gay remarks that she found the subject distasteful but at the same time it was clear that she could not see me as 'one of those'. I was her son; I was different.

In 1963, my mother married Johnnie Sim, a cousin of Lord Inchcape and the deputy Chairman of Inchcape and Co. Johnnie was a morose, pessimistic Scot. He drank heavily, about a bottle of spirits a day. A quarter of a bottle of gin would be consumed as pink gins over lunch at the City Club. In the evenings at home, he would polish off about three quarters of a bottle of scotch. He never appeared drunk, just dour and argumentative. Excessive alcohol reddened his face and marred his fine looks, his sharp brain was pickled by a mixture of alcohol and his own misery. He thought life had treated him badly. His Scottish family estate, Dunraggit in Ayrshire, had been sold during the war by his mother. He heard that the salmon fishing rights had been sold for more money than had been obtained for the whole estate. He was embittered by this and by the knowledge that, while he had little capital, nearly all his numerous cousins were millionaires. After a successful career in the family firm, Inchcape & Co., running their business in East Africa, he had returned to London to take his seat on the main board and to meet and marry my mother.

Johnnie had no close friends and he became increasingly misanthropic and morose. He hated social functions and disliked entertaining, both of which were lifeblood to my mother. They sat at home glaring at each other and bickering. Their one mutual activity was *The Times* cross-word, completed ritualistically on a daily basis. After his retirement, he became increasingly reclusive and odd; eventually his eccentricity turned to a form of madness and he was incarcerated in a home where he died at an early age. My stepsister Amanda and I developed a close loving friendship based on the feeling that we were the only truly sane people in a dysfunctional and unhappy family. We both could not wait to escape into the normal world.

Mummy survived Johnnie by some ten years and lived to the age of eighty-seven. Her last years were lonely and unhappy but financially secure thanks to his generous company pension. A wonderfully loving Moroccan girl called Fatima attended her, in her final years. She came in every day to clean and make her lunch; but more than that, she cared deeply for my mother and put up with all manner of rudeness and discourtesy as Mummy became more cantankerous with her advancing years. Fatima demonstrated the true religious values of her faith with her respect and care for the elderly. To her it was both a duty and a pleasure.

I sensed that towards the end of her life my mother became embittered with the world and her first husband in particular. She often expressed anger at the memory of how he had treated her, his frequent infidelities and his financial irresponsibility. She confessed that once she had discovered him in bed with two women at once. As the memories of her physical passions faded, so her anger increased. I made a mental note to try not to become too critical of others and angry at the world, as I get older. It damages oneself and is unattractive to others.

My mother and I kept in touch and met regularly for lunch and dinner, but the love and warmth I had felt for her dissipated with the passage of time; my regular visits were largely motivated by a sense of duty.

FATHER: ROLAND FRANK HOLDWAY NORMAN

I hardly knew my father, he was so much older than I; a remote Edwardian figure, more feared by me than loved, I am sad to say. He suffered pain both from his war wound and from his persistent ulcer. The pain made him irascible and intolerant of childish high spirits and noisy ways. Born in 1895, he had seen active service in both world wars. He was an Edwardian gentleman in style, manners and attitude, an indigent and charming dandy with a penchant for gaming, women and high society. He was at least 6ft. tall, with slicked-back pomaded dark hair and an Edwardian moustache that he meticulously waxed and twirled. By the time I knew him, he was thin, almost too thin; his beautifully tailored suits hung loose on him. A large roman nose enlivened his saturnine countenance, fixed his striking good looks and dominated his masculine features.

His father, my grandfather Horace, had disappeared or died by the time my father was two-year's old. My father and his older brother, Donald, were brought up by their capable mother, Bennie, (Ellen, Elizabeth Eeles). It must have been a struggle for a single woman of no great fortune to raise two boys in those days. For reasons of respectability, she passed herself off as a widow.

Bennie must have been a remarkable lady; she clearly had determination. Pictures that I have of her, admittedly taken later in her life, do not show her to have been a great beauty, but she must have possessed some allure as her one and only husband was undoubtedly a handsome man. She raised two boys on her own and somehow paid for her middle class lifestyle.

According to the 1900 census, she was living in a well-built,

Ellen Norman (Eeles) – father's mother

My father aged about twenty-eight – circa 1923

newly constructed, mansion flat in Kilburn close to the underground station. (The block of flats is still there.) She gives her profession as 'linguist, working from home'. I have no evidence that she ever travelled abroad, so if the term has its usual meaning, I cannot imagine where she learnt her language skills. I wondered at first if it might be a code word for some other more interesting lingual skills that could account for her high income but quickly discounted that idea for two reasons. First, on the grounds of her unexceptional looks and secondly from the fact that she took in as a lodger a respectable young man from Wales, aged nineteen, with a Chapel background. Perhaps Bennie's profession of linguist was a euphemism for elocutionist. Speaking well was considered important at that time and my father had a well-modulated and educated accent and manners to go with it. I am sure that my grandmother was determined to raise her sons as gentlemen. In manners, dress and speech at least, she succeeded well.

That nineteen-year-old was William Berry who came to London from South Wales in 1899. He found lodgings with a much older widow, Mrs Norman, my grandmother. He developed affection for 'Dear Mrs Norman' and particularly her younger son, a five-year-old, my father Roland. I know from extant correspondence that the boy's parents knew and liked 'Dear Mrs Norman', so she must have been running a respectable house.

The boy in question, William Berry, went on to become the 1st Viscount Camrose. He became one of the great press barons of the Twentieth century, owner at various times of both the *Sunday Times* and the *Daily Telegraph*. In the process he became wealthy and influential, a close friend of Winston Churchill and a major player on the political scene.

Throughout life, my father's friend and protector, Lord Camrose, bailed him out of tight corners and proved always a friend he could turn to. In the absence of his own father, Camrose became a surrogate. Camrose was not blind to my father's faults, particularly his financial unreliability and his gambling, he never entirely trusted him where money or business was concerned; but was always available to help him and advise him. It was to Lord Camrose that my father turned in times of trouble and I suspect it was through him that he had many of his glamorous social introductions. It is probable that it was from him that he learned some of the rudiments of business and deal making.

My father had a chequered career. Born in October 1895, he was a younger son of parents of modest means although both he and his elder bother were educated privately at Hurstpierpoint College in Sussex. He was a member of the unfortunate generation that were just ripe for enlistment in the First World War. He was commissioned as a Second Lieutenant in the Leicestershire Regiment, shot and badly wounded in the thigh at the Battle of the Somme in June 1916; it was three days before he got to a casualty clearing station and was eventually invalided home.

After a period of recovery (he was lucky not to lose a leg), he joined the Royal Flying Corps and trained as a pilot, graduating on 13th October 1917. He returned to France with 55 Squadron of the Independent Air Force. He joined the squadron a few days after W.E. Johns, the author of the Biggles books, had been shot down behind enemy lines; so in a sense my father was sent out to replace Biggles.

I still have his flying logbooks detailing his bombing raids behind enemy lines. The Germans are quaintly referred to as 'huns' and anti-air-craft fire as 'archie'. An entry for 3 November 1918 tells of a raid over Saarburg, the 'archie is slight and inaccurate' but the raid ends with an enemy pilot, Lt. Fleisher, and his observer nose-diving into the ground and being killed just outside the aerodrome. His wartime letters home indicate that he held strongly to the opinion that there should be no peace with Germany that did not include her total capitulation.

After the war, my father went to live in Johannesburg in South Africa to work for Sir Ernest Oppenheimer, head of the Anglo-American Mining Corporation. After three years, he somehow made money and returned home a wealthy man and a dashing wounded war hero. On his return my father must have had access to Society, perhaps through his Oppenheimer contacts, but more likely through his friendship with William Berry, who by now was the owner of the *Sunday Times* and a man of wealth and influence.

He married, in 1921, a war widow nine years his senior. Victoria (Vita) Williams-Bulkeley (born 1885, née Legge) who was a god-daughter of Queen Victoria and the daughter of Sir Harry Legge, an equerry and friend to King George V. (I have the telegram from Queen Alexandra to Sir Harry congratulating him on the engagement of his daughter to Captain Norman.) Vita's first husband had been killed in the war. She already had three children from her previous marriage, including a daughter Sylvia.

I have in my possession the gold penknife, engraved as a Christmas gift, from King George to Harry Legge in 1910. The Legge family lived at Fulmer in Buckinghamshire. I have seen their visitor's book as it was in the possession of her daughter, Sylvia Cleary when she died: it seems that they regularly entertained the crowned heads of Europe as well as the most influential people of their day in England.

Vita and Roland had a son together, my half-brother Robert, born in 1922. After an unhappy time at school, he left Eton in 1940, and was killed almost immediately, aged just 18, aboard a motor torpedo boat off the Norfolk coast.

My father had an entrepreneurial flair and exhibited a facility for negotiating profitable deals. There were times when he had been very

POST OFFICE TELEGRAPHS.

This Form must accompany any inquiry respecting this Telegram.

Office of Origin and Service Instructions.

Sandringham OHMS

Charges to pay s. d.

Handed in at 3 10 P.M., Received here at 3 64

TO Colonel Sir Harry Legge Fulmer Gardens Slough

Delighted to hear on your beloved daughters happy engagement to Capt Norman wish every happiness in her lonely life up till now best love to your dear wife Alexandra

Queen Alexandra's congratulatory telegram on my father's engagement

rich. However, by the end of the Second World War he had spent all his money. Gone were the house in Charles Street, Mayfair; the country house, Bylsborough, in Sussex and the villa in Biarritz. I know he loved my mother or at least there was a strong mutual physical attraction but I

My father and his son Bob who was killed in action in 1944

think that before they married they both believed each other better off than was actually the case.

I have come across some intriguing correspondence from my father to my mother; sadly it is undated but appears to be from pre-war days. It appears my father was imprisoned for debt in France and that his accuser, a Monsieur Filioux, refused to agree to his release until the debt was repaid. My father cashed a cheque at Cannes that was not honoured. My father describes the appalling conditions in the French prison: 'Words cannot describe the horrors of this place, bugs, filth, terrors. I am not going to attempt to tell you the details.' He complains that he cannot raise the money or conduct his business affairs while incarcerated. He asks my mother to contact friends in England and to 'ask madamoiselle to ask her uncle at Cap Juan for 200,000 francs.' He says he will get it all from Camrose on his return. He warns my mother about trying to smuggle things into the prison: 'Do not try to send any cigarettes etc. as everything is examined – the bread cut in to pieces – you did try once but it was a nice surveillant and he only warned me.' He writes to his business partner Francis, Marquis of Queensbury, asking for a loan to bail him out.

The debt probably arose at the gambling tables, one letter refers to gaming: 'You know it is absolute lies to say that 35,000 francs cannot be accounted for, I lost 500,000 playing baccarat at Cannes and the remaining 150,000 afterwards at chemin de fer, roulette etc.' The most poignant letters are notes passed from Mother on her prison visits with questions to be answered by my father about what she should do to help him. The notes are crumpled and stained and seem to have been surreptitious and concealed.

I don't think that my father's first marriage ended happily – Vita accused my father of spending all her money. He certainly had got through most of his own by the time he married my mother. After the divorce, she took the unusual step of changing her name back by deed poll and had no further contact with my father. Whilst I believe that they loved each other initially, I feel sure that Vita's elevated social position and the introductions to high society that such a marriage afforded my father, were at least a sub-conscious factor in his decision.

Vita finally divorced my father in 1944, enabling my mother to marry him on 8 March 1944.

Sylvia was my father's stepdaughter. I spent a weekend with her as a child and stayed on for a week while I recovered from a bout of measles. She lived in the same village, Clayton in Sussex, as the Van den Bogaerde family and had befriended them over many years. Dirk Bogarde in his first volume of autobiography mentions her, with affection. Dirk's younger brother, Gareth, a friend, has told me it was common knowledge that my father had had an affair with his own stepdaughter – it is hardly surprising that Vita divorced him.

We were brought up in the world of nurseries and Nanny. We were, as was traditional, brought downstairs to the drawing room at teatime. My father was not an unkind man, I'm sure he loved me, but I found his rigid, patrician, Edwardian, military masculinity both daunting and scary. I did not have to enquire, I knew the real me would be deeply

My parents on their wedding day, March 8th 1944

shameful to him. My mother told me that he had wished for a little girl as a second child but I knew he did not want to be the father of a son with feminine desires.

He was funny, often irreverent, but always appropriately and immaculately dressed, conventional only in outward ways. He loved to mimic people and accents and pull silly faces and tell us naughty limericks to amuse us. He was immensely proud of his physical courage and would show off by eating a whole chilli or putting his hand in a basin of water with electricity running through it. He was a dandy but a manly man with a huge appetite for life, loving and gambling.

The Author at age three

My father had money before the last war or at least the outward appearance of wealth. He was a member of the Carlton Club and had his own firm on the London stock exchange, Crews and Co., in partnership with Lord Queensbury (Francis). Many years later Lord Hartwell, who knew them both, told me an anecdote that seemed to typify my father's cavalier approach to life. He said that neither of the partners would dare leave the other alone in the office for fear that the petty cash would go missing. My father definitely had a rather shady reputation in business as well as with women. He was often in debt and clearly had few moral scruples but he was charming and popular with seemingly more friends than enemies.

Just how successful he became is evidenced by the fact that in 1929 he donated £500 (worth about £20,000 today) to his old school, Hurstpierpoint, to enable the school to build new squash courts. He attended the opening and played an exhibition match. He then donated a further £3,500 (£140,000) to the Chapel Tower fund. The fortune that he made was dissipated either through gambling or through injudicious investments. He died as he had lived, beyond his means. By the time we came along my father's life was nearly over and he had lost his drive and talent for business. All his money had gone although he tried in vain to make or gamble it back with ill-conceived and unlucky business ventures, and more often than not by betting on slow horses. We lived off my mother's modest private income. Life must have been a constant struggle to keep up standards and pay the bills.

During my childhood, my father was always ill; he became increasingly unwell as the years passed. The financial worry and the loss of male pride caused by living off my mother's income must have taken their toll. In addition to his war wound, he suffered from chronic duodenal ulcers for most of his life. (An affliction that plagued me from early adolescence.) As his health deteriorated, my father became increasingly thin and irascible while retaining his dashing, gaunt, good looks and old-fashioned courtly charm. A dandy, he was always impeccably and appropriately dressed by his tailor, Messrs. Wyser & Bryant of Savile Row. The paraffin burner and ivory handled curling tongs that he used to groom his elaborately waxed and pointed moustache were a source of fascination to me. I can well understand how my mother fell for him, a wounded, dashing war hero with dark, almost Spanish, good looks. I wish I could say I loved him but, in truth, I was rather afraid of him and felt inadequate; unable to live up to his exacting manly standards. I just knew I would be a shameful disappointment to him.

On one occasion forever etched in my memory, I must have been about eight years old; my mother was removing a blackhead from my brother's ear using her long scarlet painted fingernails that seemed like talons to me. Rem was shrieking in pain, probably imagined rather than real, and my turn was next. I was terrified and ran away. My father was appalled at my cowardice and chased me up a tree in the garden. Eventually he caught me and set on me in an uncontrolled rage. The sobbing interventions of Mummy and Nanny cooled him down. They managed to dissuade him from taking me upstairs to beat me properly. Normality was restored but not without lasting damage to my fragile psyche.

I did not know it then but my poor father had not long to live. In 1958, he died of a massive internal haemorrhage while on the operating table without ever regaining consciousness; I was only just eleven. Rem and I were at our preparatory school, St Andrews, Eastbourne, when we were summoned by the headmaster, Mr Liddell, and told we were going home to be with Mummy but no reason was given. We found her red-eyed and tearful; she spent much of the time alone in her room. Nanny was calm and stoic as would be expected. Rem played the little man and tried to be brave and take charge. I did not really appreciate what was happening and must confess that I did not feel any genuine sad-

With my mother and Rem

ness, at least not until the last day of term when back at school. It finally dawned on me that I would be going home and Daddy would not be there and I cried quietly in bed for two hours before the dawn.

He was buried in the beautiful little country churchyard at Clayton, Sussex, alongside his adored mother, Bennie, near where he had lived with his first family before the war. None of us, not even my mother, went to the funeral; we were not consulted. I think this was a grave mistake; it prevented us from being able to grieve properly. Burials are important rites of passage and have endured in all cultures and times for that very good reason. We were spared the ordeal, I think, because it was thought that it would be too distressing for us young boys but the strange thing was that my mother did not go and I don't believe she ever visited her husband's grave.

Dame School, Sherbourne St John – 1952–53

My first school was a dame school at the nearby village of Sherbourne St John. Dame schools were small establishments run by older women who taught young children the basic three R's. There were a few other little boys but mostly scary older girls; everyone seemed older and bigger than me. I cannot have been more than four or five years old. The girls ranged in age up to about eleven or twelve. It was a day school for girls that took a few pre-school boys. It certainly was not a play school.

The girls appeared so grown-up and it was here that I think I developed my fear of girls. I felt so much smaller and punier than they. The school was cold and draughty, inhospitable and frightening to a delicate small boy. I don't remember receiving kindness from anyone or ever having any friends. I recall the awful smell of damp and floor polish and the fear I felt of saying or doing the wrong thing. I could not wait for Mummy or Nanny to pick me up and take me home at the end of the day.

Eastacre School, Winchester – 1953–55

I was packed off to boarding pre-preparatory school at the age of six, for no good reason other than that it was 'the done thing'. My parents thought I might be lonely at home without my brother. My mother shed a tear when I went away, but did not cry as much as I did; nor did she make any protest at my being sent away so young. This was curious, since she had run away from her boarding school in Eastbourne when she was about nine. I was so frightened that I prayed for an accident or disaster of almost any sort to save me from having to go back to school.

My brother, who did not like me much and was more than two years older than I, did not even deign to know me at school. I was a 'squit' and 'Norman minor', even to him.

Mr and Mrs Beale ran the school. She was a Christian religious fanatic so I spent a great deal of time learning biblical texts by heart and reciting them in order to earn coloured picture cards of bible scenes. These were the type of gaudy sentimental art I liked at that age. Games were my worst fear. On one occasion, I peed in my pants before a football game. I was physically and mentally unsuited to team games – I found them daunting and scary. I hated being cold and dirty and was fearful of being pushed over and hurt.

I remember very little about Eastacre except the long winter walks around the streets of suburban Winchester and the rattle our sticks made on the vertical wooden slats of the garden fences as we walked in crocodile in our Sunday best. The food was of course mean and atrocious and we were forced to eat things even if they made us feel sick, in my case a bowl of puffed wheat the grains of which seemed to get stuck in my throat and clog my pallet. The damp mouldy smell of it still makes me nauseous.

I showed some early promise as a performer. I had to recite a set speech. My good memory and advanced vocabulary combined with my rich imagination came to the fore. The piece chosen for me was Mark Antony's funeral oration for Julius Caesar by Shakespeare, not a particularly suitable piece for a seven year old. But I acquitted myself well and put feeling and comprehension into 'Friends, Romans, countrymen, lend me your ears…' – so much so that another parent who was a theatrical agent actually talked to my father about sending me for an audition. My parents would hear none of it.

I recall being always cold and underfed. I liked the pleasant honey taste of the spoonfuls of Virol malt but not the cod liver oil given to fortify us in winter. Mostly, I remember the cold stark school devoid of friends where I spent so much time in fear and loneliness. I can still recall the sheer terror of putting on football boots for the hated game and trying to tie the laces with frozen fingers made red with chilblains. My legs and hands were permanently chapped and sore.

I remember vividly one particularly traumatic incident. We slept in dormitories with an older boy in charge. His name was Peter – he seemed almost grown up to me – but I suppose he was only nine or ten. He slept in the next bed to me. One night he invited me into his bed. I sensed at once that what he wanted was wrong and somehow dirty and forbidden. But I wanted to go and did. I loved it when he caressed me and touched me between the legs, then he put his hand over my mouth and pinched me hard on a sore spot on my bottom. I cried out in fear and astonishment. Why did he do this? I will never know. Can a boy of that age really have been a sexual sadist? But this remains the only plausible explanation. I screamed in pain and Matron came. I knelt by the bed pretending to pray, feeling that I had done something terrible and awaiting the punishment I felt sure would come. Of course he was the one, being older, who was punished; no one even asked me what had happened. I suppose they just assumed that he had bullied me in some way so Mr Beale beat Peter with the slipper. He never touched me again, nor was the matter ever referred to.

UNCLE GORDON JOHNSON

I left Eastacre at the age of seven to join my brother Rem at St Andrew's, Eastbourne, a prep school for boys, aged between 7 and 13. My uncle Gordon, my mother's brother, had been there as a boy and was now a governor of the school. A bachelor, he had no other close relations, so he generously paid for our education. My parents could not possibly have afforded the fees for two boys out of my mother's modest trust fund income.

We didn't see much of Uncle Gordon. He lived a rather sad, lonely life and, having no family, lived in a residential hotel. He worked in Sheffield running the confectionery business, Bassett's Liquorice Allsorts, formerly owned by the family, by then a public company and the largest employer of labour in the city. It is now a division of Cadbury Schweppes Plc.

My uncle was a shy kindly bachelor; perhaps he should have been an academic. He had wanted to stay on at Oxford where he had won a gold medal for mathematics although reading philosophy, politics and economics (PPE). His father had forced him into the family business where he had prospered by virtue of his intellect and gentle un-combative personality. He was an emotionally closed man but kind and generous to us, his only two nephews. He had a rather monastic, almost saintly, quality to him. I never heard him getting angry or losing his temper. His interests remained largely academic; politics, philosophy, economics, chess and business but also watching tennis and football. I suppose he was a true ascetic with no interest in the senses or in sensual matters; he abhorred personal indulgence and luxury. He had no interest in music or the arts; his only real loves were books and his intellectual pursuits.

If Uncle Gordon had sexual desires, as surely he must have had, I have no way of knowing what they were. One has to suspect that there may have been repressed gay desires in his life, as he showed no inclination to marry or have a regular girlfriend. I am sad for my dear uncle if he denied himself sexual fulfilment as the result of moral pressures and constraints. It is easy to forget the abhorrence with which gay sex was viewed by his generation.

He neither liked nor approved of my fashionable, flashy, gambler of a father, but would never have said so. He was also ambivalent about my mother whom he saw as vain, shallow and snobbish. I am sure she bullied him when they were children and had little time for his shy, bookish, ways. He was just a sickly younger brother and a bookworm, an embarrassment to a sexy, socially ambitious older sister.

As time passed, we started to see more of Uncle Gordon and sometimes we would go on holiday with him. He had to be cajoled into spending money on comforts or luxuries. His instinct was, when in a strange city, to buy a map and walk. When it poured with rain, I had to prompt him to hail a taxi. It was not that he was mean, he just didn't think of it. Personal comfort meant so little to him.

After retiring as Chairman and Managing Director of Bassett's, he divided his time between Sheffield and a small bachelor flat in Mayfair. He asked my mother to furnish this dull dark flat that was decorated to look like a Victorian library. It was panelled and book-lined with stained glass windows. He retired in the early 1970s, before the onset of inflation, so his pension became pitifully small. It took some persuading before Cadbury's, the new owners of the business of which he was titular Life President, agreed to buy him a new car to replace his unserviceable old banger. He saved money for both of us boys by paying into a life insurance scheme that matured handsomely on his death.

It had been his custom to return to Sheffield to attend the firm's annual dinner dance. When he was seventy-five Uncle Gordon missed the event for the first time. The new Chairman got up to speak and said that he was sad to announce that Gordon Johnson was unable to attend that year. A groan went up amongst the large assembled company of employees, as they naturally assumed he was sick; Gordon had been a popular and much loved boss. 'The reason he can't be with us today,' said the new Chairman, 'is that he got married yesterday!' There was a gasp of surprise and then the whole room rose to its feet and cheered.

No one was more surprised by this announcement than my family. He was getting married for the first time. His wife, Joan, was a widow whom he had known most of his life. I suspect the idea was largely hers, but the marriage lasted ten years until his death aged eighty-five. They proved to be some of the happiest years of his life. Joan adored him and proved an excellent and loyal wife. They sold the flat in London and bought a house on the Falmouth estuary in Cornwall. Joan was outgoing and social and soon got involved locally. She had two sons by her previous husband. The elder, John, lived nearby in Gorranhaven with his wife and two sons; so, suddenly, Gordon acquired two grandchildren. He grew to love these boys and helped with their education and left them money. It was a delight to see him playing chess with them and talking to them about football. At the close of his selfless life, he was finally experiencing the joys of love and family.

Gransie, Clarice Johnson

My mother's mother lived at 98 Piccadilly above Perkins the chemist. We knew called her 'Gransie'; in her vanity, she thought it sounded less ageing. My friend Michael Fish, the sixties fashion guru and my Greeter

Clarice Johnson (Flack), my grandmother

at the Embassy Club, lived many years later, by coincidence, in the same flat where she died. He loved black men: Gransie would have turned in her grave to think of the antics that went on in her bedroom, or maybe not? She had precipitated her divorce by having an affair with her chauffeur.

I remember Gransie as a stooped old lady with a hunched back and a liking for colourful silk dressing gowns. Her straight hair, flat face and small petite nose accentuated her somewhat Japanese appearance. She covered her thin hair in a net and habitually wore a veil, gloves and hat before venturing out. She smoked constantly, although never inhaling, through a long quill cigarette holder – very 1920s. Smoking to her was a style statement.

She devoured true detective stories and gruesome murder mysteries, a passion she shared with my mother. An outing with my mother to a murder trail at the Old Bailey was, for them, the best form of live enter-tainment. They sat, like *tricoteuses* before the guillotine, to witness the judge don the black cap and pronounce a sentence of death. Mother had some connection with the chief clerk so they always had two of the City Land seats that gave them an excellent view of the accused in the dock.

Like my mother she was, in her old age, increasingly intolerant and critical of her friends. My mother telephoned every morning to listen patiently to her catalogue of complaints. 'I never want to become like my mother,' she vowed: but of course, she did.

Gransie was a frugal Lancashire lass, often walking a mile or more in order to buy vegetables a little more cheaply. Her attitude to servants was typical of her generation; she would ask a prospective servant: 'Are you a nice, clean girl?' (Pronounced, 'gal').

Her picture shows that she had been a beautiful young girl and, like many of the post-First World War generation, was the only one of her three sisters to marry. There was little choice for girls of her generation; most of the men had been killed in the war. She never had to work although she was bright and intelligent. She played bridge well and, like my mother, managed to complete *The Times* crossword every day.

Gransie wasn't in love with her husband Percy Johnson. He was fine looking but cold, rather sexless and very rich. I can see so much of my Uncle Gordon and my brother Rem in the photos I have of him. Hers was a rather ordinary family; her father was a bank manager in Nelson, Lancashire. She was pressurised by her family into accepting the pro-posal from such an eligible bachelor. I am given to believe that she had a number of affairs both before and after her divorce.

Percy, the proprietor of Bassett's Liquorice Allsorts, owned one of the earliest motorcars in Sheffield. Gransie told us that he refused to let the chauffeur leave him alone in the car 'for fear that it might bolt'.

Grandpa Johnson's Daimer, circa 1906

My grandfather Percy died at 71, Park Street, Mayfair on 17 June 1936 and to everyone's shocked surprise left nearly all of his estate, close to a million pounds (worth about £15M today) to a hospital charity with which he had no connection. I believe he did so in order to punish his ex-wife for her infidelity

The Johnson family and their cars, Sheffield, 1925

with the family chauffeur and the resulting acrimonious divorce. My mother and my uncle were mortified. My mother was left only £50,000 in a tight trust that dwindled to just £38,000 when the trust was finally wound-up in 1968.

I fail to understand what visceral hatred must have inspired such a churlish action. Apparently, Grandfather doted on my mother and spoiled her while he was alive. He must have been embittered to hurt his children so deeply after his death. His fortune was hardly his to dispose of, it had been mostly inherited from his father, the real founder of the business. I have been told that it was his solicitor who gave him this advice; the story goes that this solicitor too had experienced a bitter divorce. When he was over eighty, I asked my Uncle Gordon what he would say to his father when they finally met in Heaven? He was not a man much given to humour; he replied, 'I'll ask him how he managed to get in?'

Gransie was stern and formal with us boys; she didn't like children much. She once rebuked me for saying OK. She said it was an unattractive American colloquialism and showed a lack of respect. She became quite angry with me and I couldn't understand what I had done wrong. Neither Rem nor I felt relaxed in her presence and I certainly don't remember her cuddling us or showing us any physical affection. Mother said that she was cold even with her when she was a child.

We went to her flat before taking the train back to school in Eastbourne and the combination of the horrid thought of going back to school combined with the rigidly formal atmosphere of 98 Piccadilly made for unhappy memories. I would stand on the balcony overlooking Green Park and wished I could go and hide amongst the bushes.

THE MAIDEN AUNTS

Gransie's spinster sisters, Mabel and Lucy, lived at 55, Park Lane in a one bedroom flat. They lived together all their lives. Husbands were hard to come by for girls of the First World War generation so many remained spinsters and often chose to live together. (Derek had a similar pair of great aunts called Eleanor and Edith.)

A smart address was clearly all-important to Mabel and Lucy. I think my uncle paid them a generous allowance that was just sufficient to enable them to rent a flat in Park Lane. We were made to visit them once or twice a year.

They were like two pantomime dames. Mabel was the elder of the two and clearly the dominant one. She made the decisions and sweet little Lucy acquiesced. Mabel was the taller and thinner of the two with a tart personality to match, rather like a schoolmarm. We never had a proper conversation; they were wholly unused to children. We just answered a barrage of slightly hostile questions fired at us by Mabel. They both spoke with the remnants of their Lancashire accent overlaid with a faux gentility. They were careful with money, as I am sure they needed to be. I remember being rather shocked at having to share a boiled egg with Rem at teatime. This was probably a hangover from food rationing. They behaved like a married couple and I think they even shared a bed.

NANNY: ROSAMUND BROWNE

Nanny was a constant source of uncritical love and devotion. I was the younger son by two and a half years, her baby. How she worshipped me and how I loved her simple soul and her constant spoiling attentions. 'Make haste,' she would say, or 'Less said soonest mended.' She had a stock of nursery phrases for every occasion, but her love was real, tender and warm. I was her baby, being but a few months old when she joined the family.

Nanny was barely five foot tall; she had suffered badly from rickets as a child and it showed in her bandy legs. Her hair was thin and straight, parted on one side and held back by a cheap Kirby grip; she could never afford more than an occasional visit to a hairdresser. She wore little make-up and looked best in plain skirts and cardigans. She possessed a homely simplicity perfectly in tune with her calling. She smelt of soap and warm water, baby powder and milky drinks. I liked her best like this; I didn't care for it when, on a few occasions, she dressed-up and wore cheap scent and imitation pearls. She desperately wanted to be thought middle-class and even invented a childhood in Bath as the daughter of a rector. We discovered that her origins were much more humble, the daughter of a bricklayer in the East End of London. I welcomed the rough caress of her calloused hands misshapen by arthritis but, above all, I bathed in the depth of her love for me that radiated from her simple smile.

Unfortunately, she was unable to disguise her preference in favour of me over my elder brother. My mother was the same but in more subtle and therefore, perhaps, more wounding ways. My elder brother, Rem, was bright and picked up on these differences from a very early age. I have no doubt that these things affected him; it certainly impaired our relationship. I can see in him the same emotional reserve of both my uncle and grandmother: he was incapable of kissing Mummy with true passion – as though he really meant it.

Nanny remained with us after we had gone to boarding school. She became our cook and housekeeper, but she was always called Nanny. It was a while before I realised that children from less privileged families called their grandmothers 'nanna'; I rather assumed they all had nannies just like me.

Nanny started to become unwell just about the time I left for university. She was scared of seeing a doctor. I think she knew she was very sick. We tried to get her to go to the doctor, but she became angry and upset when the matter was raised. Eventually, her health collapsed and so did she. She was diagnosed with advanced cervical cancer. Her last days were harrowing and her suffering prolonged. My brother Rem and I would visit her in hospital and sit by her bedside and hold her hand. She kept our photographs on her bedside chest of drawers and bored all the nurses about her boys and how wonderful we were.

Nanny died in 1970 in the French Hospital in Shaftsbury Avenue and we buried her next to my grandmother in the little churchyard in the tiny hamlet where we lived in Buckinghamshire. I was very saddened by her death.

Chapter Two

❦ ISLE OF MAN – 1954–58

For a few years in the 1950s, when I was between seven and ten, we lived on the Isle of Man. My parents decided to move there to save income tax. My mother's small trust fund income was subject to super tax at over 80% and dwindling fast. The decision was a poor one for my parents, who spent as much as they saved in tax on hotels and airfares travelling back and forth to the mainland. Our modest house was rented. Called *Couill Vane* – Manx for windy corner – it was an unattractive, pebbledash, detached, suburban villa just outside Douglas on the road to Onchan.

It was a disastrous move for my parents socially; they lost touch with many of their smart London friends. We children adored the holiday atmosphere and wide range of exciting adventurous things to do, from sea fishing to riding the horse trams on the front. The Island was a world of Celtic superstition. Little people, the local pixies, had to be saluted with 'Good luck little men' as you passed over Balaugh Bridge on the road into town from the airport. There were mountains and glens, majestic sandy beaches at Jurby with exciting sand cliffs to slide down. The climate was atrocious, always raining, and the island was often shrouded in mist. The locals said it was the cloak of the god, Manin, hiding the island from view.

We made few local friends; we were never there for long enough but we did have mainland friends to stay. The three or four years spent living on the island were largely happy ones for us children; a world of ice cream and seaside fun. Boats entranced me even then; particularly one Edwardian steam packet that had four funnels, which I felt must be superior to the modern ones that boasted only a single funnel and looked plain by comparison.

My father, ever resourceful and inventive, organised unusual outings to keep us boys amused. At least once a year we would go on a fishing trip for mackerel and pollack. We caught them in large numbers on hand lines, often four at a time. We also caught garfish, those thin fast predators with a green skeleton, on spinning rods. I remember the knarled old fisherman who took us out, his weather beaten unshaven face and his gruff, kindly manner but especially the sweet honey smell of his pipe tobacco. Smells are so redolent of childhood.

The coastline of the island was unspoiled: rendered dramatic by wild sheer cliffs and the call of sea birds wheeling on the thermals and diving into the rough waters to catch the small fry. I saw puffins and seals for the first time. I was fascinated and a bit scared by a whirlpool that appeared at certain states of the tide between the main island and the Calf of Man. In my wild imaginings, I thought we would be sucked under into a watery grave. We returned ladened with fish. We helped the captain gut the fish on the way back to port, throwing the entrails to the flock of gulls and terns that followed us home, gorging themselves on this unexpected bounty.

My father arranged for us to spend a day aboard a private yacht belonging to a Mrs Cubbin. Although tied up in port, we spent a day on board helping to repaint her bulwarks. We both thought that was glamorous and fun.

On another occasion, he organised for us to have a trip aboard an RAF motor rescue vessel, a fast MTB that patrolled the Irish Sea looking for any downed pilots from the Jurby RAF station. This was exhilarating, but quite how it was organised I will never know. I suppose my father still had contacts in the RAF from his wartime service.

The island was full of magical places for children, empty stretches of long sandy beaches, hidden glens and the huge Laxey water mill wheel. There were, and maybe still are, horse drawn trams on the front at Douglas; the last remaining in the British Isles harking back to the days of working-class trippers who came from the Lancashire cotton mills for holidays in Wakes Week.

Those days after the war were still grey and austere. My parents suspected that ice cream sold by small travelling vendors was contaminated, so we were only allowed to eat 'Walls' ice cream. Chewing gum was banned and soft drinks limited, I don't remember drinking Coca-Cola, only a disgusting brew called Vimto and fizzy lemonade.

Roller-skating was the latest craze and we would take over the local rink one morning a week for private lessons, sometimes with a few friends. This was a highlight of each week. We were allowed to roller skate on the asphalt at school so being able to skate backwards and perform other tricks gave us considerable kudos.

We made our own fun; we put on plays and charged our family a small admission charge to see them. We played detective and war games. Our imagination was fed by a continuous diet of picture comics mostly in black and white, but the art work was, in my opinion, every bit as good as any Roy Lichtenstein. I remember the excitement of a new comic that was launched in the 1950s called the *Eagle*. It featured a space hero called Dan Dare and his sidekick Digby and their arch enemy the Mekon, an alien with an oversized head. It was an attempt at a more intelligent and less violent comic and proved a firm favourite across the nation. It has now become a classic with its early issues fetching substantial sums of money.

We boys lived in the worlds of our imagination. We did not have endless toys. We had Hornby 00 electric trains and a Meccano set to build things but most of the time we played outdoors and invented our own adventures. Plastic model aeroplanes assembled with glue were another favourite and we spent hours inexpertly trying to assemble Fokker Triplanes and Spitfires. We tended to put the wings on crooked and the models soon fell to bits. The glue smelled rather nice and we did attempt a bit of sniffing. Of course, we all wore shapeless grey flannel shorts with elastic snake belts and a sweater with a coloured V-neck and a blazer for special occasions. The traditional uniform of the pre-war middle-class little boy: no jeans or trainers for us back then.

Our house was fortuitously situated directly on the route of the motorcycle TT (Tourist Trophy) course. The annual TT motorcycle races were a much longed-for highlight of the summer. We loved to sit in the window and watch the practice laps and races that started noisily early in the morning. I well remember the smell of the burning motorcycle oil that filled the air and the high-throated roar of the racing

Author, Rem and Sally Curzon

machines as they tore down the straight in front of our house. The bikes were the fastest in the world and famous names like John Surtees were our heroes. The TT course was on normal roads round the island, closed off for the event and for the practice days before hand. Quite how people got around with so many of the Island's roads closed to traffic I have no idea. The men who rode the bikes seemed like gods and super heroes, although somewhat sinister in their black leathers and helmets.

One incident from childhood sticks in my mind. I must have been about eleven years old. A friend from school, a boy called Crawford Gordon, came to stay with his parents who were to my eyes deeply glamorous. His stepfather, Eric Maschwitz, was the lyricist of the classic songs, *A Nightingale Sung in Berkeley Square* and *These Foolish Things*. His mother, a dazzlingly beautiful woman, was the owner of a night-club in Mayfair. Her sophistication and poise captivated me and formed a lasting impression. Even at that tender age, I yearned to become, like her, a nightclub owner. An ambition conceived at a tender age but which was nurtured and grew in my soul and was later to be dramatically realised through the Embassy Club and Heaven.

We children were sad to leave this holiday paradise, but our parents were only too happy to return to the more sophisticated world of London and the mainland.

Chapter Three

✹ St Andrew's School, Eastbourne – 1955–59

At prep school in the 1950s the world map was red and the British Empire covered a third of the globe. The Empire was still much admired, even though India had gained independence in 1947. Harold Macmillan's 'wind of change' had not yet reached Africa or the smaller colonies. Southern Rhodesia had still to be granted the new constitution that was to preserve white domination until UDI in 1968.

The school library had acquired few additions since the war, so our fiction was limited to Biggles, G.A. Henty and Harrison Ainsworth. It is interesting to remember that in the 1950s the First World War was far closer in time than the Second World War is now. My father had fought in the first war and it was recent history to us all.

St Andrew's bore a marked resemblance to Llanaba School as depicted in Evelyn Waugh's novel *Decline and Fall*. The headmaster was Mr Liddell, reputedly a relation of Alice Liddell of *Alice in Wonderland* fame: his interests were an easy life, gin and horses. He was a bluff outgoing man with little or no sympathy for the boys in his charge. My mother told me that if she rang up to inquire about our welfare after nine at night he was invariably the worse for drink. He lived with Mrs Liddell on the private side of the large rambling mansion that was the school; nestled into the side of the South Downs in the little seaside village of Meads, a suburb of Eastbourne.

The winters were so cold and the heating so inadequate that all the boys suffered from chilblains and boils. We slept in dormitories under thick blankets often wearing our woolly Jaeger dressing gowns in bed to keep warm at night.

There was often a sexual frisson in the dorms; nudity, playing at doctors and nurses, flicking bare bums with wet towels and other such games. Many of us had crushes on other boys. I befriended a boy called Julian Cazalet, my first crush. The adult notion that pre-pubertal boys are non-sexual is wrong. There were dorm dares such as running to the end of the corridor naked, hoping that neither master nor matron would catch you.

The boys played team games such as French and English, where two sides would attempt to cross a space trying to avoid being touch-tagged by an opponent. There were midnight feasts and dorm rags. The world of Billy Bunter was alive and well at St Andrew's. No attempt was made to curb bullying and there were some truly beastly boys who made life hell for me.

In Summer, we roller-skated on the asphalt, walked on the Sussex downs where I collected the characteristic insects of the chalk downland such as the bloody nose beetle and the beautiful privet hawk moth. I captured a pair of moths in the act of mating and the female laid hundreds of bright green eggs. They hatched into pretty green striped caterpillars, which in turn pupated and metamorphosed into beautiful moths. By a strange coincidence, they were the same colours as the school tie; purple, pink and bright green.

The grassy banks with their lofty elm trees lay behind the playing fields but inside the stout flint walls that bounded the school grounds. The long grass was out-of-bounds; but this did not stop me spending hours lying there daydreaming or collecting insects.

Like most gay boys, I was hopeless at ball games and especially at catching – I couldn't catch for toffee. Cricket was a trial and a bore; a time for daydreaming while lazing in deep field, hoping and praying the ball wouldn't come my way.

I was an emotional and sensitive child, very afraid of physical pain. I hated discomfort. I was eager to please which meant that I became rather a mamma's boy, not calculated to make me popular with others my own age. I lived my schooldays in constant fear of being beaten although I seldom risked doing anything naughty enough to merit it.

I can only remember being beaten once. I was involved in a dorm pillow fight; no doubt we were all in high spirits and making a noise, but it was the last day of term and we were going home for the holidays. Mr Harrison or 'Harry', an especially aggressive red-faced master whom I loathed, stormed into the dorm and headed straight for me. He boxed me hard around the face until I cried, took me by the ear, dragged me howling along the corridor to a side room, pulled down my pyjama bottoms, put me over his knee and spanked me hard with his bare hand. I don't know what made him so very angry. I think he just didn't like me and wanted to make me cry.

There were, of course, happy times. I longed for the holidays and Nanny's home cooking. I loved our seaside summer holidays with hours spent messing around in boats or on bicycles, with butterfly net and collecting box or just dreaming the hours away on warm summer days. I lived in my world of dreams and fantasy.

I made up stories for my own amusement and, for a while at prep school, gained a reputation as a storyteller in the dorm after lights out. I didn't have the personality or talent to be witty or amusing, so often a ruse of inadequate boys to make themselves popular. I regret that no one introduced me to music or fine art and I did not grow to love either serious music or poetry until after leaving school. Either would have provided inspiration and consolation to a lonely young boy. The prep school world I grew up in was manly, philistine and uncultured, unchanged in any material way from the boarding schools of the pre-war era.

I was conscious that I was somehow different from other boys, more delicate and fastidious, not interested in or good at games but removed from the others by aspirations and longings as yet undefined.

About this time, I developed an interest in maps and atlases that remains with me to this day. I loved the multi-coloured visual texture of them; I spent hours pouring over maps of distant places marvelling at the exotic names. Perhaps I fancied myself taking a boat up the Orinoco or visiting Blantyre, which I knew to be the capital of Nyasaland. There was so much romance in all these strange names and distant exotic places. I was given an old map of the Andaman Islands on a piece of silk. I revered it as though it were a rare map leading to a cache of buried treasure. I wondered how the boundaries of countries came to be just where they were, and I was and still am, especially intrigued by enclaves of one country that are outliers completely surrounded by a different state. I had an excellent knowledge of geography and a good memory for names and places. I suppose it was all a strange form of daydreaming and fantasising.

I had always thought that my fascination with isolated islands, colonial hangovers and enclaves was a sort of strange affliction unique to me. I have since learned that are a few other fellow sufferers. This is not some shameful, sad pastime like train spotting but an interest engendered by a vivid childhood imagination. I spent hours pouring over maps and atlases, wondering what these tiny specks of land were like and how they came to exist. I had a romantic interest in small independent states, although by now they were few in number. I thought the world, and especially Europe, the poorer for their demise. I learned with horror that San Marino had a communist government. My faith in Ruritania was shattered. What on earth was the point of a tiny pocket state if it could not boast a Grand Duke or at least a Prince-Bishop to perform high mass in a Baroque cathedral bedecked with gold chalices and high renaissance art? I fondly imagined the aforementioned Prince-Bishop hosting lavish banquets in his palace with incomparably beautiful altar boys as servitors dressed in yards of Brussels Lace. This seemed to me to be the only redeeming feature for the Papacy. I then learned that San Marino had, of all things, a football team; henceforth it ceased to exist as far as I was concerned. Colonial enclaves were decidedly more reliable. Surely they must boast at least a governor in a tricorn hat with feathers and gold braid on his dress uniform and a retinue of handsome young officers performing endless parades and arcane ceremonials in the courtyard of an old fort? The comedy film, *The Mouse that Roared*, was the embodiment of my childhood dreams. I could not understand what benefits were to be had from a headlong rush into the Risorgimento. Both Italy and Germany were immeasurably better off and safer as a collection of hundreds of principalities and city-states. The imagination of a gay child is wonderfully inventive and always intensely romantic.

At a dinner party in San Francisco recently, I learnt that a landscape designer friend, Stephen Suzman – a relative of the brave and pugnacious Helen who fought Apartheid – shared my interest in enclaves and knew all about Livia, an enclave of Spain in France, and Busingen, an enclave of Germany in Switzerland, and many other discoveries. Later, on reading Matthew Parris' autobiography and then sitting next to him at dinner, I learnt that he too shares our arcane interest. I suppose it's all a form of daydreaming and fantasizing. Whereas Matthew is adventurous and actually wants to visit these places, I dislike discomfort and have no wish to destroy my imaginings with stark reality. I am content to read about and research my finds and collect them like stamps. Never one for roughing it, my idea of slumming is drinking champagne out of a tumbler.

Many of the masters were decidedly more interested in their charges than was quite proper. They varied from the kind and gentle French master, Mr Eric Sier, to the truly terrifying bullies, Mr JIC Dent and Mr Harrison, or 'Sos' and 'Harry' as they were nicknamed. Harry, the man who had beaten me, was my particular hate. He was like an angry bull when roused. He had sparse reddish hair that seemed to stand on end when he was furious. In my memory, he never smiled and we all lived in fear of his irrational temper that could erupt without much warning. Mr Farley, the music master, never thought to play us any classical music. I think I only learnt to play the triangle. The poor man lost his job after he was arrested in a public lavatory in town.

Mr B… was probably still in his twenties although he seemed ancient to us. We were impressed with his knowledge of German, and taught us to say *hande hoch* (hands up) and other phrases that gave a certain air of realism to our endless war games. His preferred game involved putting his hands up the shorts of little boys while marking their work. We didn't really mind but we would have preferred if he hadn't. I think if any adult had found out and made a fuss the damage to us would have been far greater than the mild displeasure we felt at being touched up in this way. The masters were nearly all, I think, pederastically inclined but far too nervous to force themselves on boys who were not co-operative. The fact that they were rather too fond of the boys made an otherwise underpaid and thankless job tolerable and probably made them better and more caring masters. The same could not be said of the sadistic ones.

In common with all such establishments of that period the teaching was perfunctory and science almost non-existent. The lab equipment was ancient, left over from pre-war days and it was all broken or had bits missing. Latin prep was compulsory every night after the age of eleven. Sports were all important and home comforts and edible food absent. Like Evelyn Waugh, and those of his generation, we were also always cold and hungry. We still used a traditional slang based on Latin, such as 'cave' meaning beware when a master approached and 'quis' when someone wanted to give away something, followed by a shout of 'ego' by the boy who wanted to claim it. In spite of all this Latin, I still had trouble passing my O-level exam at Harrow. The teaching was universally uninspiring, learning was mostly by rote or instilled by fear, but we got a good grounding in all the basics. The dead languages were taught as if they had never lived.

Mr Bryan, the Latin master, had his own method of getting you to remember Latin Grammar. 'What, boy', he would say, 'is the difference between the active and passive tenses?' If you got the answer wrong, he was only too happy to demonstrate with a hard swipe of the ruler on an open hand, 'That is active and the pain you feel boy, is passive': Boy did it smart!

The only sport I liked was shooting, but the fact the range was the province of the hated Mr Dent meant that I went out of my way to avoid being noticed, even there. Mr Dent was nearly bald, red-faced and unfriendly; he was one of the few masters that did not have a prurient interest in his charges.

I buried myself in my own world of natural history and particularly the micro world of insects and butterfly collecting. I loved to idle away summer afternoon out of bounds, smelling the cut hay and listening to the distant sound of boys' voices and the sound of ball against bat, secure in the knowledge I did not have to catch or field anything. My focus on a few square inches of grass or the peeled back bark of an ancient elm tree and the insects they contained. I shared this passion with another misfit, John Scarman, son of the soon-to-be-famous Judge of the appeal court, Lord Scarman, and his sweet, gentle wife Ruth.

I left St Andrew's school early, in 1959, and attended a crammer in London (Davies, Lang & Dick) as a day boy in order to concentrate on my studies for the Common Entrance exam for Harrow. I rather enjoyed the break from the rigid discipline and horrors of prep school. Living at home again, eating Nanny's delicious home cooking, was bliss.

Chapter Four

❊ LONDON AND FAMILY – 1958 ONWARDS

After the age of eleven, and on our return from the Isle of Man, the family lived in a mansion flat in Carlisle Place, Victoria in the centre of London, close to the eponymous railway station. We boys had few friends of our own age except in the summer when we stayed with family friends at the seaside. The standards my mother instilled in me hindered my emotional development and made me appear old-fashioned and priggish to my schoolboy contemporaries; not helpful in my quest to be accepted and make friends.

London in the 1950s and early 1960s was a dirty city full of bombsites, buildings blackened with the soot of coal fires, smog and steam trains. The gas lamps in our street were still lit each night by a man on a bicycle with a long pole. There were periodic pea-souper fogs when you could hardly see a hand in front of you and many old people died from breathing the sulphurous fumes. I remember the cry of the rag and bone man as he came down our street in his horse-drawn cart, shades of Wilfred Bramble in the television comedy, *Steptoe & Son*.

The bombsites were overgrown with buddleias; rosebay willow herb and other wild flowers that attracted insects, especially butterflies, and they in turn encouraged the bird life. The evening skies were shrill with the calls of the thousands of sparrows and starlings that wheeled and turned in unison on their way to roost in Trafalgar Square and Whitehall. It was a city of drab uniform people wearing shapeless clothes and eating disgusting overcooked food. It always seemed to be wet and raining. London was a city of mackintoshes and umbrellas. Countless pigeons fed off the wasteland, as well as human rubbish. Children and visitors fed the pigeons in Trafalgar Square, so all the buildings were defaced with bird excrement.

Restaurants hardly existed. People ate in cafés, pubs or hotels, and gentlemen at their clubs. Fast food outlets did not exist unless you count eel and pie shops or Lyon's Corner House. Men wore bowler hats to work and carried rolled umbrellas come rain or shine. Everything seemed damaged or decayed, rather like the London portrayed in old black and white movies. When we were little boys we lunched at the Grosvenor Hotel at Victoria railway station, eating the hotel food of the times: soup, grey roast meat and two vegetables, followed by a steamed pudding, before catching the school train to Eastbourne.

We would often spend the day with Gransie at 98, Piccadilly, in her flat overlooking Green Park, before departure for school. Gransie's maid, an ugly fat German girl called Miss Gruby, fed us sausages and sauerkraut and taught us to sing and yodel, 'I love to go a wandering, with a knapsack on my back.' My grandmother was not kind to her. I don't know why she stayed; she was treated so badly: rather like my mother was to do with her own staff in her later years. My mother vowed that she would never become like her mother who fell out with all her friends by being hypercritical of their behaviour or punctuality. Of course, that is exactly what she did. As Oscar Wilde observed, 'all women become like their mothers, that is their misfortune'.

We watched TV for the first time at the Coronation but we were fortunate to be able to watch some of the procession from Gransie's balcony overlooking Piccadilly on the route of the royal procession. Like most children, we were giving little metal painted models of the coronation coach and commemorative coffee mugs. We waived our union flags enthusiastically from the balcony as the procession passed by.

My parents disapproved of all things American, from pushy mothers to chewing gum and comics. We were hardly ever allowed to watch television at home and when an American friend brought us a huge box of gum we had to write a thank-you letter, but the gum was immediately consigned to the waste bin. My mother particularly thought all Americans uncivilised and pushy and not quite 'our class'. It definitely made her feel superior to have others to look down on.

Chapter Five

❦ MEMORIES OF FATHER IN LONDON

I remember walking with my father and mother through the streets of Mayfair one day in about 1958. I think I must have been eleven years old. A motorcade of large black cars approached flanked by outriders. My father's looks darkened as he realised that the occupants of the leading car were none other than Bulganin and Krushchev, 'B&K', the Russian leaders currently on a state visit. In a highly uncharacteristic but instinctive action, Daddy stepped out into the street ahead of the leading car and raised his right hand in a classic V sign, making his revulsion and disapproval clear to the occupants of the car. My mother was horrified at such a display of vulgarity but at the same time, I think, secretly rather proud and supportive of my father's action. He had developed a particularly visceral hatred for Russian Communism as a result of his time spent in Russia during the war with our military mission. Unlike so many of his generation he was in absolutely no doubt as to the evil nature of Russian Communism and the pain and horrors it had visited upon its own people. The examples he saw of their inexorable cruelty, not only to others, but to their own people had made him their implacable enemy.

I knew little of my father's life or friends because he died when I was just eleven. I knew he was a businessman and what today would be called an entrepreneur. After the war he was tired and ill and had lost whatever financial acumen he had undoubtedly once had. He did not have much money with which to gamble on any new ventures anyway. For a while, he rented a small office in Ryder St in St James's. I collected exam-

My father, shortly before his death

ples of his office stationery and forms and used them to play at being an important business executive.

At the nearby Carlton Club, my father would park us with the hall porter, Bonner, who was always kind and gave us little treats. I met my Uncle Donald there, Father's older brother, for the first and only time. He pressed a warm half-a-crown into the palm of my hand and patted me on the head, as older men are apt to do when patronising the young. (It seems, on reflection, that there are many parallels with my relationship with my brother, Rem, who is similarly two years older than I.) My father had always avoided him and treated him with reserve.

Father was always devising interesting things for us to see and do, such as an expedition to a Fleet Street newspaper being printed; probably one of Lord Camrose's stable of titles. I realised, even at that age, the importance of advertising revenue as opposed to cover price. Reasoning correctly that a paper could not make money from the cover price alone. I remember making this observation to the man who was showing us around. He was quite taken-aback by such a remark from one so young.

Once we went behind the scenes at the Zoo and actually walked into the enclosure of a brown bear on the Mappin Terraces. I have a photo of me in my Sunday best with my arm round an orangutan and his extra long arm around me. During a visit to the areas behind the displays at the reptile house I noticed a lizard dash across the floor. I gave chase and caught it in my hands, much to the surprise of the keeper. In the reptile house I cradled a baby alligator and had a boa constrictor placed round my neck. I felt very special and privileged.

Father organised a trip down the river on a police launch. The police radio sprang to life with talk of a dead body floating downstream by Rotherhithe. We children felt we were participating in a real life drama. The docks looked decayed and the East End seemed to us another world from a bygone era in a pre-war black and white gangster film.

MASCULINITY AND FEMININITY

From the age of about six I became aware that I was different from other boys and that my loneliness had something to do with my lack of masculinity. I sensed I had a more pronounced feminine side to my make up. Not that I would have known much about this as, apart from Mummy and Nanny, girls hardly featured at all in my life. When they did feature, I didn't like them much. I did not seem to fit in well in the company of either boys or girls. It is not that I wanted to play with dolls and certainly not with girls. I actually liked solitary manly pursuits like shooting and fishing, but I was aware that girls did not like me much and that they were somehow rivals for the affection and attention of the handsome boys whom I so much wanted to befriend. I did like some girly things like clothes and play-acting with puppets and I had an especial fascination for soft and silky material. This I discovered early at Harrow when I became captivated by the smell of a boy's sweat on his shiny nylon shirt; the smell was intensely erotic as was the feel of the silky fabric.

As I grew up, I felt my feminine side keenly and was aware that it was something of which I was meant to feel ashamed. Part of me also saw girls as rivals for the attentions of the boys I longed to spend time with; creatures with the unfair advantages of being able to make themselves prettier and more desirable with clothes, make-up and jewellery. I never did understand why male was considered so superior to female and why feminine qualities were so wrong in a boy, but I knew I had to hide any trace of them for fear of ridicule and exposure. I felt keenly the shame I knew my father felt for my lack of masculinity.

Like other gay men before me, awareness dawned on me that there were things I might do or say or gestures that I might inadvertently make that could give the game away. I came to be guarded in my speech and actions lest my femininity should peep through. I consciously deepened my voice well before it broke and made sure I could not sing so wouldn't get roped into the treble section of the choir, which I felt

would be deeply shameful. I would have loved to wear a surplice and a ruffle and to be admired by other boys, but I daren't risk it. I longed to wear a kilt on Sundays as the Scots' boys were allowed to do, but did not have had the courage to ask; I knew there was something not quite right or proper in my interest in boys in kilts; another facet of the real me that had to be rigorously suppressed and hidden from view.

With a friend at London Zoo

Chapter Six

✹ LORD HOWE, 'F' AND ALDEBURGH – 1956–60

From about 1957 onward, we took summer holidays in Aldeburgh, Suffolk with close family friends, The 5th Earl and Countess of Howe (Francis and Sybil) and their children, including their youngest daughter Lady Sarah (Sally) Curzon. The Curzon family owned most of Curzon Street and Shepherd Market in Mayfair, an area notorious for prostitution in the 1950s. My father, much given to scurrilous and wicked rhymes, taught me – aged ten – my first naughty limerick: *When Lady Jane became a tart, it nearly broke the old Earl's heart; but blood is blood and race is race, and so to save the family face, he bought her the most expensive beat on the sunny side of Curzon Street.*

Needless to say, Lady Sarah did not become a tart but went on to marry John Aspinall the gambler; key member of the Lord 'Lucky' Lucan set. She became the chatelaine of Howletts. Before this second marriage, she was widowed tragically at a young age when her dashing and glamorous husband, Piers Courage, was killed in a motor racing accident.

My first meeting with Sybil and Francis Howe was when, dressed in our Sunday best, we were taken for lunch at their magnificent town house in Curzon Street – which later became Aspinall's Curzon House casino. I seem to recall it had a lift, which impressed me greatly, and in the grand entrance hall was a perfect scale model of an 18th-century

Sally, Sybil Howe and Author at Aldeburgh

man-o'-war of the type made by Napoleonic prisoners: correct in every minute detail down to the carved figurehead, the gun ports and black threads for the rigging. Lord Howe was the descendent of Admiral, Earl Howe the victor in the famous naval battle against the French in 1794 on The Glorious First of June.

The old Earl, 'F.', born in 1884, had been a racing

driver in the days of the Brooklands racetrack before the War. I seem to recall seeing a film clip in which he is lined up at the start only to disappear backward at the drop of the chequered flag. His love of fast cars was to remain with him. He adored his younger daughter, Sally, who was about five years older than me and was the only child still living at home. Sally was an afterthought, the child of a much older father, rather as we were. F. worshipped and spoilt her. I remember, at the luncheon at Curzon Street, that he dangled her on his knee and lovingly poured silver coins down her back inside her dress, making her squeal with delight. My mother was a close friend of F.'s wife, Sybil, a rather terrifying *grande dame* with very meaty thighs encased in large mesh stockings and a possessing a deep manly voice.

We got to know the family better during three or four years of extended summer holidays, staying with them. Their holiday house, Aldeburgh Court Cottage, was surprisingly modest but with a large paved forecourt. It must have been larger than I remember as it managed to accommodate F. and his wife Sybil, their daughter Sally and, I presume her Nanny, both of us and our parents and our Nanny. In addition, Sybil had two older daughters by her former husband, Ernest Shafto, (A descendent of Bonny Bobby Shafto who according to the sea shanty, 'went to sea with silver buckles on his knee'). Anne, the pretty one, was so kind and gentle with a divine smile that I fell for her in the way a small boy can for a glamorous teenage girl who mothers him. She had a large and boisterous older sister, Susan, whom my father nicknamed 'Trinny' after St Trinian's – the fictional academy for wayward girls depicted by the cartoonist, Ronald Seale.

Sally was closer to my brother's age. We played together and went boating on the Mere, a shallow muddy lake dotted with small islands in the nearby seaside village of Thorpeness. We were always getting into trouble for teasing Sally and splashing her with mud, which inevitably reduced her to girlish tears. We cycled everywhere but old F. was too over-protective of his adored younger daughter. We thought her a frightful sissy, as she was never allowed to climb trees or join us on our more reckless boyish adventures.

One day there was great excitement at the house: F. was taking delivery of a brand new car. The splendid futuristic beast arrived in the driveway, making a deep throated and expensive growl. Its doors lifted up like the wings of a bird; it looked as if it could fly away. I now know that it was one of the first gull-wing Mercedes two-seater sports cars. The year was probably 1959. These cars are now rare collector's items fetching hundred's of thousand's of pounds at auction.

After a couple of years, we graduated to our own small holiday cottage, Mizpah on Crag Path, rented from the Duke of St Albans. We saw less of the Curzon family and we boys sought out male friends of our own age. One of them I remember was called Rattle and I guess he must have been either Simon Rattle the conductor, or a perhaps a brother; the family lived in Aldeburgh.

Our family was not in the least musical. I don't ever remember classical music being played at home. My mother loved American show tunes and friends in New York sent her long-playing records of the latest Broadway hits. These left me cold. I missed out on that particular gay gene, always preferring history and adventure to romantic musicals which I found stilted and unconvincing; my fantasies were all in my head. My brother was later to develop a taste for classical music but where he first heard it, I can't imagine, certainly not at home. The first classical record I ever heard entranced me. It was an 78 rpm vinyl of *Die Fledermaus* which one of the masters at school played on a wind-up gramophone. I thought it the most moving and romantic thing I had ever heard. I think it was a pity that we were never exposed to good music, poetry or fine art as children. Both our parents, and most certainly all of our schools, were distinctly philistine.

Another friend was called Pin Ingre; at least that is how it sounded, I have no memory of how it was spelt. Our mothers were friends: she was either widowed or divorced so the family spent a great deal of time with us. We boys spent hours cycling on rusty old bikes hired from Mr Ede's sports shop in the High Street and doing all the usual things that pre-teen boys get up to. We used to sneak into the cinema through the exit to watch the matinees. Sometimes we got into trouble by shooting out the streetlights on the Front with our air rifle.

My happiest memories of Aldeburgh were, as so often with me then, solitary ones. Days spent with a butterfly net in the wild areas behind the beach, on the long road to Thorpeness, amongst the rushes and grasses chasing magpie moths, orange tips, painted ladies and the beautiful five spot Burnett moths. I had at last found an interest at which I could excel and one that fitted well with my solitary nature, my cataloguing mind and my appreciation of natural beauty.

These were idyllic times. I first became aware of the beauty of the English countryside in high summer. I remember the wealth of wild flowers and the butterflies and beetles that inhabited them. In my mind's eye, nature was much richer in those days and insects of all sorts more numerous and varied. Natural history, and especially entomology, became my passion. I collected avidly and spent hours pouring over

(from left) Rem, Daddy, Ernest Shafto, Sybil Howe, Sally Curzon and Francis Howe

books identifying my finds. What a bore I must have been to others, especially my long-suffering family. I longed for pets, but had to make do with crabs, lizards and caterpillars, most of which died quickly and odoriferously in my inexperienced hands. At that time, I thought I wanted to become a naturalist or possibly a vet.

One sour note was my uneasy relationship with my brother, Rem. We were always arguing. It must have been so difficult for my mother having to deal with two boys who didn't get along. We went for a long cycle ride one day, just the two of us. Rem's bike was of course larger than mine. As it had a high cross-bar, it was impossible for me to ride. We had a blazing row that ended in a fight and Rem rode off on my bike, leaving me with his. I was such a little goody-goody that I wheeled his heavy bike all the way home, instead of leaving it and walking back alone.

On one occasion, Gransie came to stay and as the house was too small for us all, we were put in a nearby hotel with Nanny. We made so much noise during one of our periodic rows that the manager asked us to leave. I seemed to be following the pattern set by my father and as I was to discover, his father, in not getting on well with my older brother.

CHAPTER SEVEN

✖ THE SCARMANS AND SALCOMBE, DEVON – 1960–63

At St Andrew's School, there was no one to help advise or encourage me with my insect-collecting hobby except my only friend, another misfit, John Scarman, the son of the Judge. I can only recall with difficulty his first name, John, as it was not customary to use first names; we were always Norman and Scarman. He and I became firm friends. We spent hours together roaming the long grass with butterfly net in hand and insect-collecting bottles at the ready.

John was a misfit for completely different reasons. He was exotic, dark, Latin-looking and physically mature for his age. He claimed to have had sex with a girl when aged eleven. I think he may indeed have done so, as by then he already needed to shave. He seemed from another planet and he had no interest in any of the other boys or in sport. He did not excel academically and was always being caught doing something wrong, like being out of bounds or smoking. He was a disappointment to his father and was to remain so.

Young John Scarman was in one way a highly suitable friend for me. His father, 'Hats' as we called him, had been at St Andrew's with my uncle and so was already a family friend of longstanding, who shared my uncle's academic and bookish pursuits. I thought of him as the father I no longer had. He was always kind and gentle with us boys. Like my uncle, I never remember him getting cross or shouting at us. For the first time I experienced normal family life.

My mother got on well with Ruth Scarman and, after our Aldeburgh days, we spent many a family holiday together at Salcombe. Ruth was highly attractive and clearly had a sensual nature, in contrast to Leslie who was all brain and little emotion. He appeared cold and asexual as a man but was warm-hearted and fatherly to us children. I believe that it possible that their marriage was a marriage of convenience, rather than a passionate love match.

The Scarmans had a house on Batson creek, a highly scenic branch of the main tidal estuary. The dense woodland came right down to the sea with few buildings to spoil the natural shoreline. Small boats lay at anchor on swinging moorings in the estuary or were tied up alongside the small stone quay. The fields were small and hilly, broken up by dense mixed hedgerows resplendent with wild flowers in summer. As often in the West Country, the lanes were narrow and steep sided, their banks pungent with the smell of wild garlic and cuckoo pint. The fields and woods were a young naturalist's paradise.

John and I spent hours messing about in boats, fishing or roaming the countryside collecting butterflies and moths. while puffing away on illicit cigarettes behind hedgerows. We had air guns and sheath knives. We were thoroughly bloodthirsty outdoor little boys. We collected adders that we placed in the bath and then put grass snakes in with them to encourage fights. We would proudly display the adder skins on our knife sheaths as badges of our bravery and prowess, but our friendship had no real basis in compatibility and did not long survive our prep school days.

I followed my uncle to Harrow. John Scarman failed common entrance and so did not follow his father to Radley. Instead, he was sent to the progressive co-educational school not far from Salcombe, Dartington Hall, where the pupils could practice free love and not attend lessons if they did not want to – and surprise, surprise, they mostly didn't.

Leslie Scarman became a renowned Justice of Appeal and shot to national prominence when he chaired the inquiry into the Brixton race

Lord Scarman

riots. He was known as a liberal but after becoming an appeal judge, his judgements disappointed the liberal cause. He denied the appeal of *Gay News* and its editor, Dennis Lemon, who had been convicted of blasphemy; a charge not heard of in the English courts for over a hundred years and thought by most jurists to be moribund. The conviction and the costs of defending the action bankrupted the only British national gay newspaper. I could not help but regard his judgement as a betrayal of liberalism. I could not understand how a man who had so sympathised with the blacks in Brixton could deliver such a reactionary judgement upholding a law that penalised free expression. I can only conjecture that there was a latent illiberal homophobia in Leslie's rather asexual make-up. This could also explain his cold rejection of my invitation to him to become a patron of the charity, Crusaid.

At some later point, the Scarmans fell out with my mother and we stopped being in touch. I contacted Leslie again after he retired, I think it was the early 1990s. He was convalescing from an operation and staying at Osborne House on the Isle of Wight. Ruth was not with him.

It was summer, so I arranged to meet him in my motorboat, named *Surfrider*, in memory of his boat on which I had spent so many happy hours as a child. He stood on the beach by the Italianate boathouse in Osborne Bay, waiting for Derek and I take him for a spin. He looked so much older, rather stooped and dejected; time had distanced us. We spent a pleasant afternoon together and he undoubtedly enjoyed the boat ride, but the close connection was not there anymore. It was the last time we met.

Chapter Eight

❀ ROOTS: TRACING MY FAMILY HISTORY

I had always meant to find out more about my family history. I finally did something about this omission in 1995. I knew something of my mother's family, the Johnsons, but I knew precious little about my father's relations or antecedents.

I had always been told that my father's mother was a widow and that her husband, Horace, had died around 1896 when my father was about a year old. My exhaustive researches in the weighty tomes of Somerset House failed to locate a death certificate or any divorce record. I knew my grandfather was alive at the time of my father's christening in 1896; he had signed the baptismal certificate – but what had happened to him after that?

I learnt that my grandmother, Bennie, was referred to as a 'penniless widow' in Lord Hartwell's biography of his father, William Berry, the 1st Viscount Camrose. Young William Berry had arrived in London in 1899, aged nineteen, from the Welsh valleys to take lodgings in Kensington with Bennie, and the biography refers to letters home to Wales, 'How is dear Mrs Norman and is the will out?' I have no idea how this family of Welshmen came to connect with my grandmother and indeed be on such intimate terms. It may have been a contact through the Baptist Church, but in any event, there was clearly an established and trusting friendship.

My next task was to find Horace's birth certificate. I knew his age as it was listed on his marriage certificate: He was born in approximately 1862. My breakthrough came when I traced my grandfather's birth certificate. Legend had it that he came from East Anglia but it transpired that there were two Horace Normans, both born in East Anglia the same year. I had to research the 1891 Census to eliminate the one from Hoxton, Suffolk, who was then still living at home; that left Cottenham, Cambridgeshire, as the birthplace of my grandfather. The 1871 census records provided me with the details of the family and their address in the village.

During one of my visits to my old university, Cambridge, I decided to cold-call all Normans in Cottenham and eventually struck lucky. From the census return, I knew that my Horace was one of six brothers and it also listed their names: Herbert; Edgar; Horace; Amos; Leonard and Clifford – the last named lived all his life in Cottenham and died unmar-

Daddy's father, Horace (second from right, backrow) with his five brothers and parents

ried, as late as 1952. After many a false start, I finally spoke to a Christine Norman who confirmed that her grandfather, Amos, had a brother called Horace. I asked if I could visit her and she kindly asked me to tea. She assumed I knew far more about our family than I did. 'You must have seen the book?' she said. My heart missed a beat. What book could there possibly be that mentioned our ordinary family?

She disappeared into her bedroom and returned holding a small paperback entitled *Mundane Matters*. This slim volume had been written by a cousin, Richard Norman (son of one of six brothers, Herbert), and was published some ten years previously in 1982. It was a memoir of life in Cottenham before the First World War based on his recollections of family life. The Normans were yeoman farmers cultivating about sixty-five acres of fertile fenland, mainly for soft fruit that they sold to the local Chiver's jam factory in nearby Histon.

The text gave brief details of each of the sons and commented, 'Horace went to America.' It was an Eureka moment. My grandfather had not died young; he had left his wife and emigrated. I reasoned that America probably meant the USA. Most remarkable of all, the little book contained a rather stylish posed family photograph; Horace looked especially dashing in a wing-collar with a carnation in his buttonhole. The photograph included the six brothers; and my great-grandparents, Robert and Harriet Norman; Robert died in 1908, so the picture must predate that year.

From what I learned from Christine, I believe Horace came back from America to see his ageing parents for one last time. Christine told me that he had to rush to leave the country when his abandoned wife, Bennie, got wind of his return. All this was news to me, and I felt excited to have gained a whole chunk of somewhat salacious history and family background.

On my next visit to New York, Derek and I spent an afternoon trawling through the microfilm records of the 1900 and 1910 census returns, state by state. Eventually Derek struck gold, finding my Horace Norman in Chicago, with his job listed as a 'motorman on a streetcar'. He had married again, a young widow called Minnie Coleman – presumably bigamously – and she had a small son, Franklin, by her dead husband.

I contacted a genealogist in Chicago who took two years to trace Franklin and his children. He found a step-grandson, Clyde Coleman, a man in his seventies, living near Lawrence, Michigan. I called him out-of-the-blue and his bemused wife answered. I established my bona fides and gradually won his trust. He remembered my grandfather vividly; Horace had, in effect, been his grandfather too. He had sat on his knee as a young boy in the 1930s – I had made contact.

Derek and I planned a visit to Chicago and hired a car to drive out to Lawrence, Michigan. The Coleman family welcomed us warmly and showed us Horace's final home, a modest wooden house and small-holding. They took us to visit the graveside where he was buried beside his second wife, Minnie. I stood beside my grandfather's grave on that cold blustery autumn day. It was the culmination of a long investigation into a family mystery. The cold wind blew and leaves swirled around the churchyard. I wrapped my coat around me and pondered on how strange life is, and how easily we can be diverted onto a totally different path. Here I was so many miles away from home in an alien continent.

What had actually happened to make Horace leave his life in England, his wife and two sons? Did he think of them or care about their fate? After marrying bigamously and becoming a US citizen, Horace lived until 8th October 1936, never as far as I know, having seen his two sons again. I wonder if he even knew that they had both survived the First World War? I will never know.

Horace's wife, my grandmother, Bennie, remains something of a mystery. According to her birth certificate, she was born in Wareham, Dorset in 1858. Her father, Thomas Eeles, was the first Superintendent of the Dorsetshire Constabulary in that town. A fact confirmed when I visited the town and bought a book, *Wareham: A Pictorial History* by

Lillian Ladle, that mentioned him by name in a caption to a period photograph of the old police station.

Although of humble origins, those who knew Bennie attest to the fact that she carried herself majestically and lived well, with a car and servants in a large house, Holdway House, in the leafy suburbs of Woking, Surrey. I found the house; it is now a private school. What remains a mystery is how she paid for all of this grandeur and managed to educate her two sons at Hurstpierpoint College. Did she have a rich lover? The recent listing of the 1901 census on the Internet told me that her given profession was 'linguist working from home', which hardly seems a plausible explanation for her wealth. She raised both my father and his brother, Donald, to be gentlemen; they dressed, spoke and acted to the manor born.

My father, who set great store by the love and respect he accorded his mother, kept her in her old age. She went to live in Clayton, Sussex, with my father's stepdaughter, Sylvia Cleary and her husband Eustace, (as mentioned in Dirk Bogarde's autobiography). His family also lived in the village. The wheel has come full circle now that Dirk's younger brother, Gareth, and his family have become friends and neighbours at our beloved weekend retreat, Needsore Cottage, on the Solent. Elizabeth Giddens, Dirk and Gareth's elder sister, knew and liked Sylvia and has told me many stories about her life in Clayton.

I was invited to a dinner by given by friends, Crispin and Shauna Money-Coutts (Lord and Lady Latymer). Shauna had also invited a young male couple, one of whom was a work colleague at Christie's. As his name was Harry Williams-Bulkeley, I asked him if he was related to the Sir Richard Williams-Bulkeley who had recently died; he said that Sir Richard was his grandfather. I asked him if he knew about Bob Norman and he told me that he had seen pictures of him and my father in family photo albums. He was intrigued to meet a relation of the – to him mysterious – Roland Norman. We worked out that his grandfather just deceased was my brother's brother (half-brothers), with an age gap between us of about forty years.

During the course of my family research, I have discovered a number of gay male relations. On my mother's side, her first cousin Kathleen Harvard Johnson had a son, Michael Walker, who adopted the surname de la Noy. An author, he wrote books about church matters and worked for a time at Lambeth Palace and became a lay representative on the General Assembly of the Church of England. He was for a time, in the early 1970s, director of the Albany Trust and secretary of the Homosexual Law Reform Society. He wrote a biography of Mervyn

Wareham – where my great-grandfather was the first Superintendent of Police

Stockwood, the gay Bishop of Southwark. On occasions, he wrote obituaries for the *Independent* and the *Guardian* newspapers. He lived with his boyfriend until his death from cancer in August 2002. I only met him briefly twice but he corresponded extensively with his cousin, my uncle Gordon, who admired his published works.

I have a cousin some years older than me who is a gay man and we meet for lunch or dinner from time to time. His brother has a grandson, an actor of about twenty, who is gay but I have yet to meet him. Another cousin has a son who is at university. He is a particularly engaging and handsome young man. He came to dinner recently and introduced Derek and I to his student boyfriend. It was adorable to see two young men so relaxed about being gay and so able to love and live their lives in total freedom. Although he is 'out' to his contemporaries, I am unable to name him, for to do so would almost certainly lead to the loss of his potential inheritance. These few gay relations are the ones I know about, there may well be others who I don't know, or who have not come out.

It is interesting to speculate to what extent there is a genetic component in homosexuality. It is certainly not either a learned trait nor is it a perverse decision. Most gay men will tell you that they sensed they were different from a very early age, and certainly they felt only or primarily attracted to their own sex from the time of their sexual awakening. I am no exception to this.

I know personally three sets of identical twins where one twin is straight and the other gay. As identical twins are monozygotic and therefore by definition genetically identical, it would indicate the cause of homosexuality cannot be purely genetic. I suspect that there is sometimes a strong genetic component; gayness does often seem to run in families, but that other factors, such as the environment in the womb, play a part. Perhaps different eggs have slightly different blood supplies, that have more or less of certain hormones. Much more scientific work needs to be conducted in this intriguing area.

One thing is clear, homosexuality is not a choice: those that are that way inclined and consciously chose not to lead a gay life are likely to be unhappy and unfulfilled.

Chapter Ten

❧ DIANA, LADY DELAMERE

I had not met the legendary Diana Delamere until I was packed off in 1964, aged seventeen, to stay with her in Kenya, to recover from an illness. My mother thought the change of scene would do me good. Diana lived in regal style on a vast ranch in the Rift Valley where the air was dry and the climate warm. I had a passion for shooting and guns and, on a private ranch teeming with wild game, I would have many opportunities to indulge this interest. Diana Delamere was a close friend of my mother, of about the same age. She had introduced my mother to Johnnie Sim, my new stepfather. My parents thought that a few months on an African farm would do me the world of good, both physically and mentally. I could heal my duodenal ulcer and indulge my obsession for hunting. I took my own shotgun and rifle with me.

I had travelled little in my short life and never to Africa, or the tropics. I soon learnt to enjoy the taste of paw-paw and fresh lime for breakfast taken on the veranda and served by silent African houseboys. Kenya had achieved independence only a year before, so little had changed in the colonial world of the Happy Valley Set. For me it was like stepping back into the world of the 1930s and 1940s.

The 4th Baron Delamere and his wife, Diana, were at the apex of colonial society and lived in a pre-war world of servants and formal black-tie dinners, every night. They received a stream of illustrious guests like royalty: the British High Commissioner and the General Officer Commanding the Kenyan army among them. A succession of titled and influential friends from Europe came to stay. I was overwhelmed and in awe. Their table veered between society gossip and political intrigue. Lord Delamere had set an example to the settler community by taking out Kenyan citizenship in a display of solidarity with Kenyatta's black government. In return, he was allowed to remove the statue of his father, the 3rd Lord Delamere, from Delamere Avenue in Nairobi, now renamed Kenyatta Avenue. It stood, looking somewhat out of place, on the farm.

Soy Sambu ranch was a collection of colonial bungalows on a low knoll in the centre of the vast estate. All the land as far as the eye could see belonged to His Lordship. In the immediate vicinity of the house, there were large areas of stables and fenced paddocks reflecting Diana's passion for everything equestrian.

Tom Delamere was short and portly, a quiet gentle older man, nick-named, after the fashion of the English upper classes, 'White Bear', by his commanding wife, Diana. She was inspiring and rather forbidding; a magnetic and forceful personality with an imposing physical presence. A masculine and dominant woman with poise and style, her voice was deep and husky with a seductive quality. She loved jewellery and wore it with panache and good taste. She preferred to dress like a Hollywood star of the '30s. She spoke in the rather glib fashion of that era, using nicknames and diminutives for all and sundry. Her pre-war nursery English style of diction was interspersed with Swahili words and phrases. 'Hughie baby, tell one of the syces to saddle-up Beauty geldi geldi, there's a poo. I want to ride over to the Plains straight after breaky.'

Nearly every morning she would go riding with a syce, or groom, in attendance, lurchers trotting dutifully alongside. She wore smartly tai-lored jodhpurs with leather pieces inserted to protect the inner thighs, a crisp white bush shirt with an open neck and a scarf tied tightly round it, cowboy style; the effect was dominated by an Andalusian-style flat wide-brimmed hat, kid gloves and a riding crop.

One evening I returned to find Diana disconsolate; one of her lurchers had been bitten by a puff adder while she was out riding. The dog had died that afternoon. She was deeply affected by the dog's death. I felt that she showed more emotion for her hound than she would have for a human friend.

I was sent out each day attended by a gun bearer, driver and Land Rover to track and shoot game from morning to dusk. I delighted in the novelty of the sounds and smells of the wild African bush. I watched the weaverbirds building their complex nests hanging from the acacia trees; I admired the strutting secretary birds parading in their isolated grandeur, looking for snakes in the grass. I relished the excitement of stalking wild animals, the ever present sense of danger and the exhilara-tion of crawling towards an alert herd of antelope grazing head down; one sentinel looking up periodically to test the air for alien smells or sounds.

The experience of Africa on foot is entirely different from watching game from a vehicle. On foot, you feel at one with the bush and not merely a spectator. You hear and smell the immensity of that world, at once silent then alive with sounds. There is time to watch and observe the minutiae; the intricacy of leaf forms; the Siafu ants with their fierce patrolling soldiers, carrying back a fat grub to the anthill to be devoured alive; scarab beetles with their iridescent colours manoeuvring enor-mous balls of animal dung in which to lay their eggs; the brilliant

Diana, Lady Delamere

orange and red of the flame tree flowers; the distant glimpse of an abandoned boma, a collection of mud huts surrounded by a fence of protective thorns; the whir of a covey of sand grouse as they take to the wing alarmed by your presence. I shot impala, dik-dik, Thompson's gazelle, waterbuck and, to my shame, zebra. I was amazed at the way the locals would appear from nowhere to claim the meat and skin as soon as a beast was shot. While stalking, I came across large spiders, snakes and myriads of brightly coloured butterflies; I sighted Cape buffalo from a safe distance – the most dangerous animal on the plains.

Sometimes, I would stop at the encampment of an archaeologist studying the Elmenteita deposits containing prehistoric implements of obsidian, a black volcanic glass, little knowing I would soon be up at Cambridge reading prehistoric archaeology. Soy Sambu, like most large estates, was still teeming with game back then. We even sighted a rhino one morning down by the shores of Lake Elmenteita, against a back-drop of thousands of pink flamingo. On my return, my bath would be drawn and my formal evening clothes laid out for me.

One day I heard a report of crop damage to an area of native shambas, or gardens, at the eastern edge of the ranch where the foothills of the vast rift valley rose out of the plains. The culprits were marauding by night and doing considerable damage to the native crops; wild pigs were suspected.

The next morning I started out well before dawn. The shamba was a large vegetable patch consisting of lines of gourd-like vines. Dawn breaks suddenly and dramatically in Africa. There is little or no twilight. I crouched soundlessly at the end of a row of squashes. Suddenly I heard a loud crashing and thrashing. I braced myself and raised my rifle to my shoulder, wrapping the sling around my arm for support, slip-ping the safety catch.

The action happened suddenly. As the light came up, I saw the head of an enormous wild boar rooting among the crops. I fired, but missed in the still dim light. The beast grunted, turned toward me, and charged; I slid the bolt back on my Mannlicher .256 rifle, ejecting the spent car-tridge and heard the next round lock into the chamber. I waited until the bush-pig was only forty feet away and fired again. I loosed off two more rounds from the clip, both hit home and the charging beast shud-dered to a halt just ten feet in front of me. My heart pounded fast with a mixture of fear and excitement. The dying animal grunted, it looked huge; it must have weighed about half-a-ton. Its thick dark skin was sparsely covered with angry red bristles and it sported a pair of huge prominent tusks. I shuddered to think what damage it might have done had its headlong charge hit home. My trusty Mannlicher bolt-action had enabled me to loose off three rounds in as many seconds, keeping calm and focused, as I had been taught to do.

Within a few short minutes, jubilant natives appeared to skin and joint the prize and take away the meat. A minute or so later, I started to tremble in a delayed response as the adrenalin cleared from my body.

There was no chance of any further action that morning so, feeling elated and heroic, I shouldered my rifle and headed back for breakfast.

Another woman lived in the house, fifty-five-year old Lady Patricia Fairweather – a sister of the 3rd Earl of Inchcape (Kenneth), and therefore a cousin to my new stepfather, Johnnie Mackay Sim. I found her both austere and frightening. I sensed that she did not like men and especially boys like me. She would bring me up short with a verbal challenge, or by correcting a mistake of mine concerning the etiquette of colonial Africa, of which I was wholly ignorant. Her manner of dress and her deportment were forbidding and severe. She imbued the term 'butch' with an entirely new resonance.

Whereas Diana, who had just turned fifty, went out of her way to make me feel at home, the older Lady Patricia seemed to resent my presence and was happy to show it. She seemed to be in charge of the household: She ordered the servants in 'Kitchen Swahili', the simple language spoken by all the different tribes when conversing with each other or their white masters.

'Kiswe, wapi bwana Lordi's?' she would demand fiercely, when a servant forgot to bring his Lordship's drink. I quickly learnt that it was not done to speak to the servants in English or encourage them to converse in our language. For a 'native' to address a European in English was considered disrespectful and familiar.

I was curious about Diana and her relationship, not only with her husband Tom, but also with Patricia. They seemed to enjoy a curious three-way relationship, dominated by Patricia. Everyone deferred to her and even Diana paid her due deference. With hindsight, it seems crystal-clear: Diana was primarily a lesbian and Patricia must have been her lover. Patricia lived with Diana at Soy Sambu until she died in 1973.

Diana had all the characteristics that I have since come to recognise in lesbians – her masculine demeanour, her liking for male homosexuals, her hard cold matter-of-fact approach to emotional matters, her love of animals and the wild open countryside and her haughty approach to straight males. This accounted for the fascination men had for her. The attraction was heightened by her insouciant disdain and her masculine allure, similar to the charisma of Marlene Dietrich (whose daughter claimed her mother had had a love affair with Garbo).

Diana had married three millionaires in succession, each much older than her and enjoying privileged positions in society. I doubt very much if she loved any of them with a sexual passion.

The first, Sir Jock Delves-Broughton, 11th Baronet, born in 1883, was a man in his late fifties when Diana married him on November 5th

1940. Diana was not yet thirty-years old. Jock was enormously rich and profligate, a gambler by nature. He was tall, arrogant and patrician. At the time he inherited, his estates comprised 34,000 acres of rich agricultural land as well as two magnificent period houses, Broughton Hall in Staffordshire and Doddington Park in Cheshire. His income is reported to have exceeded £80,000 – the equivalent of about £2,400,000 today. In White's Club, he was once asked by a friend how he managed to spend such a vast annual sum. Jock replied, 'The first £50,000 is easy, the rest is pure extravagance.'

After the murder trial and Jock's suicide in 1943, Diana married again. Her husband was another older man, aged fifty-five, Gilbert Colvile, a noted Kenyan eccentric who showed a great deal more interest in his Masai warriors (moran) than he did in any woman. He was known for his silent taciturn manner, his total lack of social graces and his lack of interest in women.

Her last husband was Tom Delamere, whom she treated with a mildly patronising affection. They developed a love of sorts that I believe was more akin to brotherly love than true romantic passion.

Diana took me to lunch with Colvile, reputedly the richest rancher in Kenya, at his home Oserian on the shores of Lake Naivasha – affectionately referred to, on account of its Moorish design, as the Djinn Palace. They were still close friends. Colvile had a reputation as a difficult man. He was monosyllabic with me but chatted easily with Diana. I did manage to draw him out on the subject of his lion spearing. He aped the ways of the Masai, who had to kill a lion with only a spear as a sign of passage to manhood. The grand hall of Colvile's house was decorated with the skins of the lions he had personally speared in the company of his faithful tracker, Swahili.

Colvile never married again and I believe left Diana all his money. This close friendship and mutual support can best be explained in terms of their mutual recognition of the other's different nature and their shared sexual secrets.

The imposing house was, curiously, the former home of the Earl of Erroll (Joss), Diana's murdered lover and the cause of the greatest scandal in the Colony's history. The book and the subsequent film *White Mischief* told the remarkable tale: Greta Scacchi played the young Diana while Joss Ackland played her much older husband, Sir Jock Delves-Broughton, Bt. Lord Erroll was played brilliantly by Charles Dance. Diana was the young and beautiful wife. Her love affair with the handsome and penniless young army officer, the 22nd Earl of Erroll, scandalised white high society. Erroll's murder, in January 1941, and the subsequent trial and acquittal of Sir Jock caused a sensation, happening as it did against a backdrop of war-time deprivation in Europe. It threw into sharp relief the decadent way of life of the privileged and spoiled expatriates of the Happy Valley set.

I have given much thought to the intriguing Erroll murder mystery. My realisation of the true nature of Diana's sexuality is, I believe, the key to unlocking the true story. Diana never had another loving, sexual relationship with a man, either before or after Erroll's death and certainly not with one near her own age. This is, to say the least, strange for an attractive and much-admired woman. Diana must have had many opportunities to fall in love with other eligible men had she felt so inclined.

I believe she loved Erroll after a fashion but more for his indifference to her, a sentiment in men she found hard to accept. He was a great prize; her lifelong hobby was literally and figuratively 'big game fishing'. He was also ardently desired by many other women and therefore represented a great prize to Diana and flattered her acquisitive and competitive instincts. Joss was also an attractive and sexy man, one of the few not to pursue her and whom she could respect and even love. He had pretty, almost feminine features and had been much fancied by other boys at Eton. She had little time for most men, thinking them weak and unworthy of her. Such a coveted trophy was a way of besting her female rivals and revenging herself on the women who may have

The Pool at Villa Buzza, Kalifi, Kenya

rejected her sexually. While every other vice was tolerated or enjoyed by the Happy Valley set, homosexuality was not. It was regarded with deep distaste. The Diana I knew was a hard, resolute and a determined woman of vaunting ambition and pride. She did not like to be thwarted. I think she was ruthless and calculating, even capable of murder.

Moreover, it is well known that she made a strange pact with Jock before their marriage; he agreed to release her should she wish it and still to provide her with an allowance. I think he knew of her sexual predilections. The marriage was not a love match, it was a marriage of convenience. She acquired a rich and titled husband and moreover one who understood and accepted her nature. He acquired a trophy wife that made him the envy of his contemporaries. If he loved her, it was as a prized possession rather than as a woman; and moreover he could not bear to be alone. He might have been upset to be so publicly cuckolded but that was hardly a motive for murder. Diana stood by him throughout the trial and afterwards, she made sure he had the best available defence lawyer, hardly the actions of a women toward the murderer of her beloved.

I think Joss found Diana exciting and adorable, but he was a serial philanderer. Perhaps he had grown tired of her and told her so on that fateful evening. He was under pressure from the others in the white community and particularly his superior officers to put an end to a scandal that had rocked their small community and was becoming a wider public disgrace. Joss was impecunious and not about to throw away his best and only chance of a financially secure future by marrying a girl with no money of her own. He may have suspected that she could not have children and he would have wanted a male heir to his ancient title. Jock may have made clear to him that he would get no money from him and that Diana had little of her own. It is also probable that Jock told Joss that Diana was primarily a lesbian; a fact that would have been deeply shameful in that homophobic society. The threat of exposure could well have been a motive for murder.

So, I believe that Diana was slighted and humiliated by his rejection and that she murdered him in a fit of jealous rage. We know that she did not like to be thwarted, particularly by a man.

The fact that she defended her husband indicates that she knew he had not murdered Joss. Jock did not defend himself as vigorously as one might have expected. He knew his wife was guilty and chivalry would not have permitted him to place her in the dock to save his own skin; he was too deeply imbued with a gentlemanly code of honour. If Diana was certain that her husband was not the murderer then she must have known who was. If so, why did she not say so? It could only be because it was she.

Diana refused to speak of the murder to anyone for the rest of her life. I believe that this was so because she committed the crime and any discussion of it might have led others to the same conclusion. An innocent woman would have been keen to discuss the murder in case she learnt of a clue to the identity of her lover's killer. She also wished to keep safe her sexual secrets.

There remain a number of unanswered questions in relation to the murder mystery. They have not been resolved by the current theories, particularly if one accepts that Diana was a lesbian.

For some years after the scandal broke, the more morally self-righteous members of the Kenyan élite shunned Diana: her marriages first to Gilbert Colvile and then to Lord Delamere ensured her rapid rehabilitation at the pinnacle of society. Diana was also one of the leading racehorse owners and breeders in the colony; racing played a pivotal role in the social world. The annual Nairobi race meeting was the centrepiece of the social season.

On my first night at Soy Sambu, I dressed for dinner and walked the few hundred yards to the main house in the pitch dark of a still tropical night. I rounded the last corner to be confronted by the alarming sight of a Masai warrior in ochre garb, carrying a spear. It took me a few moments to realise that he was one of the night-watchmen. The Masai had remained fiercely loyal to the British and shared a mutual disdain for what they believed were the indolent Kikuyu tribe that dominated the new black administration.

My two-month sojourn in Kenya went a long way to restoring my health. It was an idyllic, if lonely, period of reflection, growing awareness and maturity. I encountered many new tastes and sensations and experienced the last days of a nearly vanished world. At that time, I dreamed of becoming a 'white hunter' failing to appreciate that the very term was soon to become obsolete. Some part of me realised that there were other more powerful forces stirring within me requiring a more contemporary urban setting for their fulfilment. I had yet to attend university and begin a new chapter in my life.

I continued to see Diana on her annual visits to London, mostly for the racing season. Her adopted daughter, Deborah ('Snoo'), had been at school with my stepsister, Amanda Sim, and they had shared a coming-out dance in 1967. Diana came to dine with my mother and, like old friends, they talked mostly of old acquaintances departed and the happy times shared together before the war.

Derek at Kilifi

Some years later, I revisited Kenya, this time accompanied by Derek, my lover. Diana entertained us for a week at her house on the coast, Villa Buzza at Kilifi. We went big game fishing with her on her boat, *White Bear*, named after Tom, now deceased. Game fishing was Diana's passion and she competed in local tournaments with considerable success. By this time she had aged and drank a little too much which, together with the pills she took, made her speech somewhat slurred by nine at night. She was a generous and delightful hostess. She had no qualms about letting the two of us occupy a double bed. She had always been kind and friendly towards gay men. They are happy memories for both of us.

At no time did Diana refer to the scandal or shed light on the mystery, even to my mother. She took her secrets to the grave. I can only imagine the strain that her dissembling must have placed upon her. Not only did she lie to others about her crime, but also she probably lied to herself for much of her life about her own sexuality. I did ask her once if she would like to meet Joss Erroll's grandson, Merlin (Lord) Hay, a friend of mine from Cambridge. After some hesitation, she declined. I don't think she wished to stir old, painful, and surely guilty, memories.

Chapter Eleven

I Spy Anthony Blunt

One evening, in the summer of 1965, soon after leaving school, Hugh Montgomery-Massingberd invited me out to dinner with his gay uncle, Peter Montgomery, a conductor and musician who was over from Ulster on a visit. Peter, now well into his fifties, was a close friend, and former lover (while they were at Cambridge), of the art historian Sir Anthony Blunt, Surveyor of The Queen's pictures, who was later exposed as a communist spy and was heavily embroiled in the treachery of Burgess, Maclean and Philby.

We met at Blunt's flat above the Courtauld Institute, of which he was the director, in its magnificent Adam premises, the former London residence of the Earls of Home, in Portman Square. Hugh's uncle Peter was gentle, vague and charming. Blunt was everything I despised; waspish, arrogant and vain. He looked and behaved like a character out of a Noel Coward play, sweeping into the room in a silk foulard dressing gown. Hugh remembers him wearing a G-string but I think that must have been on another occasion; I am sure I would have remembered such an outrage. I found Blunt grand and distant and none too friendly; he certainly made not the slightest effort to put me at my ease.

Hugh knew that Blunt had been a leftie before the war but, of course, neither of us realised that Blunt had been an active Communist agent. Neither of us could understand how someone dedicated to fine art and gracious living, not to mention high society, could espouse Communism and wish to bring about the destruction of everything meaningful to his way of life. It seemed to us that socialism was the antithesis of freedom and the death of beauty.

For our post-Brideshead generation, socialism equated to the destruction of everything beautiful and historic and its replacement by concrete ugliness and conformity; a dumbing-down to the lowest common denominator. It embodied the victory of proletarian values over a higher aesthetic. We could not comprehend how economic socialism could possibly be achieved without the loss of human freedom, its very philosophy being the opposite of natural selfish instincts and therefore requiring coercion for its implementation. To make matters worse, Blunt and his kind appeared to us to be arch snobs living a life intricately bound up with all those things and people he wished to see destroyed. Not only was he enjoying the ultimate in aristocratic privilege, he wanted to ensure that our generation had neither the money nor the opportunity to benefit similarly.

As to his gay life, Blunt represented everything I disliked about his generation of privileged gay men – intensely snobbish but only able to have sex with those he perceived as real men, that is to say, working-class roughs. This implied a lack of self-esteem and a belief that all gay men were effeminates who needed to find real men for sex – what an exhibition of self-hatred. How could he or his kind hope to gain the respect of others when they clearly had no respect for themselves? While rejecting the Establishment's capitalism, he subscribed to its values in every other way, playing by their rules and accepting their values. During the pre-war period at Cambridge, gay young men enjoyed what might be described as a paradise of liberal tolerance and acceptance. They lived in a world of privilege and amongst great beauty, and yet he sought to destroy this idyll and deny it to future generations.

Blunt's sensational exposure as a spy in the late 1970s came as a shock. I suspected he had been a Communist – so many had been at Cambridge before the war – but I had no idea that he remained con-vinced by such a flawed political philosophy so alien to his way of life and so deeply damaging to his friends. For a man of the left, the greatest insult was to accuse someone of being a traitor to their class; if anyone had ever been a traitor to his class, it was undoubtedly Anthony Blunt.

Chapter Twelve

❧ PETER TOWNEND

While I was at Cambridge my school friend, Hugh Montgomery-Massingberd, started work at Burke's Peerage, publishers of the stud-book of the titled and landed classes. Hugh had always been fascinated by genealogy and family history and found the collection and ordering of so much data entirely suited his natural talents and solitary nature.

He was somewhat exasperated by his immediate boss, Peter Townend, the editor who moonlighted as the social editor of *Tatler*. The Season held no interest for Hugh Montgomery-Massingberd; Deb dances were anathema to him. Peter was seldom at work, spending too much of his time attending debutante functions and drinking excessively. In fact, he effectively ran the Season by compiling lists of debs and suitable male escorts. The mums came to him for advice on how to bring out their daughters and arrange their social calendar.

Peter was like a character from a Waugh novel: hunch-backed, with oily, thinning, sleeked back hair and a slightly camp manner. He was as creepy as a snail and as ageless as a lizard. He was deeply snobbish but had a quite extraordinarily retentive memory for names and genealogies and a genuine love of the subject. Like Hugh, he was able to read the births, deaths and marriages in *The Times* and the *Daily Telegraph* and insert the details accurately into the office inter-leaved copies of all Burke's various publications. This was all done from memory and was always accurate.

When I first met Peter at a deb dance in 1966, the year my sister 'came out', he asked me to which Norman family I belonged. He was disappointed when I was unable to name a peerage or landed gentry family. He then asked me my father's name. I answered, 'Roland,' 'Ah!' he said, 'The Peerage, Dartmouth; married Victoria Williams-Bulkeley, née Legge, for whom Queen Victoria stood sponsor.' He was spot-on, of course. The entries were there under both those families, as I was soon to discover.

I subsequently saw Peter often; he was at every deb party, usually surrounded by a group of attractive young men to whom he was inevitably drawn, and they to him – as to be on Peter's 'list' meant endless free invitations to dances and country house party weekends. Peter performed his function as co-ordinator and impresario of the Season without pay, solely for the glory of it. It had the added benefit for him of endless free lunches and dinners as aspirant mums entertained him and young men of questionable background sought to win his favour and a place on his list of eligibles. He loved to be the centre of attention; he loved to gossip about the mums and their daughters, revelling in his intimate knowledge of their backgrounds and social eligibility. He could always be relied upon to produce an amusing anecdote of a some-what risqué sort about one of the year's more characterful debutantes or her antecedents. 'Ah, Jane X, you know her mother is very pushy and she was never presented at Court; I hear she has taken up with an entirely unsuitable young man, her hairdresser. They were seen dining together at Club Arethusa, after Lady Palmer's cocktail party for her niece Stephanie Dorset.'

Peter's social calendar was a busy one. Every evening was filled with invitations to cocktail parties and Peter was not above crashing those to which he was not invited. He naturally assumed the omission was a clerical oversight. He spoke slowly and deliberately, often drawing out the last syllable of a name as though savouring it like a choice sweet-meat. His accent was as entirely indefinable as his origins, but there was a touch of sibilance to his diction. He knew the ancestry and connec-tions of everyone he mentioned but of his own background and family, he never uttered a word. He had little money but maintained a small flat in Chelsea to which no one I knew was ever invited. He seemed to sub-sist on the cocktail eats provided.

Often, he would retire towards the end of a drinks party to a chair in a corner where he would fall into a drunken sleep, to be awoken by the hostess, who as often as not took pity on him and asked him to stay for dinner. At dances, he was to be seen in an old-fashioned silk-lapelled dinner jacket much in need of a dry clean. His dyed and thinning hair was plastered across his partially bald pate. He sweated a great deal, either from a natural propensity to perspire or from an excess of alcohol and lack of exercise. Yet, Peter could be very amusing and was always a ready source of scurrilous stories, but he was never vicious or truly unkind. His style was a gently mocking one, liberally sprinkled with innuendo delivered with a knowing smile and a twinkle in his eye. As far as I am aware, he never pursued his interest and appreciation of young male beauty beyond sliding his arm around a reluctant shoulder or two.

After his departure from Burke's in the early 1970s, he took up full time employment with *Tatler* as the social editor. He had a life-long rivalry with that other social stalwart, Betty Kenward, who wrote the sycophantic and humourless 'Jennifer's Diary' for *Harper's & Queen*.

They always avoided one another at parties, and Peter loved to be able to correct her mistaken identifications or occasional lapses of genealogical accuracy, as well as mocking her helmet-like hairdo and little-girl, or as he put it 'waitress-style', black velvet bow tied primly at the back of her head. Both, however, helped to sell their respective publications largely by mentioning as many names as possible in the hope that those named would buy a copy – and they usually did.

Peter loved to be asked up to Oxford and Cambridge in term time to have dinner with his young male protégés unencumbered by the distraction of girls or their mothers. True to his usual form, he would finesse invitations when none were freely proffered; in that regard, he was utterly shameless.

Peter's early death and subsequent lavish memorial service at St George's, Hanover Square, proved just how wide his acquaintance was. Many friends and work colleagues turned out to give a worthy send-off to the representative of another age – a man for whom many had an affection but one whose inner life will remain forever a mystery.

Chapter Thirteen

THE SWINGING SIXTIES

The 1960s, as we think of them, began in 1964 while I was still at Harrow. The music came first, the ballads of the Beatles, *She Loves You*, and *Can't Buy Me Love*. Their haunting melodic tunes and simple choruses spoke straight to my heart. Every teenager believes that the music of his youth is somehow special, but we knew for sure that this was something extraordinary – revolutionary. Everyone of my generation sensed that these simple songs represented a different sensibility, a sensual honesty that was both refreshing and real. My stepfather Johnnie said, 'Believe me, no-one will have heard of these Beatles in five years time, they can't act about as well as they can't sing.' Amanda and I retorted, 'You don't understand, they are truly fab and new.' Our hearts leapt for joy, here were songs that seemed to break free from years of sensual repression and social conformity and that mirrored our desire for change.

I went with my stepsister Amanda to a Beatles concert at the Hammersmith Palais that Christmas in 1964. You could hardly hear the music for the screaming of the girls. They rushed the stage; the bouncers had the greatest difficulty in keeping the fab four from being smothered by fans, such was the mass hysteria. I wanted to scream too, but my years of self-censorship prevented any outward expression of gay desire. I liked Paul best; he was the pretty one. I also fancied Peter Noon of Herman's Hermits and, of course, I was thrilled by the savage sexuality of Paul Jones of Manfred Mann (in spite of or even because of his acne) and his sensual song, *Pretty Flamingo*.

On BBC TV, there was an explosion of rebellion against the old guard. *That Was the Week that Was* (TW3) with David Frost and his team of iconoclasts wittily demolishing the stuffy mores of the old guard with biting satire. They lampooned Harold Macmillan who looked and sounded like a dinosaur, and the pompous Judiciary, such as the prosecution in the Lady Chatterley case asking the jury if they would allow their maidservants to read the book.

Fashion started to flow from the bottom upwards instead of trickling down from the stuffy couture of Norman Hartnell and his ilk. Gone were the posed portraits of debs in white gloves and pearls; in came Twiggy leaping into space atop a Mini car. It was the street fashion of the kids that dictated the pace and caught the popular imagination. The outrageous mini skirts and heavy eye make-up of the girls and the long hair of the boys flouted convention and rendered the fashions of the debutantes and the rich irrelevant. The Antonioni film *Blow-Up* in 1966, staring the delectable David Hemmings as a fashion photographer, with its combination of gritty realism and glamorous living, captured the zeitgeist. The young had money for the first time and were living away from home leading their own lives and demanding new and exciting things to buy.

As the decade progressed and I grew older, I was still viewing the arrival of the Swinging Sixties from the sidelines. It was not until 1969 a year after my arrival at Cambridge that, in a small way, I became a participant. I, and my new-found friends, drove down from Cambridge in our sports cars to have our hair cut where the rock stars went; by Gary Craze at Sweeny's or at his other branch, Todd's, in the King's Road, next to a boutique called Granny Takes a Trip. Our long locks were wet-cut and layered and blow-dried, just like a girl's. I was entranced by the trendy atmosphere, the gay banter of the assistants and the pervasive rock music, all suffused with the smell of pot and coffee. I lusted after the gay boys who worked there and thrilled to hear them speak of boy friends and the clubs they frequented. I lacked the courage to join in, make a pass at a boy, or even enquire about their clubs. I still felt I had to maintain my disguise at all costs.

I made vain attempts to be heterosexual. I took girls out, tried to kiss them and even had sex with a few, but felt embarrassed and awkward afterwards. It just didn't feel right; it certainly wasn't fun. I recoiled at having to fondle a pair of breasts; it felt so unnatural. My thoughts always turned to boys and my eyes to the bulges in their jeans or their tight, pert bottoms. I was jealous of my sister and the handsome men that came to take her out at night. One cool guy drove a Mini Moke that had a car telephone (One-way only – you had to say 'over' before the other party could speak). She came back in the morning with tales of wild nights dancing in clubs like Tramp and the Garrison. I longed for a boyfriend to be seen out with, rather than just an occasional furtive fuck with other Cambridge boys who were mainly straight or else too drunk to care.

We went shopping at Deborah and Clare in Beauchamp Place or Mr Fish in Clifford Street to buy frilly shirts with long tight three-buttoned cuffs in sexy fabrics, voile and silk with flower patterns on them. Evelyn Waugh had made Charles Ryder in *Brideshead Revisited* declare, 'Our toys were silk shirts'; nothing had changed there. We were indeed, Dedicated Followers of Fashion. We bought our flared trousers, huge wide belts and velvet jackets in Carnaby Street or from boutiques in the King's Road.

Amanda's cousin, Jamie Mackay, younger son of the Earl of Inchcape, was at Trinity College, Cambridge a year or two before me. He was a scholarly boy with a muscular Christian social conscience and in the vacations worked as a volunteer helper in a gay club in Soho. The year was probably 1966. I asked my sister to take me along. I was burning with curiosity and latent desire. The club was a cellar coffee bar in D'Arblay Street called Le Duce. The boys were fey and effeminate, called each other by girl's names, but were also young and pretty. I was mesmerised but stuck close to my sister for camouflage and for protection from myself. The music was all Tamla Motown; the Four Tops, the Supremes and Marvin Gaye; *You Can't Hurry Love* and *I Heard it on the Grapevine*. I knew every song by heart, they were all my favourites. Jamie observed that all gay boys liked Tamla Motown music: I knew he was talking about me.

I was unsure why Jamie did voluntary work in such a place. Was he doing it for himself; to salve a social conscience by slumming it with the fallen, or had he hopes of converting queers to the paths of righteousness? Maybe he was there as bait to lure the boys off the streets; he was young and not entirely unattractive. From my observations, he did little more than clear the empty coffee cups; I never saw him talking to the gay boys.

I felt I had come home. For the first time I found myself in a room full of gay men behaving naturally, talking freely about boys and love and the music they related to. I sensed that a gay club was a private, safe world where gay men could be themselves free from censorious glances. I was not yet ready to abandon my class status and my educational advantages, but I knew I had to find a way to merge these two seemingly irreconcilable sides of my personality. I felt strangely at home in that dank cellar coffee bar with lino for a dance floor and an old juke box in the corner playing such heavenly music. Amanda and I left together; I wanted to stay all night.

We were just observers. The real makers of Swinging London in the 1960s were few in number: the fashion crowd like Mary Quant, Ozzie Clark, and Michael Fish; the photographers David Bailey, Patrick Lichfield and Terence Donovan; their models, Jean Shrimpton and Twiggy; the Media crowd like Peter Cook, Willy Rushton, Bernard Levin, Millicent Martin and all those from *Beyond the Fringe* who went to the Establishment Club; the art crowd, David Hockney, Andrew Logan and the art dealer Robert Fraser and the Society crowd; Tara

My step-sister Amanda Baird (née Sim) with her children Ollie and Lucie

Brown, Christopher Gibbs and Desmond Guinness. Not forgetting the many new rock stars like Mick Jagger and the Stones. London was burning with youthful talent and the creative desire to shock. It has been said, quite accurately, that those that made London swing in the 1960s numbered only about 1,000 and they all knew one another.

There was a sexual revolution based on the new contraceptive pill, but only for straights. Gays were still firmly in the closet and their love illegal.

These first rumblings of the volcano lead to the eruption, from 1968 onwards, of flower power and the hippy movement. The mass protests began, fuelled by agit-prop against the Vietnam war and the movements for disarmament and peace. Youth on the streets started to wear Afghan shaggy coats, flared trousers and flowered shirts; they smoked pot and experimented with LSD. As Timothy Leary advised, they 'tuned-in and dropped-out'.

Chapter Fourteen

✿ 1968 – THE YEAR THE WORLD CHANGED FROM BLACK AND WHITE INTO COLOUR

I was so excited and elated to be going up to Cambridge University; it was the culmination of a dream. I had struggled to gain three good A-level grades to gain admittance. Harrow School had written me off academically; I had left school with only two pass-grade A-levels on account of my illness. My two years as a trainee estate agent in London with Messrs Best Gapp and Partners were followed by nine months spent in London and Oxford retaking my exams. At first, I received a rejection letter and then, by agreeing to read Geography at Pembroke, I received a grudging letter offering me a place.

I matriculated late, aged twenty-one. By now I had grown into my age and my constant desire to taken for an adult, together with my somewhat Edwardian upbringing, led to my appearing, dressing and sounding older than my age. I wore cavalry twill trousers and a tweed jacket. I had values and opinions to match; I was the very opposite of hip and cool. But as a result, my fellow freshmen saw me as sophisticated, with a maturity that gave me immediate kudos and respect. I had seen something of the world and knew how to order wine in a restaurant and how to conduct myself at a cocktail party. At last, I had grown into my age, but if anything I had overshot the mark.

My arrival at Cambridge coincided with the culmination of a time of unrest at university campuses worldwide. There were student riots and sit-ins all over Western Europe and in the United States. The world was in the throes of change. (We felt that nothing so fundamental had occurred since 1848, the year of revolutions that swept away many of the old autocracies.) In America, State troopers were employed to quell the riots at Kent State University and the consequent scenes of brutality against peaceful demonstrators were shown on television worldwide. The country was in the throws of massive protests against the war in Vietnam. This, and the military draft became a focus of student protests.

In Europe, the aims of the protesters were unclear; they just wanted change and an end to the old patriarchal order with its rules and conformity. English students were imbued with a generalised but unfocused left-wing idealism. Their demands ranged from the removal of rules and restrictions, such as gate hours – the time at which college gates were locked at night – to the inclusion of student representatives on faculty boards that determined the content of the curriculum and an end to formal examinations.

In England, the London School of Economics, which had a student body drawn from all over the world, was fiercely left-wing and at the forefront of demonstrations and, thanks to the proximity of Fleet Street, always in the news. It became clear that a number of the lecturers encouraged and supported the students, doubtless because of their own Marxist revolutionary leanings. There were sit-ins at most of the major university administration blocks. The authorities were at a loss as to how to respond. Concessions were made and declarations of solidarity issued by weak dons and lecturers, who were mostly just bemused, but sometimes openly sympathetic to the broadly socialist agenda of the students. A large and ugly demonstration occurred in Grosvenor Square, in front of the American Embassy, in protest against the Vietnam war – fulfilling Oscar Wilde's prediction that 'Education of the working classes will lead to acts of violence in Grosvenor Square.'

Only at Cambridge was there a backlash by the traditional undergraduate body. A counter demonstration took place outside the Senate House where left-wing protesters had barricaded themselves inside and refused to leave. We chanted slogans on the lawn and shouted 'Lefties Out', sang *Rule Britannia* and an alternative version of the socialist anthem *The Red Flag*, with the words altered: 'The working class can kiss my ass, I've got the foreman's job at last'. It was all relatively good-natured, at least as far as we were concerned. I believe Cambridge was the only university in the world where the demonstrators caved in and retreated voluntarily, cowed and defeated.

On the whole, my friends and I were not impressed by left-wing political theory, although we did share a desire for liberal change in social matters and sympathised with the ridicule heaped upon the crusty, out-of-touch, gerontocracy that ran the country.

In Paris, the riots were of a more serious nature and a genuine feeling of political revolution was in the air. The Paris students joined forces with the striking Renault car plant workers and demanded political change. The Gaullist government's CRS riot police, in full protective armour, used CS gas and baton charges to disperse the rioters who retaliated by hurling cobblestones and Molotov cocktails at the police. Parisians were in genuine fear of an anarchist revolution, as told by Nancy Mitford in her report in the *Spectator* of *Les Evénements*.

While Parisian students and workers were rioting, their British counterparts, more subdued as always, were content to occupy the LSE in London and university buildings up and down the land. Authority was everywhere in retreat, having lost its moral purpose and will to govern. Most university dons were concentrating on saving what they could of their cherished institutions and the rules that had hitherto governed them. The sight of their pusillanimity and fawning to the so-called student representatives like Daniel Cöln-Bendit and Tariq Ali only reinforced the desire for change. For the most part they, and all those over forty, were living in a scary, noisy new world seemingly intent on throwing away all they cherished. It was my opinion that the older generation were reaping the rewards of the twin seeds that they had sown and nurtured; conservative social and moral repression and economic disaster brought about through socialism.

These social upheavals were accompanied by a sexual revolution. Young heterosexuals were having a great deal of sex liberated by the new mores, the birth control pill, illegal drugs and a desire to shock. The passing of the 1967 Sexual offences Act that decriminalised homosexuality for the first time in nearly one hundred years, did not immediately lead to a change in social acceptability. Gay men were to remain firmly in the closet for another twenty or so years. Exposure meant, if nothing else, an end to career prospects.

The visible gay world at Cambridge was both tiny and out on the fringe. My male contemporaries did have sexual interests in one another but these seldom went as far as sexual encounters, unless of course they were drunk after a club dinner – that gave them an excuse. My friends and I were all too busy trying to prove our manly credentials and appearing in public at May Balls with eligible girls. Male friendships could be both intense and romantic and we were certainly not above jealousies between friends.

The power of the Trade Unions was at its height. Shop stewards sat down with cabinet ministers late into the night, drinking beer and eating sandwiches, in a vain attempt to solve a spiralling series of labour disputes that threatened to bring the country to its knees. Socialists, and in this category I include both political parties, Labour and Conservative, could not understand where they had gone wrong. They had already conceded so much; the British Empire had been given away and punitive taxes imposed on the middle classes. Government had done obeisance to the new Commonwealth leaders in apology for our past sins. At home, the rich were taxed until, in the words of the chancellor, Dennis Healey, 'the pips squeaked'; maximum income tax was a confiscatory 98%. Unions were being given all the powers and protection from prosecution that they could wish for. There was really nothing left to concede. So why were the masses unhappy?

The economy was a shambles, brought about by anachronistic labour practices, over-manning and low productivity coupled with lack of investment and entrepreneurial innovation. There were risible attempts to institute an incomes policy by freezing the differentials between competing classes of workers whose demands for ever higher wages leapfrogged one another. Both political parties subscribed to this farce, little understanding that the only solution lay in breaking the overweening powers of the trade unions and the state-owned monopolies. The pound sterling was always under pressure, its value fixed artificially and, as our balance of payments worsened by the day, it was put under impossible pressure. Harold Macmillan, the Conservative prime minister had famously said: 'You have never had it so good.' Which was true for the mass of people in the 1950s and early 1960s. Now Harold Wilson, the Labour prime minister, was ridiculed for saying, after a devaluation of the pound: 'The pound in your pocket has not been devalued'. These were the classic problems of socialist over-regulation, high taxation combined with a large loss-making state sector.

The real problem, I felt, lay in a deeper vein and was generational. Obedience and conformity were being swept away. The surface manifestations of these trends were the revolutions in music and clothes, sex and drugs, but the deeper reality was that the young were not going to

The Author (second from left in front row) and the Pitt Club Committee, 1970

be told what to do anymore. They were not going to follow the old patterns and certainties; take the jobs assigned to them by their parents just for the sake of being able to afford a new washing machine or for a gold watch and pension at the age of sixty-five. The world of work still consisted of thousands of ant-like conformists all dressed alike in a grey uniformity with narrow, essentially middle-class, ambitions and desires. My stepfather and others like him dressed for the City in striped trousers, a black coat, rolled umbrella and a bowler hat. Not for him 'the suit of dittos' (the lounge suit) that he despised as inappropriate office-wear; it lacked the sonorous conformity he so espoused. He was fond of correcting me when I used the solecism 'jacket' to mean coat. 'Only books and potatoes have jackets', he would pompously declare.

My friends and I wanted a world of excitement and change where people worked more flexibly, if they worked at all, and worked for a more immediate and personal reward. There were greater global issues too, the war in Vietnam and perceived American imperialism being at the forefront of our concerns. Youthful idealism was at a zenith and we all wanted to change the world and, for once, we actually thought we had the power to do so.

I had a problem: I was in tune with these revolutionary ideas of personal freedom and fulfilment but I could not understand how this could be achieved by even more socialism. To me, socialism meant restrictions on personal freedom, especially freedom to make money. The left wing had usurped a monopoly on moral values and it was that part I vigorously disputed. I was, like most of my Cambridge contemporaries of that era, deeply politicised. I could find no home in either of the political parties. If I called myself anything I was a Free Trade Whig. I aspired to live in an aristocratic 18th-century world of privilege, freedom and licence. I believed that socialism was inherently incompatible with personal freedom and I realised that to create a socialist economy, it was necessary to compel people to act against their natural instincts and was therefore doomed to failure without dictatorial coercion. I was fast learning the importance of acting and living in full accord with one's natural instincts. To force people to live any other way is to force them to lead unhappy and unfulfilled lives and, as such, it is ultimately doomed to fail.

A state-owned or command economy makes no provision for innovation or invention, which is strictly the product of entrepreneurial activity. In a state-owned enterprise, innovation if successful is not properly rewarded and if unsuccessful invariably, penalised. The result is that state run enterprises are innately deeply conservative and risk averse.

People are naturally selfish and desire to provide the best not only for themselves but also their families. It seemed quite obvious to me that any form of nationalised or command economy could never be efficient, productive or most importantly provide a mechanism for dynamic innovation.

My stepfather and his colleagues typified the views of the governing classes of their generation. He knew Lord Carrington and thought very much as he did. They wanted to preserve old-fashioned courtesy, behaviour and privilege, while at the same time destroying its economic means of survival. A new way had to emerge. I had no idea from where or how it would come but in the meantime, on coming down from Cambridge, I was determined to find my own sense of fun and fulfilment and, I hoped, make some money along the way.

I was already a dedicated believer in market forces and the power of free enterprise. I was a monetarist and capitalist in tune with the ideals and ideas of the Thatcher era, way before she appeared on the radar screen. It seemed entirely natural to me that the new freedoms would come from the right and not the left. I could see no liberation in the fossilised views of the working-class political platform. Their day was done. The Conservative party had swallowed the Socialist pill and really believed that they should be knitting at the feet of their own guillotine.

1968 was the year in which the world changed forever both figuratively and literally from black and white into Technicolor. I too changed and became popular, confident and full of hope for my future.

Chapter Fifteen

✤ MY CAMBRIDGE YEARS

I arrived at Pembroke College, Cambridge in the autumn of 1968. I had romantic visions of a Brideshead world peopled by handsome young aristocrats carrying teddy bears; nothing could have been further from the truth. The University was in turmoil. The old ways were being sloughed like the skin of a snake. Gowns were no longer worn and undergraduates had become left-wing students hell-bent on destruction. Few attended lectures and the dons had become almost an irrelevance.

I found it to be true that one spends the second year getting rid of the friends you made in your first. The first year at university is one of exploration and discovery. There are so many new sensations. There is the heady freedom of being an adult with little or no responsibility. There are new friends and some new enemies to make; a new slang to learn and an entirely new way of being that is self-reliant. No one tells you what to do any more. The deep conformity of adolescence is gradually questioned and replaced by a new confidence – daring to be different. I spent endless nights sitting talking to new friends in their rooms, listening to new music, smoking dope and drinking, falling in lust, being rejected, growing and learning. Sport no longer figured for most of us. Unlike school, there were no compulsory games or hero-worshipping of sporting success. Verbal dexterity and dress sense were more admired than brawn. We tested each other endlessly, finding each other's limits. How much could we drink, what new ideas could we propound, what unheard of brand of cigarettes could we flourish around. Black Russian Sobranies were dull; scented Turkish tobacco in rainbow coloured papers were cool. Our life became a search for new, more interesting or more beautiful friends.

I had fallen in love with a beautiful blond boy who was bi-sexual and had sex with me on many occasions while carrying on serious relationships with a succession of pretty girls. The intermittent and unsatisfactory nature of this relationship made me deeply unhappy. The affair continued for a brief while after Cambridge. My lover paid little heed to my feelings and, as always, the more I wanted him the less he wanted me. He was a close friend and part of my daily life. That made his indifference even harder to bear. I found Cambridge a relative sexual desert after the easy and willing access to boys at Harrow.

In my second year, I moved out of college and into digs (lodgings) in

King's Parade. I was fortunate to obtain rooms above Peck's the Chemist, right opposite the Great Gate to King's College. The view was magnificent, if a little noisy. My landlady was the legendary Sadie Barnett. A working-class snob who only accepted 'the better sort of gentleman'. She was particularly strict about having young ladies in your room after dark, a restriction that bothered me hardly at all. Girls hardly figured in our lives, except at weekends. All the colleges, except the three for girls, were exclusively male. Undergraduate life was distinctly homo-sensual, if not homosexual.

Through my membership of the Pitt Club, a university version of a London gentleman's club, I befriended the undergraduate social élite. I hardly spent any time in my college, in fact, I even arranged to have supervisions in Trinity alongside my new best friend, Michael Waterhouse. Like me, he was reading 'Arch and Anth' – Archaeology and Anthropology. We attended few lectures but enjoyed our hourly supervisions with such luminaries as Glynn Daniel, later to become Disney Professor. I spent nearly all my time in either Trinity College or the Pitt Club. Weekends were spent staying in country houses or speeding down in London in our cars.

It took most of my first year to change from my stiff, formal tweedy self to a more relaxed, confident and cool re-incarnation. I became

The Beefsteak Club, Cambridge, 1970. (From left, back row): Hugo Slater, Jeremy Burn-Callender, Brooke Boothby, Brian Fitzpatrick, (Front row): Mathew Festing, Ian Beith, Michael Waterhouse, Michael Prideaux, the Author

much more self-assured and started to dress fashionably. My hair grew longer and my shirts more flamboyant. Trips to London honed these trends and tendencies. My new younger friends influenced me and I developed a personal confidence, style and authority. At the start of my second year, I was appointed to the Pitt Club committee and asked to organise the annual club ball. This meant that I would hold the most senior undergraduate post of honorary secretary in my third year.

By year three I was firmly established as a social figure in my chosen milieu. I rented a farmhouse at Longstowe, some ten miles outside Cambridge, on the estate of a friend, Roger Bevan. The old farmhouse was attractive, set in its own tiny apple orchard on the edge of the village. I shared the house with a friend, Michael Prideaux, destined to succeed me as Pitt Club secretary. Michael Waterhouse shared a flat in town with two other friends and we treated Longstowe as our country residence and the flat became our townhouse. I regret to confess that we were undoubtedly arrogant and rather too pleased with ourselves. We didn't play a great part in ordinary undergraduate life but existed in our own bubble of privilege and fun. As secretary, I even had my own office and telephone in The Pitt.

I had not entirely lost my contemplative side. Some mornings I would wake early and smell the dew in the damp morning air, wander alone through the sleepy town out past the Backs onto Grantchester meadows, a book of poetry in my hand. The beauty of the place and the wonders of the architecture were not wasted on me. I relished the privilege of my good fortune and the magnificence of this ancient town and university. In all ways but one, my world was perfect. I still longed for love.

Like all young men, I wondered what would become of me. My most troubling question was whether or not I would meet the dark stranger of my dreams, and find love. Curiously, I always knew with a burning certainty that I would succeed in business and make money. I even said as much at the time to my friend, Charlie Nettlefold. I also told him I would be unhappy in love, such was the force of the negative indoctrination to which I had been subjected.

I was invited to become a member of the élite dinning club, the Beefsteak, founded in 1784, a club that boasts an unbroken history of recorded termly dinners. The members wore an 18th Century livery and dined on a table laden with the club's magnificent silver donated by its illustrious members over the years. I had succeeded in fulfilling my social, if not my intellectual, ambitions. The young butterfly had emerged from his chrysalis. I had made a wide circle of acquaintances and a number of very close friends, many of whom remain friends to this day.

Chapter Sixteen

❦ KIM DE LA TASTE TICKELL

The sleepy little village of Whittlesford lies about ten miles east of Cambridge. It was at this somewhat improbable location that a flamboyant character called Kim Tickell turned the former village inn into the Tickell Arms, part public house, part restaurant and wholly eccentric establishment which was especially popular with undergraduates rich enough to have cars. It soon achieved a reputation for excellence and eccentricity somewhat similar to the Spread Eagle at Thame for the Brideshead generation of Oxford undergraduates.

The quality of the food and the theatrical atmosphere created by Kim and his much younger German boyfriend, Siegfried (Siegi for short), held an allure for us bright young things. We would drive out in convoy, usually at the weekend. The place was packed and even in the daytime candles guttered on the tables.

There was a set procedure for ordering food. Each party would be given a number and when your food was ready, Kim would shout out in a ripe, fruity upper-class voice, 'food for party number five'. He dressed theatrically in black silk knee-breeches, a frock coat and a black clerical collarless shirt. A monocle dangled on a chain at his chest. He was fiercely opinionated and held forth in a loud and contentious voice against a background of Wagner on the stereo. His political and social views bordered on the Fascist. How much he really believed and how much was showmanship I will never know.

We drank and ate at long, rough wooden tables reminiscent of a Tudor hostelry. On summer days, you could eat outside but being inside close to the action was part of the theatre. Kim always gave preference to the grander undergraduates, particularly the prettier males. He liked to embarrass those who were showing off to their girlfriends. If someone was fingering the candles, he would shout, 'Stop playing with the candles, you might get wax on your flies and give the house a bad name!' If some timid girl asked him for 'the ladies', he would exclaim, 'We don't have ladies in here, only tarts, whores and harlots.'

Kim disliked the hippy fashions then current and posted a notice on the door banning open-toed sandals and men with long hair. He could lose his temper easily and didn't like people to argue with him. It was his 'house' and he was determined to run it in the way he wanted; he didn't take kindly to criticism. His views landed him in trouble with the law on more than one occasion. He knifed a customer who he claimed had threatened him; he just happened to be carving a joint of ham at the time, so he was acquitted. His personally conducted defence in such cases was undertaken with a showmanship and wit worthy of Oscar Wilde.

On another famous occasion, he barred a black man from his hostelry and was summoned to account before the Race Relations tribunal. In his defence he proclaimed, 'I'm no racist. I've danced with Princess Elizabeth of Toro and you can't get much blacker than that!' He was a showman and a buffoon, but an amusing one. I think his whole history was a charade and his aristocratic origins a myth of his own invention. He claimed he was the squire of the village. The clue was in his assumed name of Kim de la Taste Tickell – (try saying it quickly).

Some years after leaving Cambridge and after I had come out as a gay man, I ran into Kim with his boyfriend Siegi in a London gay club. He was amazed to see me and confessed that he and Siegi had often speculated as to which of the many undergraduates they had known would turn out to be gay; my name was never even mentioned. My camouflage had obviously been a bit too good.

Chapter Seventeen

❧ The Satin and Sequinned Seventies

The 1970s (from about 1974 onward) heralded a dull decade, a sort of mass hangover after the heady excitement and promises unfulfilled of the 1960s. Society had merely exchanged one lot of geriatric politicians for another equally boring and ineffective lot; lead by Harold Wilson, a drab pipe-smoking granddad and Ted Heath, an equally boring stuff-shirt. Wilson's flair for public relations; being photographed with the Beatles and other media stars, didn't convince or impress. The Trade Unions and the working-classes smacked of the Jarrow March and cloth caps, not of swinging London and pop music. We wanted real social change, but we didn't know what or how that was to be.

London in the 1970s was indeed a dull place. Clothes fashions were alive but dire; mostly cheap, gaudy and silly – too much satin and too many sequins. The look is instantly recognisable and now appears positively embarrassing. Restaurants were few in number and poor in quality. The young frequented cheap bistros; Bistro Vino in South Kensington and the Casserole in the King's Road were typical. The décor was minimal, Chianti bottles holding guttering candles on checked tablecloths, all very cheap and cheerful with indifferent food and undrinkable wine, reminiscent of the cheap package holidays that were becoming popular. Pubs still looked working-class and were devoid of style. The lights went out at 11.30 at night and the city went to sleep. Art and creativity languished in London. The dead hand of socialism, strikes, and the three-day week killed enterprise and smothered initiative.

New York was where it was at; New York was sleazy, dangerous and cutting edge; the land of Warhol and *Interview* magazine. High taxes and grey uniformity drove many friends across the Atlantic to find excitement. Gay men idolised the USA as the land of sun, handsome hunks and sex.

By 1972, I had left Cambridge and I started my new life in London. There was still no nightlife or club scene for most people back then. Young people had to content themselves with pubs, coffee bars and the occasional night in a dance hall. The élite danced until the small hours at debutante parties to mobile discotheques and in a few fashionable nightclubs like Sybilla's and Anabelle's – mostly named after girls and ending with an apostrophe 's'. Frankly, even I found most of the sixties and early seventies music un-danceable. I felt uncomfortable gyrating alone on a dance floor or opposite a girl, trying to find a danceable rhythm in the rock music or sentimental ballads of the day.

While at university, I bought a mobile discotheque called The Desolation of Smaug, soon shortened to Smaug. My partners were Cambridge friends, Merlin Hay (now Earl of Erroll), Tim Cutler and Bill Colegrave. Bill dealt with the fathers and arranged the business deals. Merlin provided a bit of a class but soon lost interest, which left Tim and I to actually do the gigs. We had some top-line bookings and, probably thanks to Tim's exceptionally pretty good looks, were in demand by all the girls for their deb dances. In between these Society black-tie engagements, we worked for fashionable Juliana's Disco- theques when they were double booked, and we also did a Saturday night slot at a small Cambridge dance hall venue in the vacations. It was an interesting contrast working in such a place; it taught me a great deal about ordinary life, away from the rarefied atmosphere that we were used to. It was my introduction to the music business and the club world. It sowed the seeds for my later involvement in nightclubs.

Chapter Eighteen

❧ LONDON 1972: A FLAT OF MY OWN

After the success of my university social career, it was hard to start afresh in London. I was glad to move on in life, but the first months in London were lonely and full of uncertainty.

On coming down from university, my primary concern was to find somewhere to live. I felt I just had to move away from home. My mother's tiny mews cottage behind Bryanston Square was small, dark and stultifying. The presence of my mother and stepfather was intolerable to my free spirit. I longed for a place to call my own and to be able to come and go as I pleased, without having to introduce my friends.

I arranged to spend the first summer of my new life sharing a flat with Hugh Trenchard (now Lord Trenchard), a friend from university. He had the use of his grandmother's flat on Cheyne Walk and invited me to rent a room. Hugh was delightful and rather like Bertie Wooster in manner. He had an old-fashioned formality, behaving as though he were a gentleman of a former era. Although we liked each other, we were never destined to be close friends. I suspect he may possibly have disapproved of my emerging homosexuality. Hugh became a fluent Japanese speaker and lived in Tokyo for many years running the local office of Kleinwort Benson, the merchant bank.

A friend, David, at a drag party

I was now free to come and go as I pleased; wander the King's Road and savour its excitements and hedonistic youthful character. Bereft of the variety and ease of access to friends that I had enjoyed at university, the first months of this new freedom were disappointing. First, there was the problem of my sexuality and trying to understand and accept my true nature. Then there was the problem of deciding what to do with my life. I knew one thing for certain and that was that I didn't want to work for anyone else. I had the drive and ambition of a born entrepreneur. My brother and I had come into a modest inheritance from a trust set up by our grandmother. The sums involved were not enormous but were enough, if pooled, to make a start in business and to buy a flat together.

By now, I had concluded that I was homosexual and that it was assuredly not a phase. I knew I had to stop pretending and accept my sexuality and live up to my mantra; 'to thine own self be true'. I knew I had to find the courage to come out to my friends and my family. I am no actor. Too many gay people have lived double lives, become undercover subversives, dicing with discovery and exposure. I knew I valued honesty too highly to live like them.

I reasoned that my sexuality would preclude any conventional business career. I was attracted both by the city – I felt I had an aptitude for finance – and also by the world of fine art dealing. But, I was certain that I did not wish to dissemble throughout my life. The thought of having to field endless questions about when I would marry or of having to take along a compliant lesbian to the firm's annual dinner-dance filled me with horror. I was determined to be true to myself and not to lead life as a lie. I therefore concluded that I had no choice but to employ myself.

Through financial necessity, Rem and I decided to join forces and so we bought a mansion flat in Victoria. It consisted of four bedrooms, a large sitting room and a dining room that would seat ten. Not a bad start for two young post-graduates. I took on the job of decorating the flat and did so in a rather dowdy fashion that was too pompous and formal for our years. I added a few touches of modernity; I remember that chocolate-brown and orange featured, as was then the fashion. Somewhere within me lurked a latent gay designer gene. Rem seemed quite content to let me get on with the decorating but he was very much involved in the decision to buy a dull Victorian landscape painting from O'Mell's, the West End gallery; it hung over the mantelpiece in the sitting room. This purchase proved to be an extremely sound investment and was sold a few years later for a handsome profit.

We bought the flat for the princely sum of £16,750 on a long lease. I also negotiated to buy a pair of elaborate ormolu wall sconces for £20. These I placed in auction: they sold for 320 guineas; that was my first speculative coup.

In my early days in London my gay life, such as it was, was furtive and uncertain. I knew what I wanted but I did not know how to get it. Furthermore, it was illegal to publish the names of gay venues; it was classed as 'proselytizing', so no listings existed of the few secretive bars and pubs that were hidden around town.

Rem and I needed extra income to pay our mortgage so we decided to rent out the two spare rooms. I found a Cambridge friend, Hugo Slater, to rent one of them. In spite of being a cavalry officer, he had already come out after a fashion, but still felt it necessary to be discreet. I was still half-pretending to be straight and attending deb' parties and going out with girls. I was nervous about coming out until I felt secure and happy as a gay man. That meant finding a boyfriend.

Hugo introduced me two of his friends; both came to play a part in my life. As an army officer, Hugo had spent time on secondment in Northern Ireland and there had met and had a brief relationship with a BBC presenter, Sean Rafferty. The two had met when Sean presented a forces favourites programme between Belfast and the British Army of the Rhine. Hugo's other close friend was a Cambridge man, Nigel de Villiers Hart, soon to become the lover of the Conservative MP, Michael Portillo.

Sean Rafferty is a huge character; intelligent, witty and a great mimic with a broad Belfast accent when he chooses not to suppress it. He was well-known in the province as a regular voice on Belfast radio and later on television – he now hosts a regular classical music programme on Radio 3. He is highly social and involved with the arts on both sides of the border. Sean knows everyone in Northern Ireland and introduced me to Sheridan (The Marquis of Dufferin and Ava) and his artist wife, Lindy. Their magnificent house, Clandeboye, was a centre for the sophisticated arts crowd in the province. In spite of being married, Sheridan was gay, so we had many friends in common. At Clandaboye on entering the grand entrance hall and spying a bowl of Pot Pourri, Sean exclaimed in his precise imitation of Ian Paisley, 'No pot pourri here'. An embarrassed pause was followed by gales of laughter.

On our trips together through the Irish countryside we would pop in for a drink or a meal at innumerable grand houses – everyone knew and loved Sean and welcomed him with classic warm Irish hospitality – from the Duke and Duchess of Abercorn (at Baronscourt, with its David Hicks interior – very Sixties) to Lord and Lady Bangor of Castle Ward on the banks of Strangford Lough. (A house with a split personality, a curious mixture of classical and gothic architecture.) With typical Irish eccentricity the 'old bangers', Eddie and Marge, collected gaudy fairground sculpture; horses from carousels and the like. Their daughter, Lala Ward, had a staring role in the TV children's drama, *Dr Who*. You never knew who you would meet or where you would end up on a trip through Ireland with Sean.

Sean Rafferty

Rem and I decided to go into business together, reasoning that between us we could just afford to rent an office and employ a secretary. We rented a couple of rooms in the basement of 10, Manchester Square. We borrowed money to invest in London residential property and to trade in fine claret. Interest rates were low and prices seemed cheap in relation to the rental yields obtainable. So, we bought two small flats and a house, all in rather secondary locations. The most we paid was about £23,000. By the end of 1972, we had sold two of the properties at a substantial profit. London had just enjoyed its first post-war residential property boom.

By 1973, inflation had begun to bite and interest rates soared, leaving those who had over-extended their borrowings in financial distress. The property and financial markets crashed. Every property was worth about a third less almost overnight. We were left with only one flat unsold and a handsome profit with little or no debt. I had learned a valuable lesson in the dangers of borrowing too much and becoming over confident: I had experienced my first boom and slump.

With our new found confidence we employed an extra hand, a young Cambridge undergraduate, Michael Dobson. He came to help in the summer of 1973. Michael had a slow measured and unflappable manner, great charm and stunning dark good looks. I have to confess I was more than a little taken with him but kept our relationship strictly on a business level. He was bright, of course, but the work we gave him to do was hardly challenging, so I gained no impression of his real potential. By the time we met for lunch twenty-five years later, he had become the chief executive of Morgan Grenfell merchant bank.

The summer of 1973 remains memorable for a curious incident. During the course of my life, I have experienced a number of strange and unexplained coincidences but none as bizarre as this. One evening, I was driving from my office in Manchester Square back home to Victoria. Just as I rounded Hyde Park Corner, there was a jolt and a crunch: someone had run into the back of my car. I got out, rather upset and angry to remonstrate with the driver of the other car. He and I exchanged names and addresses – I hope I was polite. I think I only expressed mild anger at what had clearly been his fault, and besides the damage was quite minor. He gave me his address. It was Strand-on-the-Green in Chiswick; strange, as I was due to dine with a total stranger there that very night before a deb dance. On arriving home, I checked the details of my dinner invitation and, lo and behold, I had been 'shunted' by my host. There were a few red faces when I arrived in black tie at his door that evening. The incident had of itself no consequences or point that I can divine, but it has taught me that coincidence is a reality and not to dismiss the play of chance in our lives. Never assume that the man you are off-hand with one day won't be your host at dinner.

We tried our hand at estate agency and called our fledgling effort, Square Feet. We only ever sold one property and the seller, an acquaintance, never paid us our commission. My brother Rem meanwhile was developing the interest he had acquired at Oxford in fine wine. He had realised that an arbitrage existed between what wine merchants and hotels were selling vintages for, and what the same wines were fetching at auction in Sotheby's. Rem has an excellent academic brain and a love and knowledge of fine wines; indeed, he has since written a number of well-received books on the subject. He decided to make a living trading in vintage clarets and I was dispatched to buy from Berry Brothers and other well-known merchants. His face had become too well-known. In those days the wine trade was old fashioned and slow to adapt to new circumstances. Wine was bought and laid down then marked-up by a fixed percentage, so that the sale price three-year's later bore no resemblance to current market price. I don't think we made much more than a modest living out of this exercise and we had to venture ever further a field to make attractive buys.

Our lease at Manchester Square came to end and we decided not to renew it. I had noticed a small advertisement in *The Times* for a furniture business for sale in Chelsea. After some negotiation, we purchased the shop business and lease of Ruth Bellord Ltd of 56, Walton Street and moved in to learn a new trade. The shop was on its last legs and I had neither the imagination nor flair to become a retailer. My days behind the counter were not without interest. Some of our more outrageous customers were diverting and right opposite the shop was La Popote, a camp restaurant run by a notorious character, Christopher Hunter, a linchpin of the nascent gay scene.

One morning, as I was walking my dog, I noticed an attractive young Italian waiter coming out of the restaurant. He stopped to talk and pet my dog; the rest as they say, is history. Through him, I learnt the ways and mores of the gay world as it then was. It was my first relationship with another gay man and the first affair where my interest was truly reciprocated. I now felt able to confront the issues involved with declaring my sexuality to others, i.e., 'coming out'.

Being stuck behind a counter was hardly my idea of fun and, in my snobbish way, I thought it rather demeaning. Although the furniture business was not a great success, we had bought a good lease cheaply. Rem wanted to expand the wine business and so we turned the ailing furniture shop into La Reserve, a fine wine merchant specialising in high-end clarets and wine brokerage. I think we were one of the first businesses in London to promote wine as a serious investment. The look Rem gave the shop was an innovation too. The wines were displayed in their original wooden crates and the shop had some of the atmosphere of a genuine French cave. The young assistants were all educated public school types keen to learn about wine, and so our well-heeled Knightsbridge customers could find someone attractive and knowledgeable to buy from.

Rem and I bickered a lot and did not really enjoy working together. We had made a modest living and increased our capital through our property investments, so we decided to go our separate ways. He ran the wine business and I ran our newly acquired publishing business, Burke's Peerage from the offices above the shop. From this sedate and conventional base, I was soon to branch out into the entirely different world of nightclubs and fast living.

I moved out of our shared flat and bought a house on my own in Pimlico. At last, I felt free of my family and able to lead my own life. As my circle of gay friends enlarged, I became more confident, both sexually and socially. I was going out to clubs and bars, such as they were, almost every night and enjoying and exploring my new-found sexual freedom. I soon abandoned the Italian waiter.

My next boy friend was a handsome dark haired boy, half-Peruvian and half-French, named Guillaume de Brou; his mother had abandoned him in Switzerland at the age of eleven. She sent him to a boarding school, La Gruyere, and then left him there for a number of years while she sought refuge in a nunnery. I don't think my friend ever truly got over this early traumatic experience of abandonment, even though the headmaster and his family looked after him in the holidays and showed him much love and kindness.

Guillaume was a social boy and through a mixture of boyish good looks and old-fashioned courtly charm he made many friends. He was especially charming towards older people and many women felt the desire to mother him.

He introduced me to Stephane Grappelli, the famous jazz violinist, by then in his late sixties. One evening Stephane invited us both to dinner in London. It was quite clear that he was somewhat taken with Guillaume and that he wanted to get to know us better. He was wearing a rather unsuitable brightly coloured and patterned silk-shirt; it would

Guillaume de Brou

have looked better on a twenty-year-old girl. We sat entranced while he played a solo for us; George Gershwin's *Summertime*. The privilege of being serenaded by such a virtuoso will always remain with me. In his skilled hands, the violin seemed able to express subtle emotions speaking directly to my heart. We failed to repay the heavenly experience by performing a duet for him, as he so clearly wanted. I now regret that we were too prudish and selfish to afford him such a small thing that would have given him so much pleasure. Such is the arrogance and ageism of youth; it is truly wasted on the young.

My relationship with Guillaume drifted on for a year or so, but we both knew it was going nowhere. We parted friends, and he now lives in Paris.

ALAN TAULBEE – A FRIEND WHO FELL OUT OF LOVE WITH HIMSELF

I first met Alan Taulbee while I was still an undergraduate at Cambridge in the spring of 1971. He had come to London as agent for Nancy Oakes, an eccentric Bahamian heiress, and was charged with organising a debutante ball for her daughter, Patricia (Patty), combined with a 21st party for her son, Sacha von Hoyningen-Huene, at the Savoy Hotel. Patty happened to be the girlfriend of my roommate, Michael Prideaux. In my final year at university, he and I shared a country house together about ten miles outside Cambridge on the estate of a friend, Roger Bevan, in the village of Longstowe.

Nancy was the daughter of Sir Harry Oakes who had been murdered in Nassau during the War, when the Duke of Windsor was Governor of the Bahamas. The ensuing scandal and trial caused a sensation comparable to the murder of the Earl of Erroll in Kenya. The Oakes murder remains to this day one of the great unsolved mysteries.

Alan Taulbee

Nancy's husband, the young, handsome and ambitious Alfred de Marigny, was tried and acquitted of the gruesome killing of his father-in-law. Sir Harry was a rich man, one of the so-called Bay Street Boys, the controlling clique of Nassau businessmen. He made many enemies and had a reputation as a ruthless bully. Few mourned his passing, but society was intrigued by the mystery surrounding his death. Conspiracy theories proliferated; one of them implicated the Duke of Windsor with a putative Nazi plot.

Nancy had been raised rich and spoiled; used to getting her own way. Alan had met her in Mexico during his time there in the 1950s and 1960s. She lived in great splendour with her husband, an Englishman, Patrick Tritton.

Alan, properly attired in hunting pink, rode to hounds in Patrick's hunt, Mr Tritton's Hounds. Mexico City, although densely populated, was but a small town for rich or well-connected expatriates. Alan was firmly of the latter category: gay, charming, and impecunious. He drifted from one job to another, none of them amounting to a career. His siesta hours were spent languishing in a Turkish bath, being massaged by young Mexican studs. The alcohol flowed freely in that expatriate world and gossip ran alongside the endless drinks parties and the bored leisurely existence. Jobs were easy to come by for a man of charm and sophistication, who had the correct residence papers, spoke Spanish fluently and had all the right connections. At the first hint of criticism or boredom, Alan would move on to something else. He even tried his hand at running a hotel in Yucatan, but he had little patience for the day-to-day detail of such an enterprise.

Nancy had taken a shine to him and eventually employed him as her secretary and 'walker'. Alan needed the money but resented the somewhat demeaning role of companion to a rich and demanding woman. He particularly resented being told what clothes to buy or wear.

Nancy's daughter, Patty, had coincidentally, been a friend of my step-sister Amanda at Heathfield. She had a sassy, confident demeanour, not unlike the heroine as portrayed in the film, *Love Story*. Most boys found her daunting but Michael liked a strong confident girl who was not obviously bowled over by his exceptional good looks. 'How does it feel to be ideal fag bait?' she once teased him. To my eyes, she was not particularly pretty, but then I was not a little jealous. Michael found her indifference to him captivating. She wore little make-up and had a powerfully masculine drive and confidence; there was nothing girly or frilly about her.

Michael, by contrast, had a poetic Rupert Brooke quality to him. As well as dark good-looks, he was erudite and well-read. He often appeared soft and gentle and, with Patty, supine in his devotion. The only times he showed irritation were when dismissing the adoration of others, myself included. Sexually, he was a tease: he flirted outrageously with boys. Girls flirted with him. Once, he kissed me in front of some of our friends just to see how I would handle the embarrassment. He adored Alan and would sit enraptured at tales of his exotic life, laughing at his jokes, always eager for more.

Alan was 6´4˝ tall, elegantly and fashionably dressed with an upright, almost military bearing. He walked with a stick following a riding accident and a hip-replacement operation. This served to accentuate his air of authority. At fifty-one, he had white hair and a pointed white moustache; he could be described as looking like Colonel Sanders of Kentucky Fried Chicken fame or more accurately as a distinguished diplomat. His educated and well modulated mid-Atlantic accent commanded attention. He was fluent in Spanish, having been brought-up in Puerto Rico where his father had been stationed while an Army officer; this added to his air of international sophistication. He was not in the least bit camp or effeminate but he was bitchy and vastly entertaining.

He had a fund of witty and amusing stories, usually of a scurrilous nature and about well-known people or those in London society. He liked to shock, using language that was direct and overtly sexual. In a typical letter from America, having spent a page haranguing 'The Duchess of Beverly Hills', whose only crime was wishing to buy Alan a new wardrobe of clothes from Neiman Marcus, he wrote, 'Can't she get it through her thick Louisiana head that I don't want her shitty neckties? It will all end by my telling her where to take her menswear and stuff it. FUCK HER! Pas moi – TOI.'

Alan loved to smoke dope, and would sit for hours with us stoned and giggling like a teenager. At heart, Alan was still a boy: he longed to be one of us. He was emotionally immature, much given to moods and sulking. He sometimes let the act slip and became a petulant child when thwarted. To us young undergraduates he was a man of mystery and allure. He made little secret of his sexual proclivities and was charmed and amused by the company of intelligent and aristocratic young Englishmen. The admiration was mutual.

After the war, Alan had spent a few years in New York where he became a radio announcer for the *New York Times* radio station. I was entranced by his recollections of those days and especially gay life in New York in the 1950s. He had three brothers, one of whom was also homosexual. Woodson Taulbee had been immensely good-looking and

Alan Taulbee and Author in Hong Kong

the lover of the celebrated interior decorator, Billy Baldwin, who remained a friend of Alan. Alan kept a black and white photograph of Woody taken by the Vogue photographer, George von Hoyningen-Huene in the 1930s, that left one in no doubt about his striking male beauty. Alan was not himself a particularly good-looking man. In some respects, he could even be considered ugly; his nose was too large and he had poor skin. I suspect he suffered greatly from always being thought of as Woody's brother.

Alan took an immediate shine to my housemate, the wickedly handsome Michael. He wasn't gay but with Alan, for whom hope sprung eternal, the process of seduction was more important than actual success. Although Alan fell secretly in love with Michael, he was too experienced and worldly-wise to intimate the extent of his adoration. He enjoyed playing games with us and being sexually provocative. He was the first openly gay man I had ever met and one I could admire; he was so unlike the camp, stereotype of a gay man then prevalent. I formed an admiration and attachment to him.

He was living in Nancy's flat at Carlton Gardens that he decorated for her stylishly, after the manner of Billy Baldwin. Alan was glamorous and sophisticated, with a fund of amusing stories. He liked to recall how, when Lady Edith Foxwell came for tea at Carlton Gardens, she asked to borrow his bedroom for an hour in order to entertain her handsome black chauffeur. No adult had ever talked to us like this before: he was a revelation.

After the glamorous party at the Savoy, Alan stayed on in London. First as an employee of Nancy, looking after her affairs and properties over here, then, after the inevitable row with her, living independently. He rented, from Kenneth Neame an antique dealer, a tiny basement flat in Hans Place. This he decorated to look like a New York Upper Eastside apartment in dark chocolate gloss paint, lots of mirror, down-lighters in the ceiling and wicker basket potholders, resplendent with light-green ferns. Simple elegant modern furniture made the one room both comfortable and seductive. His collection of photographs in silver frames, the illustrated volumes on art and decorating, completed the look and feel of urbane sophistication.

I continued to see Alan for some years. I would meet him for drinks and dinners, often taking young male friends along. All the time we grew closer and more intimate but never sexual; our tastes were both for young men. Eventually, Alan decided to move back to Mexico. His brother, Woody, was dying of cancer and had offered to buy him a prop-erty in Puerto Vallarta. Our friendship continued via an exchange of cor-respondence; Alan was a particularly fine and witty letter-writer with an intimate conversational style. With the distance provided by these letters, I was able to tell him that I had homosexual feelings and Alan advised and counselled me through a difficult period of adjustment.

His years in Mexico were a disaster for Alan, emotionally and finan-cially. Woody died and left Alan some shares that soon became worth-less. He lost his house over a legal problem and was left almost desti-tute. He decided to return to London, where he was happiest, and moved into a small flat above my offices in Walton Street, Chelsea. He wanted to be near his London doctor in whom he had so much trust. Given to bouts of melancholia, there were times when Alan went to ground and would see no one. When he emerged, he was the greatest fun to be around; generous to a fault and extravagant with taxis, restau-rants and clothes. He had his suits tailor-made at Blades, next to the back entrance of Albany in Savile Row. Nevertheless, he would com-plain to friends that I was stingy, even though I charged him a ludi-crously low £10 a week rent.

In the early days of my nightclub, the Embassy, Alan would prop up the bar entertaining his fan club with his stories while drinking away on my bar tab. Many people believed he was the *éminence grise* behind the club: its rich mysterious backer. Nothing could have been further from the truth – darling Alan was increasingly reliant on the kindness of strangers.

As I got to know him intimately, I became aware that like so many gay men of his era, Alan was a snob, deeply attracted by titles and fame. He loved to drop names and appear to be in-the-know. He had a capacity for friendship with men but was always suspicious of the motives of women. 'She's trying to ensnare me,' he would say. 'The bitch is out to own me.' There was more than a streak of misogyny in his fear of women.

I think he had always been disappointed in love. He so mistrusted long-term intimacy with anyone and was often catty and critical of close friends usually to other friends; in doing so he often risked exposure and the loss of cherished friendships. His ploy was to reject people before he could be rejected; it was safer and less painful that way. The result was that he became lonely in old age. This unfortunate trait was not helped by his frequent moves, not only from city to city but also of countries. Long-distance correspondence was a much safer bet.

Some months after the opening of the Embassy Club and its initial success, Alan thought I needed a break away. A friend of his, Max Reed, the son of Sir Carol Reed, the film director, offered him the loan of his flat in Cannes in the South of France. Alan asked if I would like to join him and bring a friend. It was understood that I was expected to pay all expenses. I prevaricated as to whether I should ask Derek Frost, a divine and talented young interior decorator, or Ben, a cute young actor whom I fancied and whom I felt sure would be hot sex. Luckily, I decided to ask Derek. It was on this memorable weekend that we fell in love with each other – and in a way with darling Alan. From this moment onward, he became our surrogate parent and lifelong responsibility. In many ways, particularly financially, Alan was a child and he drifted through life certain, like Mr Micawber, that something would turn up and of course it always did.

Derek and I vowed to each other that, no matter what Alan said or did to drive us away, we would never abandon him. There were many times when he tried our patience and resolve sorely, but we never reneged on that promise.

Eventually, Alan found that he could no longer afford to live in London, besides he found the winters too cold. Reluctantly, he moved back to America, first Miami, then to Key West where we would visit him twice a year. He soon got bored and made too many enemies in that small town, so he moved on again. At one point, he returned to Mexico for two years in order to try to salvage something from the debacle of the house. He lived in Guadalajara, where it was cheap. His health deteriorated and his hip was giving him trouble. His finances dwindled. We worried for his sanity and even more for his solvency. He developed a sentimental friendship with the teenage boy who cleaned his apartment and Alan came to look on him as a son. He smoked more and more dope; it dulled the pain of loneliness and the worries over money. The dope gave him highs but increased his tendency to paranoia. We persuaded him to return to America, where at least he had access to Medicare. He decided, for reasons that still remain a mystery, to settle in the tiny coastal town of Bandon, Oregon. (He was truly abandoned in Bandon.) The year plus that he spent there was a period of healing; his sanity and equilibrium returned, probably as he was unable to buy his beloved 'Mary Jane' (Marijuana).

I decided that his friends had to rescue him and so I clubbed together with a couple of close chums and decided to make Alan a monthly allowance, in order to enable him to live with a modicum of dignity. When he felt strong enough, he moved to San Diego where the easy climate further aided his recovery. He went for days without seeing anyone but protested that he was not lonely. He read voraciously and listened to classical music on public radio. He possessed neither a car nor a television and wanted neither. He was now well into his seventies and barely able to walk. He agreed to move to Los Angeles where another friend, Richard Mytton-Mills, was on hand to keep an eye on him.

He took a small one-room apartment that he decorated with his usual éclat, retreating further into his world of books and music. His routine consisted of reading and housework in the mornings, followed by a light lunch and an afternoon rest on his day bed. He would awake about 5pm and have a joint, open a bottle of wine and prepare dinner. He

Alan Taulbee and Derek

loved his food and used to send us endless recipes. He delighted in the literary works of MFK Fisher, the elegant food writer, and would salivate at her glorious descriptions of Mediterranean picnics. At 6pm he would switch on the radio and listen to the news; he remained well informed on the subject of politics. He loved to rail against the iniquities of Reagan and the Republicans. By 6.30pm he was stoned and a little drunk, he gave himself over to listening to a classical concert. He would conduct his orchestra with brio or dance with himself round his apartment like a thing demented.

Alan stopped writing letters about his time and from then on, we spoke at length on the telephone. He came to stay once or twice in Key West but found the journey too tiring and felt sidelined by the mad round of fun that characterised our life in that party town. His tendency to show off was often an embarrassment as he strove ever harder to be the centre of attention. Our love for him never wavered, even as he became more childlike and reliant on us for all the important decisions in his life. We visited him in LA about once every other year, and watched his inexorable physical decline. We loved our visits and the pleasure they gave him, but there was usually a brief episode of childlike self-pity and tears before we left. He kept our pictures in a place of honour by his bedside. We were his children.

He could just manage to stagger from his apartment to his local grocery store. He noticed a fine young black guy at the checkout. With his quirky seductive manner, Alan managed to persuade the young man, Derwin, to help him home with his groceries. They sat and talked and drank a cup of tea. A most unusual and touching friendship arose between this eighty-year-old white, gay man and the basketball-playing, church-going, twenty-something straight black man.

Alan came to love Derwin. Tears appeared at the corner of his eyes when he spoke of him. I think it was the only fully requited love Alan had known since his mother died. Derwin, and his fiancée Tasha, cared deeply for Alan and his whole family accepted this strange relationship for what it was: Two people who delighted in each other's company and looked out for one another without any expectations or hope of material reward. We spent one last weekend together with Alan and Derwin in a rented cottage in the desert near Palm Springs. We came to know and admire this straightforward, honest young man and delighted to see Alan's happiness in his company.

Alan died in 2003 after a relatively short illness. Derwin and Richard took his ashes to be scattered in the desert at Joshua Tree; sadly, we were unable to be there. Alan had left his last $10,000 to Derwin in his will but Derwin said he wanted us to have it, as by rights it was our money that we had given to Alan. Naturally, we refused and were happy to view the money as a wedding gift from dear Alan to Derwin, the only real love of his adult life.

Chapter Twenty

❈ NIGEL AND THE PORTILLO AFFAIR

Nigel de Villiers Hart, a friend from my Cambridge days, was one of the few out gay men at the university. In 1970, the university gay scene was tiny and I was not really part of it. I was more interested in hanging out with the beautiful people and the social élite in the Pitt Club, than mixing with those on the fringes of society, although I had a sneaking admiration for their courage.

Nigel was not only openly gay but highly politicised as well. He managed to retain a certain social acceptability in spite of his louche connections, and I admired his adroitness. After Cambridge and a spell of guiding tourists round Europe on coaches, he became the full-time information officer for the newly formed Campaign for Homosexual Equality (CHE) and as a consequence moved to Manchester where CHE had its base.

Nigel was a good-looking man, but had a tendency to take life too seriously. He was earnest and intelligent but found it hard to lighten-up and relax. His earnest manner detracted from his sex appeal; he had no idea of how to flirt. He had deeply held left-wing political beliefs, especially on social issues. I shared many of his aspirations but believed that the best way to achieve social integration for gay men was to be open and relaxed in everyday life with everyone one encountered, rather than to make public protest. My creed is that people take you at your own evaluation of yourself. Appear embarrassed or ashamed and people will assume you have something to be embarrassed about. If you are open about your sexuality, it leaves no space for salacious gossip or sniggering innuendo.

Nigel de Villiers Hart

Nigel persuaded me to accompany him on the Gay Pride March through London in 1974. It was only the third such march. I am so pleased that I found the courage to go. There was a great sense of camaraderie and mission. The march was small, only a few thousand people as I remember. Some of us were reticent lest our pictures should appear in the press, while others revelled in their flamboyant exhibitionism. We still had so much to achieve in the normalisation and acceptance of gay men and women. At first, I felt uncomfortable in the company of drag queens and leather types, but by the end of the day I had learnt to accept their difference and rejoice in their ability to express themselves without shame – but how the people stared.

Nigel's one claim to a sense of humour was the invention, with a friend, of a satirical version of Polari, the traditional camp slang. This involved initials to indicate sexual preferences or to denote jesting disapproval. NQOCD, for example, meant 'not quite our class, dear' and NTBG 'not the butchest thing going', when referring to some poor limp-wristed queen. Un-chic areas of town, where our less fortunate friends were forced to live, were upgraded; thus Clapham became 'Cla'am' and Battersea, 'Batt-er-see-ah'. This poked fun at the silly, faux upper class pronunciation so often effected by those who wanted to be thought smart. Our private slang language seemed to cement our small group and it gave us confidence and solidarity; we revelled in our difference.

One weekend Nigel asked me to stay with his parents at the family home, Huntworth, in Somerset. His father was an old-fashioned squire and country gentleman much involved in local politics, for the Tory party naturally. Lt Commander Michael de Villiers Hart (Royal Navy Ret.) was a leading campaigner against the Common Market, locally and nationally. Nigel was his only son and I think his father found him hard to comprehend, and so they preferred silence to angry political exchanges. It was not an easy weekend. The conversation was stilted and the atmosphere tense. I don't believe his father was ever reconciled to his son's sexuality.

Together we discovered the emerging world of London gay life and rather sad it proved to be – a few grubby pubs and some tiny basement coffee bars. There was one club we both frequented that was great fun. It was on Kensington High Street below the El Sombrero restaurant but its real name was 'Yours or Mine'. A fearsome bitchy queen with a sharp tongue guarded this underground cavern of delights. He revelled in his powers over the door and his control of admissions to his den. It took a bit of courage to go down those steps and face his inquisition, until he knew you and made you welcome as part of the family.

The club had an illuminated dance floor and a 2am licence. It was full of hairdressers and waiters and a smattering of more glamorous people – shady aristocrats, minor actors and a few drag queens. Elmir de Hory, the notorious art forger, was a habitué when over from his home in Spain.

A curious character called Vikky de Lambray held court there every night and was lavish with champagne. He had numerous aliases including Vicky de Rothschild; he was the first man I ever met who wore make-up. He masked the truth of his life equally as well. Such fantasists, as I was to discover, populate the clubs and demi-monde of London nightlife. I heard he eventually killed himself – I suspect that his permanent acting and life of subterfuge took its toll.

It was at Yours or Mine that I first started on my regular nightclubbing and eventually found the courage to take boys home with me. Soon, I became completely immersed in the gay world of London. Nigel was much bolder and more secure sexually than I. We were unlikely friends and eventually we drifted apart; his move to Manchester did not help. Our only real point of cohesion had been our homosexuality and our Cambridge connections.

I started to see less of Nigel. He had begun a love affair with an aspiring Conservative politician, Michael Portillo, whom he had met at a party at Peterhouse in Cambridge. Their love affair began at Cambridge, but did not last initially. However, the pair re-encountered one another by chance in France, underneath the Eiffel Tower and their affair recommenced in earnest. I heard Nigel on the radio and occasionally on television as spokesperson for CHE. Unfortunately, his innate shyness of manner made him in turns aggressive and then defensive when speaking for that organisation. He totally lacked the relaxed confidence and assurance of his lover, 'Polly' Portillo.

For some reason I was never introduced to him; possibly because Michael Portillo was by then engaged to be married. We heard a lot about him from Nigel when we did get together. It proved unfortunate for the future Conservative Party leadership contender that he had chosen a gay political activist with whom to have a six-year sexual relationship, but then Jeremy Thorpe, the leader of the Liberal Party, chose the unsuitable Norman Scott as his boyfriend with disastrous results.

My mother (a *tricoteuse*), loved to attend sensational trials at the Old Bailey. One day in 1979, I accompanied her to the Thorpe murder trial. We were sitting in the City Land seats facing the accused in the dock. One of the three accused, David Holmes, kept looking at me, so much so that my mother asked me if I knew him. I blushed with embarrassment. I believe that I was actually being cruised from the dock. Jeremy Thorpe, with his customary insouciance, had his feet resting on the rail in front of him. He seemed entirely confident of a successful outcome.

In his final days, before his premature death from an AIDS-related disease, Nigel gave a highly controversial interview to a tabloid newspaper about his relationship with Portillo. He told me that he would never have outed him, but felt incensed that in outing himself, Portillo had belittled their long affair by reference merely to an early student homosexual encounter, or words to that effect – whereas in Nigel's eyes they had had a long and important relationship, lasting six years.

Michael Portillo had neglected to mention that when they first had had sex, Nigel was below the then age of consent of twenty-one. Considering Michael had voted against the lowering of that age, this made him at the very least, a hypocrite. Nigel believed that once Portillo had outed himself, he, Nigel, had the right to set the record straight about the true nature and intensity of their affair. Nigel was convinced that he was not Portillo's only gay lover and that he was, at that time at any rate, by nature more gay than straight. It was a sad finale to what had clearly been an important and loving relationship, extending over such a long period.

Chapter Twenty-One

✖ Hugh (Massive Snob) Montgomery–Massingberd

It was with some trepidation that, in 1960, I approached my first term at Harrow. I was starting rather younger than was customary; my thirteenth birthday was during my first term. I was a small boy and under-developed for my age. The only other new boy at my house, Rendalls, was Hugh Montgomery, as he was then called; a tall, thin shy boy with a love and knowledge of cricket but no particular talent for playing games. Although we were un-alike in most respects, we formed a bond in adversity. We were literally thrown together, as we had shared a tiny study-bedroom in the new boys' annexe. When my mother took my brother and I back to school in a taxi, the taxi driver helped carry my trunk into the house. On returning to his cab he exclaimed in a rich cockney accent, 'Blime m'um, is that (H)arrow? I wouldn't let a child of mine go to a place like that! It's worse than Wormwood Scrubs.'

Hugh and I had in common our devotion to our respective nannies; they still looked after us at home. Harrow was not a happy time for either of us. Hugh gained popularity through his knowledge of cricket and his endless mimicry of television personalities, especially comedians. The age stratification of the school, together with the prohibition

Gunby Hall, Lincolnshire

on forming friendships outside one's own house, kept us closely together. Hugh's shyness was such that it prompted our housemaster to exclaim as Hugh tried to avoid him, 'Montgomery, I don't know if you are really shy or just plain bloody rude?' I suspect that, even at this early date, there was something of the subversive anarchist in Hugh. He loved to send up institutions and pompous people, while always maintaining a seeming deference to the status quo. His inner core was torn between wanting to succeed on establishment terms and a need to prick the pomposity and stupidity of the rules; he could identify both with the school monitors and the rebellion typified in *If*, the film by Lindsay Anderson.

By the mid-sixties, after Harrow, Hugh worked as an articled clerk for a firm of London solicitors. He was no happier there than I was as a trainee estate agent with Best Gapp & Partners of Sloane Square. Most of our contemporaries from school lived away from London, which left us both rather friendless. Hugh often came to stay at our family flat in Victoria. We shared a romantic view of the world based on an attraction for the manners and mores of pre-war life. We liked to imagine ourselves in a PG Wodehouse world of servants and country houses. We both felt we were misplaced aristocrats fallen on hard times, he with perhaps more justification than I. He had the more illustrious ancestors but I had more ready money. Hugh had a strange but engaging turn of phrase, a combination of Wodehouse, Waugh and Anthony Powell, with a bit of *Private Eye* thrown in. When on form, and amongst friends, he was entertaining but always eccentric. His mind was quick and alive and his memory phenomenal.

Hugh Montgomery-Massingberd

Hugh's sexual tastes had, after leaving school, become decidedly heterosexual: he had taken to visiting the sleazier parts of Soho. He lived in a fantasy world and was fascinated by satire and the world of television. He spent hours in front of the box in his suburban family home at Cookham in the Thames Valley being overfed by his nanny, Biddo.

Hugh's natural propensity for hero worship led him to befriend a fellow clerk at his firm, Richard, a good-looking, cock-sure dandy whose addiction to high living led him to spend way in excess of his modest means. I didn't like him and resented his Flashman-like manner, his arrogant heterosexuality and his influence over Hugh.

Hugh and I spent some weekends at his old family home, Gunby Hall, in Lincolnshire, now the property of the National Trust; referred to by Tennyson as 'a haunt of ancient peace'. It is a particularly beautiful but severe William and Mary manor house built of plum-coloured brick with dressed stone quoins. The house is tall and rectangular with little or no decoration, just perfect proportions lending it an understated grandeur. The grounds included a formal garden, a walled flower and vegetable garden and a romantic pond path known as the Ghost Walk. A stately park dotted with mature oak trees surrounds the property. In short, a seat fit for the Field Marshal that was his great-uncle, Sir Archibald Montgomery-Massingberd, Chief of the Imperial General Staff in the 1930s.

As a condition of inheriting the tenancy of Gunby, Hugh's father had changed the family name to Montgomery-Massingberd. Hugh was secretly pleased at this noble-sounding addition, but he was saddened by the absence of the baronetcy that he felt to be its natural and deserved adornment. The new name stood him in good stead in his journalistic career as a writer on the subjects of heritage and aristocracy.

In 1966, unable to concentrate on academic work at my crammers in London, I took myself off to a tutorial college at Oxford. Hugh joined me there, having also decided to try for Cambridge. We took digs in the Banbury Road, a primitive place with one gas ring.

I studied hard but, with only one tutorial a week in each subject, I had to be self-reliant. My days were spent in the Oxford public library at Carfax or in the Pitt-Rivers Museum, that dusty compendium of savage tribal objects arranged by typology. I love old-fashioned museums with their collector's cabinets filled with serried rows of collectibles and labels inscribed in neat copperplate handwriting.

My leisure time was spent wandering alone by the river Cherwell dreaming of what it would be like to be part of the University, and have a group of young male friends. My other favourite place was the romantic ancient forest of Wychwood near Cornbury. Hugh and I were once expelled for trespassing by Lord Rotherwick's officious gamekeeper. In the haste to escape, all my revision papers flew off the roof of my car where I had unwisely placed them. Wychwood is also near Blenheim Palace. Little did I know what an important role the Spencer-Churchill family would come to play in my future life through my friendships with Michael Waterhouse, grandson of 'Bert' Marlborough (the 10th Duke) and Lord Edward Spencer-Churchill, son of the present Duke.

Eventually I managed to obtain three A-levels: two A grades and a B. As a result, and after an interview, I was offered a place at Pembroke College, Cambridge, to start in the autumn of 1968. Hugh decided not to take up his Cambridge place as he had already started work at Burke's Peerage; he had found his metier.

Chapter Twenty-Two

❋ BURKE'S PEERAGE

In 1971, the owners of Burke's, Mercury House publications, became fed-up with Peter Townend, the editor, and sacked him replacing him with Hugh Montgomery-Massingberd, his assistant, aged only twenty-four. Hugh was brimming with enthusiasm for his new task and had many ideas for expanding the list of publications into new but related areas. Few of these fantastic schemes found favour with his employers. They published trade directories and had no interest or feel for this arcane area of endeavour. So, in 1973, Hugh approached me with his proposals. I liked his plans and recruited a small band of investors. We were able to buy the imprint, started in 1826, for a few thousand pounds. I duly became the chairman and managing director of this august publishing house aged only twenty-six. Hugh was the editorial director.

(From left, back row) David Williamson, Charles Kidd, Hugh Montgomery-Massingberd, Patrick Lichfield, Mark Bence-Jones (Middle Row, from left) Hugo Vickers, Remington, Author, Suzanna Osman-Jones, Peter Cook (Front row) Emma Clifford-Browne

It is hard to imagine the power and mystique of the name Burke's Peerage then still held. There was no chief executive or person of importance who would not take a call from us. 'This is the chairman of Burke's Peerage' was an open sesame. But how could we turn it into profit? We never did discover that golden key. On reflection, perhaps we were too honourable and timid. At the time we took over, I made a pompous statement to the press saying, 'It is absolutely not a vulgarising exercise.' We had high ideals, perhaps ideals more appropriate to a bygone age. We should, I suppose, have been prepared to be more ruthless in exploiting the name and prestige of Burke's.

We considered publishing a rival to *Who's Who* with a broader-based appeal by including fashionable names from the arts and the new younger society. But we funked the opportunity and now Debrett's publish *People of Today* to some acclaim. We also had a bash at a popular book to mark The Queen's Silver Jubilee in 1977, but we published our effort after Debrett's and it was probably too sycophantic, formal and not gossipy enough. Debrett's book, though admittedly even more sycophantic, went on to be the best-selling hardback of the year.

We might perhaps have foreseen the enormous popular success of *Hello* magazine and popular picture books about royalty. About this time, The Queen permitted a documentary television team to film her family life, depicting such scenes as a relaxed family picnic at Balmoral.

Burke's Peerage Ltd, Colophon

This helped to withdraw the veil of secrecy and mystique that had until then surrounded the Monarchy and, together with the Silver Jubilee, fuelled the popular hunger for royal gossip. Yes, we were undoubtedly inhibited by our scholarly pretensions and our patrician disdain for the popular. This insistence on old-fashioned standards was Hugh Massingberd's greatest disadvantage as a commercial publisher, and I accepted his judgment without sufficient question.

We made use of the vacant flat above the wine business owned by my brother Remington and me, La Reserve, in Walton Street, as our offices. The four rooms were just adequate to accommodate our editorial staff: Hugh Montgomery-Massingberd, his deputy Charles Kidd, and two female assistants, Suzanna Osman-Jones and Camilla Binny; supplemented by two contributing editors: Hugo Vickers and David Williamson, as well as me and my secretary, Isobel Clive-Ponsonby-Fane. After a few years, Felicity Mortimer joined the firm. She took over as managing director after I left to become a full-time nightclub owner. She is still a close friend and lives happily back home in Malta where I visit her from time to time.

Hugh and the team set about expanding the list and working on a new edition of the *Landed Gentry of Ireland* now re-titled by us, *Irish Family Records*. We had lofty ideals about making the books more contemporary and relevant without losing their mystique and cachet. We included more anecdotes, of which Hugh had an inexhaustible fund, and included literary, business and academic families while dropping those dim dynasties who had either lost their landed seats or whose members were of little interest to others. Sir Ian Moncreiffe of that Ilk, the great genealogist, was a regular visitor to our offices to advise and proffer historical insights into his numerous royal descents. He was a true eccentric of the old school, a strange mixture of childishness and scholarship. He was also the father of my Cambridge friend, Merlin Hay, now Lord Erroll.

While producing our book *Irish Family Records*, we had to deal with many a knotty political conundrum. We were keen to include families from both sides of the border and all faiths and political persuasions. Traditionally, the landed classes in Ireland were from the Anglo-Protestant ascendancy. We included de Valera and other Catholic families. Some die-hard Protestants protested that they were English not Irish. When I said to one man that his family had been in Ireland for over three hundred years; did that not make him Irish? He countered, 'Some American families have lived over there for just as long, it does not make them Red Indian.' Another scion of a well-known Catholic

Dublin family told me his son was in the Diplomatic Corps. He was proud to call himself Irish and strove to be politically correct on that subject. I rejoined, 'Does Ireland have many embassies worldwide?' He looked puzzled and explained that his first-born son was, of course, a British diplomat.

The fact that the Burkes and Fitzgeralds had been living in Ireland since Norman times, indeed some were even Catholic, did not prevent their houses and persons being attacked by the IRA as hated English invaders. In Ireland, I was quick to learn, nothing is as it seems and in politics you can never win. I heard a clever joke that helped to explain it all. It is best told in a Belfast brogue. A man is stopped in the street by an armed terrorist and asked what religion he is. The wrong answer could mean a bullet to the head. He has a clever reply, 'I'm Jewish'. 'Yes,' says the terrorist, 'But are you Protestant Jewish or Catholic Jewish?'

During our time at Walton Street, we heard IRA bombs go off. Terrorists threw the bomb into Walton's restaurant completely destroying the interior; sadly, a number of the diners were killed. We learned to live with IRA atrocities; we also heard the bomb go off behind Harrods one Christmas. We were all angered by the lack of American help for our country's anti-terrorist efforts and by the support given to the IRA by prominent Americans, the Kennedy clan in particular; and also the fact that NORAID, a front for the IRA, was permitted to fundraise openly on the streets of New York.

The days at Burke's were spent in laughter at Hugh's endless witticisms and mimicry; photocopying pedigrees to send out to family members; selling and delivering books to John Sandoe, Heywood Hill and Hatchards, or answering the queries of eccentric family members who sometimes came to call at the office. Every post contained amazing, vainglorious, endearing or sometimes just plain dotty correspondence. The funniest of these letters were pinned up in the loo. Thanks to Hugh's enthusiasm, we knew Peter Cook and Dudley Moore's sketch about *Burke's Peerage* by heart: 'This Burke had a clever idea, Dud, put the names of all the grandest people in the land together in a book and flog it to them!' Never has a job been such fun, but sadly we didn't make much money and the new series of titles proposed by Hugh proved to be more costly to produce than expected. Throughout the 1970s, as elsewhere there was massive price inflation in the cost of book printing and publishing.

We were all young and having fun, riding a great adventure and following a dream. The press were calling us all the time: we were excellent copy. Hugh was always ready with a scurrilous or amusing anecdote.

We recruited The Queen's cousin, Patrick Lichfield the photographer, to our board. He took a group photograph of our team that was published in *The Times*. Another board member, co-opted to give us academic gravitas, was the convivial John Brooke-Little, then Richmond Herald at the College of Arms, who snored his way through several post-prandial meetings.

Our first truly moneymaking venture was to be a book on American Presidential families, published to coincide with the bi-centennial of American independence. The idea had originated from our contributing editor, the redoubtable David Williamson, a rotund, camp gay man and Ronnie Barker look-a-like, with a well-stocked brain and a ready wit. All of us in the office loved David; he never took himself too seriously. Genealogy, I quickly established, attracted a great many older gay men. Every family seemed to have a bachelor uncle who was the family historian. It was often these men who returned the galley proofs of our books accurately corrected and updated, and they were the ones who bought the books. Snobbery dictated that it was noveaux riches to have the latest edition of any Burke publication; it was far grander to have an edition that was at least twenty-years old. This attitude proved disastrous for sales.

During my ten year's reign as proprietor (1973-1983) we inaugurated a number of new multi-volume series and titles; Burke's *Royal Families of the World* and Burke's *Guide to Country Houses*, to name but two. The former was a comprehensive reworking of the royal section of the *Almanac de Gotha*, long since out of print; the latter, a regional directory of houses of architectural and historic importance, every one of them illustrated and with anecdotes about the families that had lived in the house and references to where their pedigrees could be found in the Burke's series. If I have one regret about having to sell the imprint, it is that neither series was ever completed.

Hugh handled all the British and European publicity. It was decided that I was to promote the new Presidential Families volume in America, hence my first trip to New York in 1975. Our smoothly

David Williamson

oiled and effective machine only slipped up once when we, like many others, fell victim to the Henry Root spoof letters. The writer, William Donaldson, had the clever idea of posing as an eccentric retired wet fish merchant, offering £1 and right-wing advice to gullible notables and establishment figures and then publishing the letters along with the, hopefully, sycophantic replies. In our defence, we always replied politely to all letters received, however mad or implausible.

After ten years of struggle against rising print costs and too few sales, we finally were forced to sell up. I had moved on to other things and Hugh Massingberd was ready for a wider challenge. Charles Kidd and David Williamson left to work for Debrett's. Our other contributing editor, Hugo Vickers, has become a well-known biographer of, among others, Cecil Beaton.

Prospective purchasers of the imprint often contacted us, most of them proving to be less than serious: one, an American, even proved to be an elaborate confidence trickster. In the early eighties, we received an approach from a rather dubious East End character, David Haring, claiming to be representing Baron Frederik van Pallandt. (A genuine Danish aristocrat and the Frederik of the Nina & Frederik singing duo.) He produced what transpired to be a genuine power of attorney. We negotiated a price with him and a contract of sale was duly signed. The day appointed for completion came and went, but no completion monies arrived at our solicitor's office. After some weeks, we decided to issue proceedings to force the Baron to complete. In those days, one had to serve the papers in person on the defendant: in this case David Haring, the man with the power of attorney. With the help of a private detective, Felicity Mortimer and I tracked him down to an office in Pall Mall.

We sat in a car outside and laid in wait. After a couple of hours, he emerged talking to no less a person than Terence Stamp, the actor, who lived nearby in Albany on Piccadilly. We learned that they had been friends since their school days in the East End. Stamp was, we were led to believe, a close friend of the Baron. (We could only speculate on the nature of the curious and unlikely relationship between these three men.)

The court papers were duly served. On the last day before the court hearing, we heard from the mysterious Baron himself. He arrived at our solicitor's office, immaculately dressed, and carrying a briefcase containing the completion monies in cash. In a theatrical gesture, he emptied the case on the desk saying: 'There is your money, gentlemen. I am here to save my reputation.'

❦ NEW YORK – 1976

My first visit to New York was in the year of the American Bicentennial. I went ostensibly to promote *Burke's Presidential Families of the USA*: I also burned to discover the excitement and glamour of New York nightlife. For a European gay man, New York held endless possibilities. It was the world before AIDS where no holes were barred and New York had the best clubs, bars and the hottest men.

I arranged to stay with friends of my mother, Mr and Mrs Dudley Johnson. They were a moneyed upper-eastside family with a brownstone house on 68th Street and a large mansion in the centre of Edgartown, on Martha's Vineyard. They looked after me beautifully and arranged for me to meet lots of eligible girls, but I could not wait to escape from their stuffy dinner parties into the anonymous world of the night.

I had a few contacts in the city. Mark Shand (brother of the Duchess of Cornwall) was a friend and he introduced me to Warhol's crowd at the Factory, and particularly Catherine Guinness, Warhol's then assistant. One visit for lunch at the Factory was enough to convince me that they were not for me and I think the feeling was mutual. Warhol hardly said a word throughout lunch; he spent the whole meal taking snapshots with a cheap camera. Catherine talked about the hard-core gay bars she had visited like the Mineshaft and the Toilet, where men urinated on one another. I can only imagine that she gained admittance to these men-only bars because of her close association with Andy Warhol. I was shocked and found the thought of such places too unattractive for words. I was still a bit of a prude.

Author's passport photo, 1975

Another introduction was to a strange German man, Freddie von Meirers. He was gay and intensely social but a little secretive and sinister. He seemed to know everyone and was pleased to show me around. He lived in a tiny elegant bachelor apartment on the East Side heavily decorated with mirrors everywhere, especially in his bedroom. He took me to a party given by the legendary hostess, Bobo Rockefeller. I observed a US Senator snorting coke and young male models behaving in a louche manner with each other. I felt I was in a scene from a Fellini film. It was all heady and exciting.

I spent time in Edgartown on the Vineyard being shown off by my hosts to all their smart friends. There was boating to enjoy and lazing on the beach in the summer sunshine. There was still gossip on the Vineyard about Mary-Jo Kopechne's death on Chappaquiddick Bridge in 1969, in a car driven by Senator Edward Kennedy. Many believed that there had been a cover-up by the powerful Kennedy clan. I relaxed with my English friend, Tim Cutler, who was a guest of Nancy Oakes's sister, Mrs Shirley Butler and family, on the opposite side of the island.

I longed to get back to New York where there was so much new to explore. I spent an evening at the Continental Baths where Bette Midler used to perform with Barry Manilow, accompanying her on the piano. I visited the Empire State Building and the Chrysler Building and marvelled at their grand public spaces. I checked out the new Trump Tower with its incredible shops and boasting an imposing atrium many stories high; all covered in gold and brass with even a waterfall and mature trees. The skyline of the city at night, with the lights left on in all the buildings, seemed both wickedly wasteful and magically enthralling. London seemed penny-pinching and infinitely dull in comparison.

I ate hamburgers at Mortimer's bar, run by a young Anglo-Irishman Richard Beamish, where the smart Euro-trash crowd like Egon von Furstenberg and Harry Fane hung out. I knew many of them from London or through friends and was introduced to loads more in the heady few weeks I spent in the city. Mortimer's was pretty much like many other New York bar, part drinking bar and part restaurant. For the first time in my life, I discovered a bar where I felt at home. The atmosphere was so unlike the seedy, beery, smoky British pub that I so detested. The place was young and fun, dominated by one long bar where the young barmen were welcoming and poured drinks free-style: that is without use of mean-looking optics favoured by pubs back home. Optics also meant that the barman had to turn his back on the customer, whereas by pouring free style, the barman faced the customer all the while he was pouring and mixing. The bar staff actually looked you in the eye and engaged you in conversation, while making your chosen drink. The mixers came from a bar gun, so once again the barman continued to look at the customer. In a British pub, the barman would hunt around under the bar for a mean-looking micro-sized bottle of mixer to add to the already parsimonious-looking drink. Post-mix soda guns simply did not exist back in 1976 in London, and I had to fight hard to get my brewery to install them at the Embassy Club.

The bar surface was uncluttered by naff-looking beer pumps; it was clear and level with a comfortable leaning rail, plenty of room for the customer's drink and with a foot-rest that encouraged customers to sit and linger at the bar. The barman made a show of pouring generously sized measures by hand and used plenty of ice to make a tall generous drink; so unlike the British mean gin and tonic with one lump of half-melted ice from a cheap plastic bucket and a dry-looking slice of lemon – if you were lucky. The bar itself was properly ventilated so it didn't smell of stale beer and smoke. The beer, of course, was sold ice cold in bottles. I discovered that in America, bar staff and waiters lived off their tips that ensured their service was both friendly and efficient. The contrast with service back home could hardly have been greater; none of the surly, grudging condescension and half-remembered orders, but slick smiling faces and instant action. The music was great too; no jukebox in the corner, but a proper sound system playing continuous hits at a decent audible volume.

I was making mental notes all the time; comparing and contrasting the New York way with the ways back home and finding New York way ahead in every area; presentation, drink size, customer service and hi-style. Going out for a drink or a simple hamburger at a bar like Mortimer's was a fun youthful experience – the place was welcoming to both singles and couples alike. In my mind, I was creating the blueprint for the style of operation I intended to run back home. When I eventually opened my own bar and club, The Embassy, I incorporated the lessons that I had learnt in New York.

Through the publishing world, I met Charles Ryskamp, the director of the prestigious Pierpont Morgan Library; through him, I was introduced to the Grolier Club, a private club for bibliophiles; a strange mixture of gentleman's club and academic institution; something that could only be conceived on the East Coast of America.

I had some more down-to-earth contacts through the gay friends in London and it was at this time I was introduced to Greg James, a gay guy and small town DJ, from the Pocono Mountains; we became friends. Greg came to London to work for me at the Embassy Club.

I was given an introduction to Leon Danelian, ballet master of the New York Theatre Ballet Company. With trepidation, I telephoned him one Friday afternoon. He was very polite, but said he was too busy to see me as he was leaving for the Hamptons for the weekend. He called back fifteen minutes later and asked me to pop round immediately for a quick drink. I think he was intrigued to meet me. He ushered me into his apartment and after a short chat asked me, 'Do you like girls or boys?' I was somewhat nonplussed. I blushed and hung my head and answered in a small voice, 'boys'. He picked up the telephone and called one of the boys in his corps de ballet.

Half an hour later, a gorgeous lithe young hunk arrived and whisked me off on a twelve hour-long magical mystery tour of the New York gay scene. After a late dinner and some illegal substances, we started on the tour. First, we visited the bars, then on to Le Jardin, the hippest club in New York. (This was a couple of years before Studio 54 opened.) I was entranced by the music; Barry White, *The Hustle* by van McCoy and George McCrae's *Rock Your Baby* were big at the time. As for the club, I was in paradise. The music was seamlessly mixed; the lighting mesmerising and original; the cocktails seemed huge and had ingredients that I had never heard of, like blue Curacao; the waiters wore the sexiest satin shorts that were silky and revealing. They were all stunning-looking boys and very flirtatious with both of us. Not only did I have fun, I observed carefully and made mental notes of the elements that went into the heady mix, planning ahead to when I would own a club of my own. (On a subsequent visit to New York, after I had become a club owner, I spent a day with the owner of Le Jardin, John Addison. He could justifiably claim to be the father of contemporary dance clubs and the inspiration behind Steve Rubell and Studio 54.)

Just when I thought the evening was coming to an end, at about 3.30 am, (London would have been fast asleep by then), we jumped into a taxi and headed downtown. We rounded off the night exploring the gay dance clubs in the meat-packing district near the West Side piers, places like 12 West and the legendary Flamingo. There were no signs on the street, just an anonymous doorway and a flight of rickety stairs leading to a cavernous warehouse interior. I experienced gay dance heaven for the first time. Hundreds of beautiful young gay guys dancing in a trance, half-naked, to underground disco music that was mixed by top DJs. There were no tables or seating, just a rough and ready space that was all dance-floor. The atmosphere was both heady and intensely sexual. Men were touching each other's oiled, sweaty muscled bodies or kissing on the dance floor. Torn and worn jeans, in fashion now, were the uniform even back then. At about 6.30 am we rolled home and into bed together, had sex, slept a while then had a late breakfast of coffee, a doughnut and a cigarette. We parted with a lingering kiss, an end to a true-life fairy tale. I knew what I had to do on my return to London, start a club like those I had experienced in New York.

Chapter Twenty-Four

❧ THE EMBASSY CLUB, OLD BOND STREET

It took me two years to find a suitable site and a business partner and backer for my nightclub venture. Duncan McLaren, a young friend, who was well connected and worked at Sotheby's, initially agreed to be that person, but for whatever reason, he eventually got cold feet. He introduced me to the head of the Sotheby's Old Master picture department, a young genius still in his twenties, Derek Johns.

Derek and I had an instant rapport; with his multi-faceted renaissance mind and entrepreneurial spirit, he related immediately to my vision. He agreed to become my one and only partner – I was in business.

Derek went on to have a stellar career as an art dealer and discoverer of many sleepers (works whose attribution and identity remain lost or hidden). Derek has made a number of such really important discoveries and new attributions. He was also the first man to win the television amateur cooking competition, *Master Chef* – a truly renaissance man.

The club site, at 7 Old Bond Street, near the junction with Piccadilly, had been for much of the century the most famous nightclub in London – the Embassy – but was now sad and abandoned. The last tenant had run a topless bar; now the basement was flooded and the place in disrepair. He had gone bust, owing back rent. The Embassy was reputedly the place where Edward, Prince of Wales, first wore black-tie for dinner thus relieving gentlemen of the requirement to change into white-tie every night. My mother had known the club in its heyday. She even remembered exactly where Prince Ali Khan had his regular table.

There were only three years left on the lease: a mad proposition for anyone without my burning vision and crazy youthful confidence. I

The Club logo in neon

Derek Johns, the Author & Michael Fish toast the club's success, 1978

signed the lease and found a decorator to help me, Mike Crosby Hogan, who had been responsible for the Way In boutique at Harrods, and had mastered the blend of modern and traditional that I was looking for. I already had a clear vision of what I wanted – a radical departure from the traditional club with its tables round a small dance floor and a DJ who talked between discs. We made the main room upstairs, which was architecturally rather like the ballroom of a 1930s ocean liner, into all dance-floor with a bar along the wall at one end. The seating was car- pet-covered banquette staging that could be moved around to change the scene and the feel of the room. Railings separated the sunken dance floor from the standing area around the bar.

The club had a dramatic double-curved staircase leading to a balcony overlooking the ballroom floor, giving the space an elegance and drama that was breathtaking. The whole space was to become a huge dancing area; we laid a sprung wooden floor. We put our speakers into metal towers and created a scaffolding grid to hold the lights in the ceiling. The effect was entirely novel and dramatic, totally in keeping with Disco, which was becoming all the rage.

Downstairs we created a restaurant and a long quiet bar for the seri- ous talkers and drinkers; that was where most of the money was taken. The avant-garde artist, Andrew Logan, of Alternative Miss World (a drag send-up of the tacky Mecca Miss World contest) fame, a friend of Michael Fish, was commissioned to make two 'Trees of Life' on a Garden of Eden theme. They had large apples and snakes made from broken glass pieces, crude but effective and very striking. I still have a couple of the glass apples at home to remind me of those heady days.

Michael Fish, the well-known 1960s men's clothes designer, and the new friend I had made in New York, became our front-of-house 'greeter' and was the other name the public came to associate with the Embassy Club. He knew everyone from that era, from Princess Margaret to Mick Jagger: Ozzie Clark the dress designer was his best friend. If a thousand people made up Swinging London in the Sixties, then he was certainly one of them.

We had three days of opening parties in May 1978. An Ozzie Clark charity fashion show kicked off the proceedings, a glittering affair attended by Margaret, Duchess of Argyll, Lady Diana Cooper, Bianca Jagger and a host of other notables. Deriding my passion for disco music, 'that thump-thump disco music will never work,' both Michael Fish and James Fisher, the music guru, prophesied its swift demise; but I stuck to my guns and was soon proved right.

The club became the haunt of the fashionable and the 'in' place for the beautiful of both sexes – especially the best-looking gay boys. It was the London equivalent of Studio 54 in New York. Steve Rubell paid a visit on one of his trips to London, accompanied by an entourage of heavies and hangers-on. When I paid a visit to New York, I soon realised that, as a club owner, they assumed I had 'mob' connections just because they all did.

Other opening nights were dedicated to our long list of founder members and their friends, a heady mix of the A-list gay crowd and a mailing list of the glitterati and the fashionable; cafe society meets high society, with sex thrown in to jazz up the cocktail. *Saturday Night Fever* – the film staring John Travolta – opened in the same week as us. It

The Dance Floor, Embassy Club

seemed everything was in our favour, the club was instantly a massive hit. Everyone wanted 'in'.

We wanted to invite a few older people who had known the Embassy in its former glory days. These included my grand elderly 'Aunt' Magda Bouchel. Her friend, Henry Crichton-Stuart, escorted her on the opening night and found the mixture so enticing that he left his wife. From the very first week, the club took off and we were busy every night with lines of limousines and Bentleys outside the club.

We promoted our first party night, in what is now the classic fashion, by means of a glossy flier posted to our membership, 'The 4th July, King George III's biggest loss', as the invitation announced. We were taken completely by surprise to find there were queues round the block.

Our doormen struggled to keep out non-members and aggressive punters whose line was invariably, 'Don't you know who I am?' More than one man swore to my face that he was a friend of the owner. There were a few fights and numerous heated altercations. Such was the price of being, for a brief moment, the hottest ticket in town.

I developed, in a small way, a public profile. My new boyfriend, Derek, and I found that we were quite often in the gossip columns or our doings catalogued in the newly emerged gossip magazines such as *Ritz* and *Tatler*. Richard Compton-Miller, the gossip columnist, decided to make me one of his characters whose social and business career he chronicled in the *Evening News*. Richard Young, one of the first London

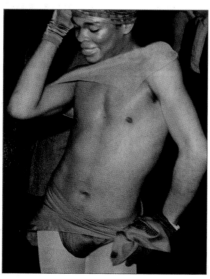

A Dancer at the Club

paparazzi, cut his teeth at the Embassy Club and was one of only two press photographers permitted to take photographs inside the club, (the other was John St Clair), subject to restrictions to ensure the privacy of our celebrity guests – a privilege he could not resist abusing and on at least one occasion he had to be ejected. But, of course, we needed the oxygen of publicity to promote the club and keep us in the public eye.

The Embassy was full of beautiful boys and model girls dancing and carrying on in a sexually charged environment to ecstatic Disco music and revolutionary lighting effects. The club became a cultural crossroads. Notables from the worlds of music, arts and letters partied alongside beautiful unknowns. To that exotic mix, we added well-known names from the peerage and parliament – a recipe for success. It is my observation that innovative nightclubs are gay run: Le Palace in Paris, owned by the late Fabrice Emaer, opened in 1978; Studio 54 owned by Steve Rubell in 1977 and of course, John Addison's Le Jardin was the earliest of them all.

Steven Hayter, the club manager, was a colourful showman and used many New York tactics to generate hype and excitement. One evening while things were temporarily flagging, he got three of our most provocative and sexy boys to jump up on the bar and dance with spotlights trained on their crotches. The crowd went wild and the bulges in their shorts got noticeably bigger. This was something entirely new and hugely exciting for London. Every hip cool young Londoner was there plus a few older groovers, who should have been at home in bed but wanted to party and boogie the night away – night after night.

The club held about 600 people and was full, even on Monday nights. Thursday was our most glamorous night, as quite a few of our rich and famous clientele, such as Lord Montagu and the late Earl of Pembroke would leave for their country seats on Friday for the weekend. If you wanted to spot the stars, then Thursday was the night. The weekend saw queues down Bond Street long into the night, but the crowd was gayer and more 'bridge and tunnel', as New Yorkers say. (A derogatory expression denoting that a person lives in one of the suburban boroughs and has to enter the fashionable city from across the water.)

Every night was party night – and how we partied! People who had never gone to clubs before came to dance with us night after night. A membership card was like gold dust and many were turned away. London saw its first wild dance venue dubbed by one journalist 'a trisexual club, a place where you could try anything sexual.' – hedonism ruled. 'There were so many people and so many parties at the Embassy that it is impossible for me to chronicle – it would be a tome the size of the Bible' commented *Ritz* newspaper. Everyone who was allowed in had something to contribute to the party, whether it was looks, style, fame or fortune, but most of all sex appeal. Come closing time, no one wanted to leave, or the party to stop.

Were there drugs at the club? Well, yes there were, as in any nightclub the world over. The police, in those days, hardly knew what cocaine was and its use was limited to a select few. It was also horrendously expensive, costing about £50 a gram – a vast amount in the 1970s. The recently issued, new £50 note was colloquially termed a 'coke voucher'. (I am told the substance still costs the same, twenty or more years later.) There was also a worrying trend amongst the young straight set for 'chasing the dragon', or smoking heroin from silver foil. The tell-tale burnt foil would be found in the loos in the morning by the cleaners. Gay men danced while high to 'uppers' and 'downers' and would use 'poppers' or amyl nitrite for both dancing and sex: the heady rush from poppers add to and heighten the transient pleasures of both.

On many nights, after the club closed around 3.30 to 4.00 am, we all wanted the party to continue and the staff would repair to an all-night café; we would go on to a private house to continue the fun. Elton John and his then manager, John Reid, were regulars. John had bought the former home of my friends Julian Gibbs and Martin Stephens, the portly gay Tory MP, in Montpelier Square, near Knightsbridge. We had a few late night parties there that often got out of hand. We were young, rich, hot and horny and out to have fun.

The club generated huge amounts of money but the financial controls were rudimentary. These were the days before modern tills and computer stock control. I realise now that we were robbed blind at every level, but even so the club generated considerable profit in the first couple of years before the sudden and dramatic death of Disco in 1981, which saw turnover dive overnight and profits turn into sharp losses.

Edward Wood, a friend and former flat-mate, was employed as our

'Bubbles' Rothermere about to devour a Busboy

accountant and bookkeeper. Sadly, the relationship turned sour and we parted not the best of friends. It was perhaps all too heady for us young guys unable to cope with the pressure while we were up all night having fun. Edward was the son of the Conservative Minister for Overseas Development, Richard Wood (later Lord Holderness), and the grandson of Earl of Halifax, Viceroy of India.

One weekend while staying in Yorkshire with the family, we went over to visit his delightful old grandmother, Lady Halifax, in her modest country cottage – quite a contrast for a former Vicerene of India used to living in a palace. My life was an intriguing mix between my gay and club life and my friends from Cambridge and traditional London Society.

Among the galaxy of celebrities who partied at the Embassy Club were: Rod Stewart and his manager Billy Gaff; Elton John; Robert Stigwood and Alan Carr (the producers of *Saturday Night Fever* and *Grease*); Piers Brosnan (James Bond) and his wife Cassandra; Mick Jagger; Ayesha Rajmata of Jaipur; Jennifer Little (brother of John Aspinall); Earl Jermyn (later The 7th Marquess of Bristol) and his boyfriend Robin Hurlestone (later to become the boyfriend of Joan Collins); Lords Bath, Hertford and Pembroke; the Earl and Countess of Snowdon; Catherine Guinness (Andy Warhol's assistant); John Siddeley (Lord Kenilworth); Mark Shand; Lord Burghersh; Rupert Deen; Richard Compton-Miller (the gossip columnist); Lady Diana Cooper; the beautiful sisters Charlotte and Mary-Gaye Curzon; Nicky Haslam (the Boswell of the 'B-list'); Lionel Bart ('Aunty Li', composer of the musical *Oliver*); Tony Galliers-Pratt (Decibelle); Viscount Newport (now Earl of Bradford); John Schlesinger; Twiggy, (the Sixties muse, model and actress); Claire Hambro; Danny La Rue (the drag queen who ludicrously claimed to be straight); John Bowes-Lyon, ('Bosie', a cousin of the Queen Mother); public-school boys out of bounds and many models of both sexes and none.

Jeremy Fry, the man who was to be Anthony Armstrong-Jones's best man on his marriage to Princess Margaret, until his bisexual past was revealed, was a special friend and supporter. His glamorous and handsome children were regulars. Cosmo, his eldest son, chose the club for his 21st birthday party, the hottest party of that year. Two regulars were the very cute Prince Stefano Massimo, universally fancied by both boys and girls and his pretty wife Atalanta, daughter of Lady Edith Foxwell. The artists Craigie Aitchison and Patrick Procktor were often to be seen, as were many from the worlds of sport, pop and show-biz and all the Sixties crowd who were friends of Mr Fish. Everyone who was anyone wanted at least to come and look and usually wanted to stay long into the night, such was the atmosphere of fun, sex and fashion.

We employed cute young guys as waiters and barmen. Sadly many were later to contract AIDS and die while still in their twenties and thirties. Most, but not all of these boys were gay; their uniform was an outrageous pair of nearly sheer tight white satin shorts and nothing else. With their taught, hot, smooth young bodies, they drove both boys and girls wild. I think we were perhaps one of the first businesses to flaunt the beauty of the naked male body and use it in an overt way to promote and sell, in the same way that girl's bodies have always been used. Now posters frequently depict sexy naked young men – the male body sells. It has always been acceptable to objectify women as sex-objects, now young males suffer the same fate and don't seem to mind in the least.

Amongst our brigade of waiters were four young Peruvian boys of good family, all gay and the best of friends. They were dedicated party people and had fun-loving personalities, even if their waiting skills left a lot to be desired. One of them was the young Mario Testino, now celebrated as a fashion photographer and Society darling. Together they rented an abandoned ward in the old Charing Cross Hospital – God knows how they came by it. Visitors had to push through the dossers on the ground floor to arrive at their stylishly dramatic apartment furnished on the cheap, in an eclectic mix of over-scaled found furniture and redundant hospital equipment, all put together with flair and

Mummy's 70th birthday at the Embassy Club, 1979

panache. Mario was one of our most popular waiters, when he could be persuaded to desist from socialising with our members and actually serve a drink. It seems that everyone was a waiter once.

The Society PR operator and fixer Liz Brewer, her husband John Rendall, and Roddy Llewellyn (the sometime boyfriend of Princess Margaret), opened a rival club called Bennett, in Battersea, in the same week as us. This provided the press with a field day; the papers had fun building up the rivalry between the two clubs. I knew Roddy slightly; Liz and I had, unbeknown to her at the time, shared a boyfriend in my Cambridge days. With jealousies long forgotten, she has since become a friend. Bennett, despite these illustrious progenitors, was not a success. It was a thoroughly old-fashioned style of nightclub in a secondary location. Even with the much-publicised piranha fish beneath the glass floor, it could not drum up much interest from anyone but their most loyal friends.

Elaine Paige and cast members of various West End hits were regulars at the Embassy who added glamour and hype – and caught the interest of the press. I was invited to almost every opening in town and was even pictured in the evening papers dancing with Derek Frost, my beautiful young boyfriend, at the opening of Regine's Club at the Roof Gardens in Kensington. Poor Nandkishor Ram, her backer, wept as the bills mounted and the profits failed to materialise. Regine, a Parisian legend, was unable to make her magic formula work in London, but this did not ameliorate her endless requests for chauffeur-driven cars to drive her around and other extravagances. Her style of club just did not work in London, its appeal being mainly to young rich Arabs – not the high-society crowd that Regine hoped to attract.

'Burgie' (Lord Burghersh, heir to the Earl of Westmoreland) and Dai Llewellyn (Roddy's elder brother) both ran Wedgies Club in King's Road, Chelsea; one after the other. This club lacked a hip edge and catered to a certain breed of older 'Sloanes'; it eventually turned to the young Arab market, then a new feature of the London scene. The older straight patricians and aged rockers still frequented those small fashionable hangouts: Tramp, run by Johnnie Gold, and Annabel's, Mark Birley's perennial dine-and-dance place for the old grand county set, notorious for its staid music policy – *Tie a Yellow Ribbon Round the Old Oak Tree* and *Lady in Red*, etc. 'Where the middle-aged meets the Middle East', as we used to say. For two amazing years, the Embassy remained the place for anyone hip to be seen.

It wasn't until the early 1980s that any serious rivals to the Embassy came on to the scene. An Asian businessman, Campbell Palmer, an

Embassy regular, was always asking if he could buy the club. Eventually he started his own club, Legends, round the corner in Old Burlington Street; it has now ironically been renamed 'The Embassy' but it has no connection with my old club. Unfortunately, Legends gradually started to share the cream of our business.

What really impacted on our success were the sudden death of 'disco' and the emergence of a new Soho underground scene led by the so-called 'New Romantics', the prime movers of which were Steve Strange, Marilyn, Boy George and Philip Sallon. They became the leaders of a new set of sexually ambivalent, pallid and emaciated night-people. Their new music, bands like Visage, and their use of make-up and theatrical costume inspired both a new look and a new nightlife fashion. They invented a series of one-nighter events in small Soho clubs like Blitz to which only their crowd were admitted. Although mostly gay boys, the scene was full of sad anaemic-looking girls with satanic make-up and other strange night creatures wearing fanciful clothes. Their cultural heirs are the 'Goths' of today. It appeared to us to lack excitement and to be profoundly non-sexual, but none the less, it eventually became mainstream, seducing away many of our younger members. The Disco scene rapidly died. It was left to Heaven, my second big dance club, to create a new mainstream gay scene, together with a new genre of dance music.

Chapter Twenty-Five

✤ STEPHEN HAYTER – THE QUEEN OF THE NIGHT

It is said that one should never speak ill of the dead. English libel law does not agree and neither do I. This adage has now been comprehensively debunked in the obituary columns, thanks to the breath of fresh air breathed into those dead tombstones by my old school-friend Hugh Montgomery-Massingberd. He first did this in Burke's Peerage publications in the 1970s, but because they were buried in so much print, the revelation was lost to all but a select few. He then became obituaries editor at the *Daily Telegraph* and Middle England received a jolt, as the former boring hagiographies of dead brigadiers blossomed into humorous and scurrilous anecdotes about the more interesting and amusing departed.

Whatever the prevailing ethos, I am happy to speak ill of Stephen Hayter. He was without doubt one of the most pernicious and evil individuals I have ever encountered. His cocaine addiction made him increasingly erratic and paranoid. Cocaine renders its addicts voluble to excess; he would often talk manically for hours about nothing of real importance.

Stephen Hayter was introduced to me by the art dealer, Francis ('Fanny') Burne and Lord Montagu of Beaulieu. He was good-looking, on the surface charming, hard working, but loquacious. Stephen was fresh from the bar world of New York and had worked for the legendary John Addison, proprietor of the seminal club Le Jardin – the club that started it all – the place where I had gained much of my inspiration. Addison was the man who had inspired and taught Steve Rubell of Studio 54, although they subsequently became the greatest of rivals.

Stephen seemed the ideal general manager for a nightclub and so, in many ways, he proved to be. He was an excellent and energetic promoter with, if anything, a tendency to over-promote ruthlessly. What I did not know then was that he was a thoroughly nasty piece of work, and our huge success, together with large quantities of drugs, went straight to his head. He had a ruthless side and had been literally run out of New York by his enemies. He was a sex and cocaine addict who used drugs to blackmail and control his friends and enemies. His addictions and ambition made him a dangerous and unpredictable enemy. Paranoia led him to suspect and mistrust his work colleagues; one moment he would be charming and friendly, the next he would sow the seeds of mistrust or cast aspersions on the honesty or good-intentions between friends. His insecurities led him to become both bitchy and scheming. Sad to say, I have since met others in the club world just like him.

His favourite game was to tell Michael Fish that I had spoken ill of him and mistrusted him; he would then tell me much the same about Michael. It was not long before we discovered his game and the two of us became allies. The younger more insecure bar staff were less empowered to resist these malicious attempts to undermine their confidence. Their jobs were at stake and they lived with an entirely unfounded fear that either Michael or I were out to get them. Hayter wanted to be seen as their friend and protector, and gain kudos for having saved them from the sack.

This was my first encounter with a truly amoral person. My naive public-school innocence was severely challenged. Until then, I had trusted people and assumed they had good intentions; the club world put me right. Then, and more so today, it is a world largely inhabited by evil, avaricious and deeply damaged people. In all his appetites, he was intemperate and excessive.

I soon learnt that my self-effacing attitude to personal publicity left Stephen to grab the limelight; so much so that he began to believe that he was primarily responsible for our success; conveniently forgetting that it was I who had the vision and Michael Fish who had added the glamour. By talking indiscreetly to the press, Hayter usurped more of the, often embarrassing, press coverage the club garnered. Our early favourable coverage deteriorated. From articles in the quality glossies, we descended to less favourable portrayals of his cheap stunts in the tabloids. The image of the club slipped from glamorous to sleazy.

Elaine Page, Stephen & Olivia Newton-John at the Club

Hayter, with his coke-driven manipulative and divisive ways, increasingly became a thorn in my flesh; so, I eventually arranged for him to buy me out of the ailing Embassy. He readily assented to this; it was the fulfilment of a dream to own his own club. He recruited the 'Disco Dowager', Lady Edith Foxwell, a frankly unsavoury old lady with a penchant for promiscuous sex and late-night parties, a mode of life quite unsuited to her advanced years. She was an embarrassingly undignified spectacle who wore too much make-up and too few clothes. Another investor was David Shaw, who had had a successful career as a showbiz accountant, but was now short of money. He even tried to become a producer of musicals, a role for which he had no talent whatsoever. He produced an ill-stared musical entitled *Fire Angel* that lasted for about a week. He then commissioned Lionel Bart to write a new musical based on the life of Robin Hood, called *Twang!* That didn't last very long either. Poor Lionel (Auntie Li) had sold his rights to *Oliver*, his great success, to Max Bygraves for literally a song. He was now living in penury; his talent had deserted him and his simple cockney ditties were simply not sophisticated enough for current tastes. Both were regular patrons at the Embassy and keen to participate in the glamorous world of the night.

Hayter was plausible but ultimately dishonest. It proved difficult to get him to honour his contract: in the end, it required a lengthy legal battle. None of his backers seemed willing to assert any influence over Hayter to induce him to behave decently. I was learning about the world of business and the old truth about money and friendship. I was growing up fast.

Hayter continued to run the club for a few more years until the landlord terminated the lease for redevelopment. He spent his last years organising parties and promoting bars and restaurants for other people.

He organised a camp and lavish wedding party for the gay young Earl Jermyn, another drug addict and louche wastrel; a man whose swine-like behaviour perfectly complimented his porcine appearance. He was adept at using his sharp tongue and ready wit to put down those in no position to answer back. He thought such behaviour aristocratic, whereas it was arrogant and demeaning; the conduct of a parvenu, not that of a gentleman. It was hardly a surprise that the marriage did not last long.

Eventually, Hayter succumbed to AIDS, protesting to the end that he did not have the disease, even threatening to sue a newspaper that dared to suggest the contrary. He was always a man who believed that if he told a lie loudly enough and with enough threat of coercion, others would believe it.

Chapter Twenty-Six

✖ Mr Fish

I visited New York for the first time in 1975 in order to promote my firm's latest publication, *Burke's Presidential Families of the USA*. Burke's specialised in works of genealogy and social history, and in particular produced the definitive guide to the British Aristocracy, the eponymous *Burke's Peerage*.

The American Bicentennial of 1976 seemed like a suitable occasion to bring out a book of American Presidential families. I had naively under-estimated the interest such a work would command, especially when published by someone so young. My editorial director, Hugh Montgomery-Massingberd, had provided me with a crib sheet detailing some of the more bizarre Presidential family relationships and descents. Nixon was, for example, related by marriage to both Hoover and Taft. Franklin Delano Roosevelt was related to both Winston Churchill and to Charles de Gaulle, his wartime colleagues – Churchill through his American mother, Jennie Jerome, and de Gaulle through the French Delano connection.

As a consequence of all this interest, I was interviewed at some length by the *New York Times* and asked to appear, not only on various televi-sion chat shows, but also on a popular game show called *To Tell the Truth*. The format of this show was that a panel of celebrities asked questions of three contestants in order to establish which one was the genuine curiosity. In my case, they needed to find two other Englishmen in New York to impersonate me. One of those chosen was Michael Fish.

Michael had been famous in London in the 1960s as both a designer of men's clothes and as a member of the core group that made London the 'swinging' capital of the world. He knew everyone and everyone loved Mr Fish. His boutique in Clifford Street, Mayfair, was the 'in' place to buy your shirts and ties. Its labels read 'Peculiar to Mr Fish'. It was Mr Fish that put Mick Jagger into a white leather mini-skirt for his wedding to Bianca.

His shirts were extravagant confections in silks and lace, often with ruffles and long tight three-buttoned cuffs. His basic formula was to use outrageously feminine fabrics on men's shirts, which was totally in keeping with the peacock men's fashions of the time. His greatest con-tribution to male sartorial elegance was the famous 'kipper' tie: a very wide and showy necktie that complemented the extra-wide suit lapels then current.

One of his backers, Barry Sainsbury, asked the accountants what could be done to stem the mounting losses; the weary reply came back; 'Tell Mr Fish to buy the strongest padlock he can find and put it on the back door.' Even when sales had been high, stock was pilfered and extensive credit given, while debts remained uncollected. By 1975, his shop had gone into receivership and he had largely been forgotten as London faded into relative obscurity at the close of the swinging sixties, becoming a rather dull place.

After the closure of his shop, Michael took up an offer of a job in New York to work for the old-established firm of Sulka, makers of extravagant foulard dressing gowns and beautiful traditional silk shirts. He had descended to become a glorified shop-assistant once again.

One of Michael's greatest qualities, as I was to discover, was his total absence of false pride. He came from a poor North London working-class background and felt he had been lucky to have enjoyed fame and money whilst young: he had no air of resentment or regret. Life was always as good as the next party.

His new reduced status did not mean he was without friends. He had a fund of amusing anecdotes and a disarmingly engaging diffidence that he combined with an ability to converse easily and naturally with all types and conditions of people. Celebrities loved Michael; he put them

Michael Fish

at their ease. He showed them due deference but never fawned or appeared to be impressed by their fame. He employed exactly the same manner with doormen as he did with duchesses.

His appearance with me on the television show, *To Tell the Truth*, caused some consternation. One of the panellists, Kitty Carlisle, said that she would have to stand down as she had dined with one of the three of us the night before. That was, of course, Michael Fish.

After the show, Michael and I talked and we found that we had many friends in common in London. I also learned that, bizarrely, Michael had lived in a flat at 98 Piccadilly above Perkins, the chemist; it was the very flat that my grandmother had died in. I dread to think what her ghost would have thought of the antics he must have got up to in her bedroom. We had lunch a day or two later and I outlined my plans to open a new style of nightclub in London. Michael said he was planning to return home to work for Sulka in London, and we vowed to stay in touch.

Michael was tall and wiry but surprisingly strong. He was extravagant and louche, but not fey. He touched people a lot and had the gift of engaging intimacy on early acquaintance. His diction was curious; one had to concentrate hard to follow his train of thought. This may have been because his mind was never very logical or organised, or maybe it was because he was always spinning off at a tangent and could not follow his own train of thought. His unkind friends might have said it was because he was too stoned to concentrate. The overall effect was one of confusing charm. He seemed to be imparting something profound or interesting even if one couldn't quite grasp what it was. I suppose his education had been somewhat rudimentary, but his accent was hard to place and definitely not obviously 'common'. He was the true embodiment of the new classless society of Swinging London. In the best theatrical tradition, everyone was 'dear' or 'darling', regardless of the sex or status. He had that disarming quality of concentrating entirely on the person he was talking to, so as to make them feel interesting and special. Michael invariably dressed to disarm, often in a kaftan or loose cotton harem pants. He would team these with something bright and flowing, a silk scarf or a cravat. His hair was extravagantly long and wavy, after the best male '60s fashion. He was a creature of his time and locus, more Marrakech than Milan.

Back in London, I eventually managed to find a site and arrange finance for my new nightclub. The Embassy Club opened at 7, Old Bond Street to great acclaim and instant success. Michael Fish (Myrtle Poisson) became my front-of-house man, or as Americans would have it, my 'greeter'. Michael garnered most of the initial publicity, and a superb job he did. Journalists not only loved him, they thought of him as a friend. The Embassy Club was featured in the gossip columns and all the influential glossy magazines: we had a double-page spread in *Harper's & Queen* the month we opened.

Michael's close friend, the dress designer Ozzie Clark, staged a glamorous charity fashion show for our opening night; it was attended by, among others: Bianca Jagger; Margaret, Duchess of Argyll and the legendary Lady Diana Cooper. We got off to a glamorous start. But even then, it was clear that all was not well. Once again, Michael Fish exhibited a trait that had hastened the demise of his former business, his unending generosity. He would grant credit to all and sundry and, worse, he would be lavish with complimentary bottles of champagne – not just the ordinary non-vintage, but Crystal and Dom Perignon. He was always sure that his important friends were just about to book a private party or bring down a major international star; but mostly Michael just did not know how to say no. Generosity came naturally to him, even if it was with other people's money.

One of his most endearing qualities was the love and loyalty he had towards his elderly mum. I employed her, somewhat reluctantly, as the coat-check girl. In fact, she was a great success in this capacity and became a much-loved feature of the club, until her need for a few early nights forced her to retire.

Michael had no concept of saving money or investment; his whole life had been lived for the moment. While he was earning good money at the Embassy, I persuaded him to buy a house, instead of renting. He was at first reluctant to take on anything as adult as a mortgage. He had always had a particular penchant for black men, so Brixton had a special appeal for him and property there was cheap. He was able to buy a large townhouse for a few thousand pounds. At the time, he had a black American boyfriend, Tyrone Brown. The two of them moved into the house and took in paying lodgers to help pay the mortgage. Michael Fish became a 'landlady'. The lifestyle suited him well, except that he allowed some of his lodgers to become badly in arrears with the rent.

After the demise of the Embassy, Michael faded once more into relative obscurity. He had another try at the fashion business but he had lost his touch; he was too much in tune with the '60s and couldn't adapt to the eighties. The income from his tenants was providing him with something to live on, as well as paying the mortgage.

With each successive boyfriend, Michael changed his religion. After Tyrone returned to New York, he became attached to the Muslim religion but soon moved on to chanting and to Buddhism. I think he fervently believed in each successive change or perhaps, rather like the Vicar of Bray, his conversions were simply practical expressions of his latest carnal passions. In any event, they gave him something to do.

He was not by nature energetic; his days were spent lounging around or having lunch in smart Society restaurants with old friends, always at their expense. He was known and welcomed at such society watering holes as San Lorenzo in Beauchamp Place, Knightsbridge, where Princess Margaret, an old friend, could often be seen. I don't think he ever took any deliberate exercise but, like many gay men, he liked to have a lot of sex. His other interest was gardening; his Brixton house had quite a large garden for London. His preferred crop was not altogether conventional.

As the years advanced, his health deteriorated. He suffered from a bad back that gave him much pain. When I asked him what he was doing these days he replied, 'Well dear, I spend a lot of time lying down.' He would stir himself occasionally in order to give a dinner party. The usual cuisine was Caribbean. It tasted fine but was not particularly prettily served. His domestic sense of priorities did not extend to over-fastidious cleanliness: the house was frankly a mess. It was interesting to note that much of the table setting, including the napkins and cutlery was of Embassy Club vintage and provenance; a fact of which Michael was rather proud. He did not appear in the least bit reticent about having 'liberated' them from the club; I don't think it had ever occurred to him that he was doing anything wrong. His naivety was perhaps the essence of his universal popularity.

While writing this chapter, in 2005, I tried telephoning him. The telephone rang but was never answered. I asked around, but no one had heard from Michael for some time, so I went round to his house in Brixton. I found it locked and bolted and all the furniture missing. A neighbour told me that Michael had suffered a major stroke. His sister, Lesley, confirmed that he was now in a home but had lost his memory and can hardly speak.

Yet the memories of our Mr Fish will linger on. The joy and pleasure he gave to so many will not be forgotten; even if to younger people his name is more readily associated with the other Michael Fish, the unprepossessing figure who used to give the weather forecasts on BBC television.

Chapter Twenty-Seven

❦ HEAVEN

The success of the Embassy Club in the late 1970s inspired me to fulfil my real ambition to create a huge, exclusively gay, dance club. The Embassy provided me with the confidence and funding to fulfil such an ambitious dream. The press eagerly anticipated the new venture. I gave an exclusive interview to *Harper's & Queen* and they published an article on Heaven with colour photos of the pre-launch interior showing our massive lighting rig. After the opening nights, the *Evening Standard* published a full-page article with photos. 'Heaven Ultradisco', wrote Peter York in *Harper's and Queen*, 'will be for the '80s what the Finsbury Park Astoria was for the '30s – a total mass fantasy.' All this publicity was not enough; we experienced a worrying few months during which our new baby was nearly empty on weekday nights. We were unsure what to do.

Fortunately dear, dotty Kenny Everett put us firmly on the radar screens. He recorded an edition of his immensely popular prime-time TV show, *The Kenny Everett Video Show,* at the club. The vast space looked glamorous and throughout the transmission, our neon logo formed the backdrop to the stage set. We were suddenly hip and cool!

Even before the Embassy, I had had the site for Heaven in mind: 21,000 square feet 'underneath the arches' at Charing Cross in Villiers

The Club Logo, circa 1980

Street. These gloomy brick railway arches had a number of advantages. They were of sufficient size to accommodate more than 1,500 revellers; the space was already licensed until 3.00am, (the latest alcohol licence available in London at the time); and, above all, they were in an amazing location at the epicentre of London, close to all the night buses.

The space was still trading, but only just, as Global Village. Soon it failed financially, and the club lease of 21-years was for sale. I realised that a great deal of money was needed to turn Global Village into my vision of Heaven Ultra Disco.

At this time, gay clubs in London were discrete cellar bars holding a couple of hundred people apologetically hidden from public view. There was a brave 'one-nighter' at the Astoria called 'Bang' which was drawing a crowd of about 1,000 every Monday – traditionally the hardest night to fill. That gave me confidence that the right gay product would achieve capacity at weekends. Experience had taught me that if you fill a club for two nights, you pay the overheads; every other busy night is profit.

Naturally I turned to Derek Frost, to undertake the design of this somewhat daunting space. We decided to move away entirely from the traditional club design of tables round a dance floor. Heaven was all about being young, sexy, bold and raw. I wanted something startling for a new decade. Derek came up with an outstanding 'hi-tech' design, an innovation at the time. All wires, pipes and conduits were exposed and painted silver; walls were painted all black and surfaces hard. The three huge vaulted brick arches were exposed and remained unclad. We hung hard-hats on the walls, and the bars were constructed out of industrial materials. There was scaffolding everywhere, supporting the lighting-rig and the sound towers. Our patrons could be forgiven for thinking they were entering a factory or a construction site. The ethos created was of a downtown warehouse space in an American city, totally appropriate and in tune with the style and feel of the new decade.

America was a promised land for gay men at that time. A land of sexual opportunity and where the men were men and the boys, beautiful and available. From the perspective of a tired and socially backward London, San Francisco and New York represented a promised land of liberation.

We employed an East End lad, Dave Bailey (no relation to the photographer), as our builder. Dave gutted the entire space right back to the brick arches. He made so much money out of the job that he achieved his ambition to buy a Rolls-Royce. I used a jobbing electrician, Wally (Basher) Barrett. He and I had worked together many times before on smaller jobs, but he found this job too much for him. 'Blimey, mate,' Wally exclaimed, 'I've used over four miles of bleeding copper covered pyro on this job. How you going to pay for it?' Pay we did. Everything was paid in full, including the bank loan, in nine months, mostly out of cash flow. But I had woefully underestimated the cost of refurbishing 21,000 square feet of club space; at the time, one of the largest club venues in London. It was completed just in time for the succession of opening nights.

There was a last minute, near-fatal mishap. One of the workmen left the fire hose connected, but turned off only at the nozzle. The pressure built up over night and the hose flooded the new wood dance floor. With only a few days to go before the opening night, we had to replace the entire floor and had to work all through two nights to achieve it.

Although it seems almost impossible to believe today, Bang, and indeed all other clubs, still had DJs that took record requests and chatted away between records. To me this was an outdated concept that killed the atmosphere on the dance floor. I had proved at the Embassy just how heady and seductive mixing records with a properly trained DJ could be. By using twin variable-speed turntables and the latest mixing techniques, the beats per minute could be altered to segue one track seamlessly into the next. I had imported a DJ friend, Greg James, from America to give form to this vision, but now he had been seduced away by the success of the Embassy to go freelance.

We eventually found a relative newcomer who shared my vision, Ian Levine, (latterly nicknamed 'Miss Piggy'), and together we developed 'High Energy' (Hi NRG) music. Ian was soon playing to packed houses with mixed sounds geared to the mood of the dance floor. The trick was to build up gradually to achieve a crescendo of ecstatic, sweating, sexually charged humanity, before bringing the crowd down by reducing the tempo. Then, by interspersing some chilled tracks, there would be a cool-down period before the next high. This style of music was effectively the start of contemporary dance music and the precursor of Acid House and Rave. I believe that we can claim to have invented 'Rave' some six years before it broke out into the mainstream, to become the bedrock of youth culture in the late eighties.

For gay men, the dance floor was truly a place of liberation: a place where we could feel free to express our sexuality and the unity of our tribe. The dance club was, in a sense, our cathedral; the music our liturgy and Disco our religion – a truly ecstatic and visionary experience. Gay guys have told me how their first visit to Heaven liberated them, making them realise that they were neither alone nor a freak, but one with thousands of other like-minded souls who were handsome, fun-loving, well-adjusted and happy. We were not the sad camp queens that the straight world had tried to make us believe we were destined to become. I firmly believe that no single experience is more liberating to a gay man than his first night spent dancing in a large gay club; it gives him the courage to be himself – what a revelation!

The cornerstones of my new concept were exceptional sound quality, total sound immersion coupled with 'trip' quality lighting effects, and a vast dance floor. Accordingly, Tony Gottelier of the firm Illusion Lighting, who had worked with me at the Embassy, was given a brief to create a lighting experience unique in London. I had spent a lot of time in America going to clubs and studying their sound, lights and décor and we drew from that experience. The lights were linked to the sound pulse so that the two complemented each other, in its day a new idea. We used neon as lighting flashes to create drama. The old standby mirrored balls were given a new twist with high-powered spotlights and lasers, directed on to contra-rotating balls of different sizes. We introduced a 'Curtain of Light', a rotating bar of powerful pin spots that swept the floor. Other gimmicks, such as police lights, strobes and lights that could be raised and lowered in among the dancers, all served to heighten the drama.

These innovations gave the GLC Health and Safety inspectors kittens. They were all for banning everything; this seemed to them the safest policy and the least risk. Luckily their inspectors liked an early night, so many of the effects could be safely used after 12.30 am; anyway, I had seen all of these same devices used in America, so I knew that they were safe.

The sound system at Heaven was awesome for its day and capable of delivering a huge wattage. I knew just how much sound massed bodies would absorb. As well as massive bass bins to give a physical thump that could actually be felt by the dancers, we had tweeter arrays in the ceiling to give an overhead sizzle of treble that is electrifying. One of the most exciting moments was the first time we turned on the sound and cranked up the volume. There were just a few of us alone in that vast space, and our spirits were uplifted. We were confident that our target audience of gay men would not fail to respond to the thrill of our creation. We had an entirely new product for a new decade, and a mission to liberate the spirit and realise the fantasies of thousands of gay men. We permitted ourselves the fun of playing some Beethoven loud over the mighty sound system to test its resonance, and give us courage to persevere with this daunting enterprise.

as usual, but her performance was electric. Playing to a packed house of disco-crazy men she walked to the top of the stairs and, in full view of the crowd, took a pint of lager from a man's hand and poured it over his head on to his naked sweaty torso; the crowd went wild.

The notorious dog-shit-eating American trans-sexual Divine (voted 'the filthiest person alive') performed for us. So too did Boy George and his friend Marilyn on a nightly basis, but as paying customers. Heaven played host to live performances by Madonna before she was famous; she was still trying to build her career. Like so many canny pop performers she appreciated that, by appealing to the gay market, she could launch her career. Gay men are always at the forefront of taste and trends in entertainment.

The experience of owning two of the hottest nightclubs in London at such a young age was heady and exhilarating. The press courted Derek and me; we were included on every PR guest list in town. Our mantelpiece was stacked high with invitations to celebrity functions – art-gallery openings, restaurant launches and fashion promotions. Our social life became, for a brief while, the subject of press coverage. We were photographed for magazines and newspapers. We were essentially private people and, although flattered by the attention, we wanted our private lives to remain our own. It would be untruthful to deny that we enjoyed our moment of fame, but we were conscious of the downside that comes with celebrity. The moment in the sun didn't last long and within a few years, we were thankfully forgotten and slipped back into welcome obscurity. 'Today's peacock is tomorrow's feather duster.'

Once Heaven really took off, I realised that I had spent five hedonistic years at the pinnacle of the club business and, frankly, I was burned out. I had also my relationship with Derek to consider. He was an interior designer with a career ahead of him. He needed his sleep to do his day job. I had all my money tied up in Heaven. I knew clubs were a risky business.

My business partner, Derek Johns, knew Vanessa Devereux, a picture-dealer who happened to be Richard Branson's sister. Branson expressed an interest in acquiring Heaven for Virgin. The negotiations took place on his hippy houseboat on a canal in Little Venice. Richard suggested that I sign a one-sided option that gave him the right to buy, but with no obligation on his part. I quickly disabused him of the notion that I might be an unsophisticated pop entrepreneur. I told him firmly that we had a deal only when he signed a binding contract; he was welcome to do his due diligence beforehand. Once he realised that he was dealing with a savvy businessman we got on famously.

I knew that I had to sell cheaply; I reasoned that not many business-men would buy a gay club for a large sum of money. If I didn't sell to him, I might wait for years for another opportunity. After much hag-gling, we agreed a fair figure. In addition, I was to be paid a consultancy fee of £25,000 per annum for four years; a good deal of money in the early 1980s. Bill Frankel, my wise lawyer, warned me that Virgin were short of cash (the music industry was going through one of its periodic recessions), so we insisted on a bank guarantee for the twelve quarterly instalments. It was time to move on.

❧ JOHN GALLIHER – THE DUCHESS CHASER

A certain type of gay man just loves the company of older women, the grander the better. The love affair is mutual. Grand ladies love the company of artistic gay men who are often good-looking, younger and entertaining company; best of all, their husbands won't be jealous. They can go to the opera and ballet together, the latest exhibition at the Royal Academy or a private gallery opening, events that bore many straight men. The accomplished Duchess Chasers (DCs – Americans call them 'walkers') will always remember to compliment his lady on her latest outfit or new handbag. Husbands only remember to notice such things when they have a guilty conscience. Apart from sexually, gay men make the perfect partner for a woman of style and taste; nearly everything that interests her also interests him; decoration, gardening, fabrics and clothes. Indeed one is tempted to wonder what straight men really have in common with their wives?

Some DCs make a career out of their obsession: others are merely enthusiastic amateurs. A country house party is a stage on which the DC truly shines. He will know the date and history of the house and the

Dicky Salmon (left) with John Galliher at the Embassy Club

amusing stories associated with the family history, not to mention all the gossip about current family members. He will remember to spend time talking to the retired family nanny, who lives in a cottage on the estate; she too will have stories to tell about when His Lordship was a toddler and said something highly embarrassing to the Prince of Wales. He can be relied on to dance with all the older women at the hunt ball for he is never a wallflower, nor is he attached to anyone in particular.

The Duchess, or indeed The Queen, is the archetypical gay man's drag persona; larger than life, overdressed and impossibly self-important: the mother that many gay men either had or wished they had had. The Duchess type is personified in Lady Bracknell or in Alan Bennett's character in *Forty Years On* who, on feeling chilly, puts on another rope of pearls. Perhaps this love of the grande dame is what gave rise to the nickname for gay men – Queens.

It is for reasons of his social life, or so he will tell you, that the dedicated DC has no permanent boyfriend; it would be too inconvenient socially, and besides the invitations might dry up. Sadly, there is often another reason too; however much a DC might be attracted to another man, he is a potential rival or if not, he is bound to be less glamorous than his current favourite society lady. The perfect man for him would have to be beautiful, titled and gay – an almost impossible bill to fill. This type of gay man seems to want to segregate his life into compartments; one part lives in the drawing rooms of the rich and social where rank is carefully assessed, the other half lives in a classless society of gay men. The schizophrenia involved causes mental tensions and often a conflict that remains forever unresolved.

It is little wonder that DCs work for the major auction houses. Single men are always in demand and DCs display impeccable manners and have dress sense. They are always *au fait* with the latest society gossip and are clever and witty guests at a cocktail party or formal dinner. If they are accomplished flatterers, they are always to be found on the best guest lists. Their knowledge and love of fine art ensures that they can easily introduce the topic into the conversation, landing a juicy deal in the lap of their employers. Rich widows are particularly good prospects; they might want to downsize their collection or perhaps they have estate duty to pay. They might be in need of a new diamond necklace.

DCs have a fascination for the rich and important; titles are a big turn-on. Sub-consciously DCs award points for social clout based on title, lineage, husband's position and wealth. Duchesses and Royalty are especially prized, even if impecunious. The practiced DC will be a walking encyclopaedia of genealogical connections and will be instinctively able to rank people in order of precedence, giving just the right level of deference to each.

Women are always preferred to their husbands or similar high status males; after all, they are much more fun to talk to and they share the same interests. Straight men, by contrast, are wary of forming close relationships with gay men: people might talk. They are happy to be convivial when in the company of their women but are uneasy if left alone too long with a DC. A straight man is never sure what he should talk about to a gay man. Dresses and fashion somehow seem inappropriate and gay men seldom know the name of a single football team, let alone the finer points of the game.

There are DCs to be found working in the art and antique trades and a significant number are interior designers. Many gay men just love the company of older women, particularly the Belgravia tweed skirt brigade of grand widows. Playing bridge is often a shared passion. Older women can be great company; they have lived a long life and have a fund of stories to tell. They appreciate an audience and love to gossip. Their own children treat them as a duty, whereas the DC hangs on their every word, thrilled by the social intrigue of yesteryear.

One such DC played an important role in my life by introducing me to Derek. John Galliher was an enthusiastic amateur, only in the sense that he was never employed. He dedicated his whole life to being an accomplished international socialite. He would turn up at the grandest house parties all over the world: if Peggy Guggenheim was in Venice or Lady Sarah Churchill was in Greece, John Galliher was there. If Diana Vreeland needed an escort to a charity function at the 'Met', she was on John's arm. Always wickedly entertaining, he was scrupulously careful never to offend. He always eschewed the subjects of religion and politics, or indeed anything controversial. His stories, although enjoyable, were never cruel or derogatory. He kept his conversation light and witty. If a serious subject arose around the dinner table, he would deftly deflect it into something less dreary. Polished would be too rough a word to describe him; he was honed to perfection.

He spent hours at his toilette, particularly as he got older. His age was, like any grande dame, a closely guarded secret, as was his source of income. He was rumoured to have been a boyfriend of a Mr Bloomingdale in his youth and he must have been a strikingly handsome young man. In truth, no one knew precisely where his money came from and I think there probably wasn't a great deal of it. With John, it was always style before substance.

He was tall and almost as thin as the women he escorted. His suits were subtlety stylish but plain enough never to shock; black was his favourite colour. He was always fashionably late when appropriate, but on time for the opera. In short, he could be relied upon. By the time I knew him, there was just a hint of rouge on his cheeks and an artificial brightness in his eyes. He never appeared drunk and made sure he had enough beauty sleep. When he asked you to dinner, he made it clear when he wanted you to leave.

Like so many gay men of his generation, John kept his young males entirely separate from his grand society friends. We were asked to 'boys only' meals, often luncheon. He kept a small flat on the Upper East side in New York and, for the summer months, a basement flat in Chester Row, off Eaton Square in Belgravia. I suspected he habitually rented one to pay for the other.

One day in 1975, he asked me to lunch. One was asked promptly for 12.30 pm and drinks were served in his stylish drawing room. Then at 1.00 pm, the telephone would ring and we were summoned to the dining room, where an elegant but simple meal was laid out and served by our host. We never actually saw a servant; their existence was always implied. I concluded that the telephone call was a prearranged alarm call. Apart from admiring the clever and stylish decoration of the flat, the attractions were the other guests. John invited only the most interesting and pretty people. Across the dining table from me sat a vision, Derek. I was dazzled.

As you can imagine, John became an important person in our lives. We were always sure to call on him when we visited New York. He was our fairy godfather. In the latter part of his life, John sold the flat in Chester Row and lived solely in his New York apartment.

A much younger friend, Billy McCartey, had died of AIDS. He had been the lover and heir of the pugnacious Douglas Cooper, the celebrated collector of 20th-century art. Billy had auctioned most of fabulous collection that comprised his inheritance, so was worth a great deal when he died. Generously, he left John Galliher enough money to move apartments. He didn't move far, just across town a few blocks, still on the same street in the Eighties, but from Third Avenue to Park.

In January 2003, we arrived in New York and as usual, gave John a call. By now, he would have been well into his eighties. His machine answered the telephone with a message in his distinctive clipped New York patrician voice: 'John Galliher here. I'm out now so leave a message'. We left a message, but never heard back. A few days later we were lunching with David Kleinberg, a smart decorator friend, who told us that he had seen John in high spirits, shopping on Madison a few days before Christmas, but that he had died on New Year's Eve. He left the world as he had always lived in it; making sure he caused the minimum of inconvenience to others. I feel sure when he died, he was dressing to go to some glamorous soirée.

The elegant John Galliher

Chapter Twenty-Nine

❋ JOHN SCHLESINGER

When I first met Derek, he was spending many nights with the celebrated film director John Schlesinger, at his house in Victoria Road, Kensington. John was larger than life. He was quite short, overweight, thickset and balding with an attractive face and personality and naturally, as a distinguished film director, he had many glamorous connections. He was a close friend of Alan Bates and Michael York, and a host of other stars. He had won an Oscar for his greatest success, *Midnight Cowboy*, starring Dustin Hoffman and Jon Voight. In 1977, he was at the height of his career.

To start with, I was somewhat jealous of John and he of me. He had the irritating habit of mimicking my public-school accent, which annoyed me, particularly as he himself had been educated at a public school and had a mellifluous, theatrically-trained, voice. Derek was having a sexual relationship with John, despite John having a longstanding boyfriend, an American called Michael Childers. He was seldom around. They had been lovers for many years, but Michael preferred their Hollywood house and spent most of his time living there. Michael's photographic work was mostly in America. They had an open relationship that satisfied their prodigious sexual appetites.

Derek moved out of his own flat to live with me almost as soon as our relationship started. We continued to see a great deal of John, and often had dinner together. John gave glamorous parties at Victoria Road to which we were invited. We met Joan Collins, Zoë Wanamaker, Bill Devane, Julie Christie, Twiggy and a host of others. Twiggy was always a favourite; she was wonderfully natural and unaffected, quite unlike so many other self-important stars. In real life, she was just like her slightly scatty and childlike film persona. I found most film stars to be mainly or only interested in talking about themselves and their own little world.

John made us laugh. He had a fund of stories and anecdotes and an impish, scatological sense of humour. He referred to Elizabeth Schwartzkopf as 'Betty Blackhead' and Herbert von Karajan as 'that old Nazi'. He was full of scurrilous tales of the sexual exploits of the stars: 'She was a good friend of Mrs Rimmer,' he would say about a certain well-known male actor, always with a twinkle in his eye.

He was not particularly fond of Dirk Bogarde and he told us the reason why. On Dirk's return from his long exile in France, John decided to give a dinner party for him to re-introduce him to many old friends. On arrival, Dirk took one look at the opulent surroundings at Victoria Road and exclaimed, 'Why John, such a magnificent house, and I thought all your films had been flops.'

John himself could be cutting and even cruel, especially towards those who thwarted him in the film world. His final film, *The Next Best Thing*, starred Rupert Everett and Madonna; he had hardly a good word to say about this demanding diva. According to John, she was high-handed and dictatorial and in effect usurped directorial control from him, especially with regard to the editing. The studio bosses would always defer to her wishes rather than his; she had more clout at the box office. John held her responsible for ruining the film and ultimately its commercial potential.

John loved opera and was called upon to direct at La Scala and Covent Garden. Classical music and especially opera was always playing in his house. John had a great musical ear and talent. Some of his finest work, into which he put the most love and concentration, was for the operatic stage. Music always figured largely in his movies and was always carefully and appropriately selected. Music expressed the passion in his life. He was aggressive and forceful in all his artistic endeavours, always determined to see his precise vision realised.

John Schlesinger

Numerous boyfriends came and went. They were always gorgeous and sexy: 'Americans are star fuckers, my dear, unfortunately the Brits are not,' he would explain. He adored the adulation of Hollywood, but was keenly aware of the capricious nature of the place – 'You're hot one minute but after a failure the telephone goes dead. You're only as interesting as your last success.' He truly loved England, and his English friends with whom he could have a giggle and who stood by him through triumphs and failures. We shared the view that Americans are often fickle in their friendships and only a very few can ever be close friends in the way other Englishmen become. We don't share the same sense of humour.

John was a greedy man, and partook of all life's pleasures to the full, regardless of the health implications. He was driven in his work and found it hard to relax. He was a perfectionist. His brilliance as a director depended upon his minute attention to detail and his constant striving for perfection in his art. He was often deeply frustrated by producers and the money-men whom he felt did not understand what he was trying to do, and were always tailoring a film to a budget and not out to achieve the best result. The studios would ruthlessly drop a film within days of its failure to perform financially. John would often be on the telephone to Hollywood, cajoling and haranguing studio executives to try to get them to see things his way. Then he would slam down the receiver and launch into a torrent of invective on the iniquities of Hollywood.

John and the Author

John was generous to a fault. He was rich by many people's standards but was not an accomplished manager of his own resources. He had a long list of dependants that included his old friend, Noel Davies. Noel lived in John's house in London and as he became increasingly infirm, his needs became more costly; a lift had to be installed because he could not manage the stairs.

Noel was an accomplished casting director and worked on a number of John's films, and also for Warren Beatty on *Reds*. He was a misogynist and scathing about most women, but he was also entertaining and frequently had us all in stitches with his stories and his theatrical delivery. John loved him as a friend and came to rely on his companionship. Noel was always short of money – I don't believe he ever paid John any rent.

During the filming of *Yanks* in the late 1970s, John invited us up north to visit the set. It was my first real glimpse of how a film is made on location. There were hours of tedium. I could never understand the reason for the interminable delays. John was too busy to look after us, so we had to make our own fun. We left the set to explore the wild countryside and enjoyed romantic lunches at tiny village inns. I did get to meet the stars of the film: Richard Gere; Bill Devane; Vanessa Redgrave and Lisa Eichhorn – John's beautiful new discovery.

John had liberal, even left-wing political views at odds with my own. However, he believed his friend Vanessa Redgrave was extreme in her views, and even a bit unhinged. He hadn't quite the courage to refuse to support her when she called up to ask for money for one or other of her hare-brained schemes. He put the practicalities of maintaining a good relationship with her before his principles.

John made some truly fine films. Derek and I especially loved *Madame Souzatzka,* starring Shirley Maclaine, and we went to see some of the action being filmed. One scene was shot in Pimlico School, right behind where we live. The music he chose for it was both sublime and apposite. The character vignettes, such as Peggy Ashcroft as the owner of the London townhouse full of letting rooms, were moving and funny. Twiggy gave an endearing performance as one of the lodgers.

He also did some outstanding work for television, most memorably *An Englishman Abroad,* starring Alan Bates as the traitor, Guy Burgess. It tells the true story of the marvellously catty Australian actress, Coral Browne, who played herself in the film. While in Moscow on tour she encountered Guy Burgess in her dressing room. He asked her to lunch in his dingy flat. It transpires that he wants her to buy him a new wardrobe of clothes in London, and especially a fresh Old Etonian tie.

The dialogue, written by Alan Bennett, contains some of the cleverest and funniest lines imaginable; the film was a critical triumph.

Another television piece was his production of Stella Gibbon's classic, *Cold Comfort Farm*, a dark comic tale centred on a mad farming family, the Starkadders. The elderly female lead was brilliantly played by Sheila Burrell, a friend and, curiously, related both to Derek and to me. She is Derek's mother's first cousin, and she is connected to me through her marriage to my stepfather's brother, David Sim. We only learnt of this curious coincidence after having lived together for some years.

John never disguised his gay life from those who knew him, but he was reticent in his professional and public life, in spite of having made an autobiographical film, *Sunday Bloody Sunday* about a three-way relationship between a handsome young man (Murray Head) and his simultaneous male and female lovers (Peter Finch and Glenda Jackson). He only came out fully late in life when he co-signed a letter to *The Times* supporting a knighthood for Ian McKellen, who had starred in *Cold Comfort Farm*. I wonder how differently he would have led his life and managed his film career had he felt able to be more open about his sexuality sooner. He believed that Hollywood was *au fond* a deeply homophobic place and that any revelations would damage his career.

In spite of much critical success, John did not have many financial successes – he certainly had his share of failures such as *Honky Tonk Freeway*. This film had the dubious distinction of being one of Hollywood's ten greatest loss-makers of all time. Making comedy was never John's strongpoint, although he had an excellent sense of humour and was a polished raconteur. He loved black humour and being Jewish himself, loved Jewish jokes. His ironic style did not find favour in America. The scene in which a deceased's ashes are snorted like cocaine went down especially badly.

Derek decorated John's house in Victoria Road and latterly his last flat in Old Brompton Road, South Kensington. John loved and appreciated Derek's prodigious talent as a decorator. This was a great compliment from someone of such taste with a sophisticated and developed visual sense.

In spite of many health scares and warnings from his doctors, John never let up. He could not conceive of life without work. He did not have much internal life, and only loved and valued himself in terms of his work and the prestige it brought him. He had one illness after another, until sadly dying far too young. His love of life and his great sense of humour are sadly missed by us all – especially, of course, by Michael Childers.

Chapter Thirty

❧ The *Marchioness*: The Pleasure Boat that Sank on the Thames

My friend Antonio de Vasconcelos, had invited Derek and me to join him, and some hundred or so of his friends, on a riverboat to celebrate his 25th birthday. The boat was a Thames cruiser called the *Marchioness*. The year was 1989.

A recent experience of being trapped on the Isle of Eigg in Scotland on a holiday from hell – wanting to leave but unable to do so because there were only two boats a week – was to have a direct bearing on our decision to refuse an otherwise tempting invitation. We were doubtful if we would know many of the other guests, except our young friend Luis de la Huerta from Miami, who was staying with us in London. Instead, we headed south to our cottage by the sea in Hampshire for the week-end.

A few years before, my Cambridge friend, Richard Mytton-Mills, had brought Antonio to stay with us in Key West. The house was already full to bursting with boys out to have fun. There was a special magic about that old house tucked away down a quiet lane in Old Town. A

Richard Mytton-Mills

rather pompous friend called it 'The Cuban Shack' and shack it was; a cigar-roller's shotgun house over a hundred year's old, built of white clapboard with a pitched tin roof. The magic of the place was its secluded garden, lush with banana, papaya, avocado and lime trees; a veritable fruit salad of tropical delights. Every houseplant in Europe became a tree in that lush tropical oasis. We lived mostly outside on the wide deck strewn with sun loungers by the swimming pool. Although the shack had only two proper bedrooms, there were two loft spaces in the eaves reached by stepladders and an additional bed in the enclosed porch, so the house could sleep ten if everyone doubled up.

Antonio had joined Samuel Montagu, a City merchant bank. At the bank, he had met my Cambridge friend and contemporary, Richard. Antonio arrived in Key West as a rather shy and studious young man. His polite formality was more appropriate to the City of London. He was overdressed for casual Key West, where a T-shirt and shorts were customary and then only about town. Inside our private world, clothes were optional and bathers constituted formal wear. After a week, he left relaxed and happy, with a grin from ear to ear. The tropical shack had worked its magic.

That mad spring of 1989 there were ten of us on many nights. Our guests went out to the clubs and bars and often came home on their bicycles, with a new friend walking along beside. There was always at least one new face for breakfast. Sometimes the new addition would stay on for a few days and swell our numbers. Few who experienced the special charm of the place, and the relaxed atmosphere of love we created wanted to leave. That house had a special magic.

Luis, a charming and handsome 25-year-old Cuban boy, came down from Miami to stay for a long weekend. We knew him from previous visits to Miami and he had been down to visit before. He had an engag-

Reine & Luis Huerta

ing and attractive personality, as well as being easy on the eye. Judging by those we met in Miami, Cubans must be the gayest race on earth. Miami was full of gorgeous gay Cuban boys, all of whom loved to dance and party.

One evening he returned from the Copa, a huge dance club, with a sweet, ash blond, blue-eyed young German boy called Reine. Reine was backpacking round America and had arrived in Key West with a couple of German friends all about the same age, nineteen. He was seductively dressed in lederhosen, but I don't think he realised quite how cute he looked. For him it was just the way boys dressed in Bavaria. It was clear that Reine was not accustomed to gay life; his innocence of dress mirrored his innocence of manner. He abandoned his straight travelling companions and stayed on with us for about a week, in fact until we were due to leave. In that short space of time, Luis and Reine fell deeply in love and spent every moment together.

Back home that autumn we declined Antonio's party invitation. The next day, we woke up that fateful Sunday to a brilliant autumn morning. Looking out over the Solent from our bedroom window, we looked forward to a quiet day. We tuned into BBC Radio 4 to listen to the morning news. The fateful events of the previous night were the main headlines and we realised that the party on the Thames could only be Antonio's birthday cruise. It seemed that fifty of so young people had drowned the night before in the freezing cold, dark powerful currents of the River Thames. A dredger, *Bowbelle*, had rammed into the *Marchioness* from the rear, cut her in half, and pushed her under the water. Even before we heard the name of the boat, we knew it must be Antonio's party.

On returning to London, we had a call from the police. They wanted us to attend and identify the body of a young man, one of the first bodies to be pulled from the water. The police were kind and considerate, but the experience was harrowing. The body was Luis's. He looked peaceful and intact; he had not been in the water too long. I had the sad duty of calling his family in Miami to tell them the awful news. Over a week later came the sad news that they had found Antonio. As befits the perfect host, his was the last body of all to be retrieved.

Out of intense sadness friendship can bloom, and we came to know the other members of Luis's large Cuban family. His sister Maria, in particular, became a friend and we dined with the whole extended family on subsequent visits to Miami.

About six months after the accident a memorial service was held at Southwark Cathedral on the banks of the Thames near where the disaster had occurred. Coming not long after the Lockerbie plane crash, where there had been criticism of the lack of official representation, there was a full turnout of public figures at the reception afterwards. Luis's siblings had never travelled to Europe before and this was a moving occasion for them, as well as a rather daunting experience.

After the service, at which there were many tears, we gathered in a large hall in the Cathedral precincts. Various strangers came up and talked to us, beginning with an impressive-looking short older man, who turned out to be the deputy prime minister, Sir Geoffrey Howe.

Antonio de Vasconcelos in Key West

The highlight was a five-minute chat with Princess Diana, who came representing the Royal Family. She was everything her reputation led us to expect – elegant, demure, charming, relaxed and friendly. You can imagine the impression that this made on my young visitors. As we left the hall, Cardinal Heenan, the Archbishop of Westminster, was waiting by the door. He took the exceptionally beautiful Raquel by the hand and held it. Looking into her eyes, he said: 'My child, I noticed you in the Cathedral and joined with you in your suffering.'

Next spring we returned to the house in Key West to find, tucked inside a book, the draft of a poignant letter written by little Reine to his new love, Luis. It was the first love letter of a young man smitten, written in broken English: 'I thinking about us and it's hard to describe what I feel for you, all I can say is that I have never felt so strongly about anyone before. I hope you feel the same for me. I miss you, your new good friend Reine.' The letter is now pasted into the back of our photo album as a sad reminder of a young life, lost at the very moment of blossoming. I had no contact address for Reine and so I do not know if he ever knew why he never heard from Luis again.

Chapter Thirty-One

✹ CRUSAID:

A NATIONAL FUNDRAISING CHARITY FOR AIDS

In 1986, Derek and I went to see the Larry Kramer play, *A Normal Heart*, at the Royal Court Theatre in Sloane Square, produced by a friend of ours, Derek Grainger of *Brideshead Revisited* fame. The play was very angry and powerful and full of foreboding of the crisis to come. I was so moved that I felt obliged to start raising money to combat the tragedy that became known as AIDS. My friend, Richard Taylor, introduced me to David McFarlane and Geoff Henning: both had come to the same conclusion after the death of their close friend, Kit Woolcott. Together we decided to start the charity Crusaid, and they invited me to be its first chairman.

The launch of the charity took place at Leighton House by courtesy of Stephen Jones, the curator. I made an impassioned speech to a capacity crowd of more than 300 friends. It was well received, although some of those present thought I was being unnecessarily alarmist about what they viewed as an overblown American scare. How I wish they had been right.

Unfortunately, both Lord Scarman and the Marchioness of Dufferin and Ava declined to become patrons of our new charity; such was the stigma then attached to this new deadly disease. I was hurt and disappointed in both cases. In the case of Lindy Dufferin, her husband Sheridan, an art dealer, was a friend who had recently died of AIDS. I felt that her endorsement of our efforts would have been a fitting memorial to her husband and a positive contribution to the fight against the disease.

As for Leslie Scarman, I had known him and his wife Ruth, since childhood; we had spent many happy summer holidays together in Salcombe, Devon. After my father died in 1958, Leslie had become a surrogate father to me as well as being a renowned liberal Judge. I had felt sure he would not refuse me, but as ever, I was to learn a great deal about human nature, true friendship and moral courage. Most people are more concerned with their public image and what others will think, rather than about doing what is brave, right and decent. Leslie's refusal was formal, polite but distinctly cold.

It is sometimes said that the rich often don't give, but the poor can be generous. How true this was to prove in some cases. A few rich friends made public promises of financial support only to be found wanting, whereas quite hard-up friends donated generously and without fuss or expectation of thanks. Fundraising for charity from one's friends is an emotionally draining business. The generosity of a few is heart-warming but it goes hand-in-hand with the bitter disappointment when close friends fail to support your efforts. I found it hard to suppress the anger I felt when friends made ostentatious and public promises of financial support, and then never gave a penny. In at least one case, an acquaintance in this category went on to contract AIDS. I have to confess I felt a wholly uncharitable sense of *schadenfreude*.

Princess Diana at the opening of the Kobler Centre

On a visit to New York, a friend Bill McDermott, introduced me to the playwright Larry Kramer, the author of the play that had inspired me. We had dinner with him, so I was able to tell him how his play had given birth to my new charity. His pleasure and satisfaction were evident and a joy to see.

Freddie Kobler, a gay man, and co-founder with Maxwell Joseph of Grand Metropolitan Hotels, died and left a legacy of £500,000 to be used for charitable purposes. His executors, Andrew Stone and Antoine Schwareb, decided it should be given to Crusaid. It was our first major donation and it enabled us to part fund the Kobler AIDS/HIV treatment centre at Chelsea and Westminster Hospital. Derek undertook the interior design for no fee and involved the artists Patrick Procktor and Howard Hodgkin in the window designs. The Princess of Wales opened the Centre.

We instituted a hardship fund to give respite breaks to patients and their carers and also to pay for extras, such as a special invalid bed or even to settle an overdue electricity bill. We provided fridges in the AIDS wards so that patients could have their own food brought in to tempt their poor appetites. We raised money to benefit London Lighthouse, the AIDS hospice for the dying; the Terrence Higgins Trust, the leading AIDS information and counselling charity, as well as many other AIDS-related projects across the nation.

After about a year and a half, I decided to resign to concentrate my efforts on the newly formed National Aids Trust. Although the resignation was amicable on my part, I felt that some of the founder committee members were not so well disposed toward me. Charity committees are well known for infighting and inflated egos, and Crusaid was sadly no exception. On the tenth anniversary of the foundation of our charity in 1996, Crusaid hosted a celebration dinner which to our sadness, neither Derek nor I were invited. I am proud that Crusaid continues the fight

www.aidsark.org

and raises large sums of money to help the battle against the disease at home and abroad.

In the early years of the new century, Derek and I started a modest new charitable venture, AIDS Ark, a UK-registered charity that seeks to provide life-saving, anti-retroviral treatment for about a hundred or so named patients, accessed through doctors working in the field, in India and parts of Africa. The inspiration for AIDS Ark was *Schindler's Ark* (or *List*). As Schindler said, 'To save one person saves the world entire'. Schindler saved only as many Jews as he could afford, because he believed it is better to save a few than do nothing and let them all die. We hope we can find others, younger and more energetic, to take on and grow this charitable responsibility for the future.

Chapter Thirty-Two

❧ GEORGE DESIPIO

For some gay men, their mothers are the only women in their lives. All men love their mums, but few mothers are as loved and cherished as by their gay sons. In my case, my close relationship to my mother turned sour because of her refusal to accept my sexuality and my chosen partner in life. In spite of Derek's loving kindness to her, especially as she grew old and infirm, my mother never felt able to embrace him as a member of her family. I felt the loss of our close relationship was an even greater loss for her than for me.

It is my experience that gay men fall into two distinct categories in their attitude to the opposite sex. There are those that seek out and enjoy the company of women and there are those who mistrust and dislike women and are largely, or mainly, misogynist. George de Sipio was of the former type. He was open and friendly to all in the way that only a social New Yorker can be.

He was terminally ill and wanted to see London one more time before he died. He decided to make the visit accompanied by his adored mama; he needed help to get about and look after himself. We were

George Desipio and Author, rafting in Idaho

friends from time spent together in New York and, only the year before, we had shared an exhilarating adventure, rafting down the Salmon River in Idaho for six glorious days together with half a dozen friends. He was then the picture of good health.

George was a big man both physically and in personality. He weight-trained obsessively and had a football full-back's manly torso. Now his hair was thinning, but his face was lit perpetually with a radiantly wide smile. He had a New Yorker's ready wit but I never knew him to be mean-spirited or cutting. He loved to chat to everyone. On our rafting trip, he had spent time explaining to a suburban stockbroker's wife why he shaved his legs and comparing methods of depilation – this was a surreal spectacle on a sand bar by some raging rapids in the Wild West.

By now, AIDS had ravaged him; he was skeletally thin and walked on crutches, such was the pain from the neuropathy in his feet. He suffered most acutely from the facial lesions of Kaposi's sarcoma, a vicious and deadly skin cancer that left its purple stigmata all over what had been a beautiful manly visage. For a gay man who was vain about his good looks, this disfigurement was the final indignity.

In London, George insisted on seeing the sights and wanted to go to all the 'in' places. I booked a table at the recently revived Conran gas-trodome, Quaglino's, in Bury Street. I chose it because it was large and anonymous. I was certain that we would not be turned away. The general manager of the whole Conran restaurant group, Joel Kissin, was a friend.

On arrival, George, his mother, Derek and I made our way painfully slowly down the celebrated staircase to our assigned table. Walking was difficult for George and he was tired after a full day. I was horrified to see other diners staring at him as though he were a freak; I had expected better of my countrymen. During the meal George laughed and joked, but ate little.

The loving attentions of his mother were a delight to see. As the other diners continued to stare, she reached up and lovingly stroked his damaged cheek and looked with love into his eyes. He was still the most beautiful man in the world to her. Truly, a mother's love is like no other; she loved him with a burning intensity that could not be extinguished by any disfigurement. I know that her love was returned in full measure.

I saw George again one last time in New York, just before he died. I stayed in his apartment while he spent his final days in hospital. I sat by his bedside and held his hand; by that stage, he could not move much. His smile lit up the room; the nurses loved him. I could not bear to stay around for the funeral of yet another close friend taken in his prime.

Chapter Thirty-Three

✖ FERDINAND COUDERT

Ferdinand was the living embodiment of the cartoon character Mr Magoo. He was both myopic and diffident with a lovable vagueness of manner that instantly endeared him to all who crossed his path. He was immensely rich and loved to entertain. Although American, he was an Anglophile, or should I say a Europhile, for he was naturally of French extraction. He was learned and an especially accomplished linguist, not only of French and other living languages but also of the classics: he could read classical Greek and Latin and was familiar with the ancient texts. A lawyer by profession, his family firm of Coudert & Partners was one of the most respected New York law firms with an international practice that boasted the Government of France amongst its prestigious clientele.

I came to know him well through the sleepy tropical island town of Key West at the southernmost tip of Florida, where Ferdinand had settled in his retirement and had his winter home. What a house it was, a grand old white-painted, wooden, sea captain's house; one of the largest properties on the island, situated in the historic part of Old Town. The lush tropical garden was extensive and was Ferdinand's

(From left) Author, Scott Masters, Chas Fitzgerald, Trey Bartosh
and Richard Taylor; Key West, Florida

pride and joy. The climate in Key West ensured that eating outside was the norm for most of the winter, and Ferdinand would host memorable dinner parties al fresco under a specially constructed logia in the garden.

His cook, Sophie, a matronly soul who had been in his employ for many years, would prepare dinner beautifully. She cooked delicious meals and the wines, well chosen by Ferdinand, complemented her cuisine. The table was artfully dressed with candles and bedecked with magnificent flower arrangements of heliconias, orchids, jasmine and tropical lilies. In the background, the swimming pool glistened with softly reflective light and the sweet smell of the night-blooming cactus filled the air. Frogs croaked loudly by the pool and the sound of insects filled the tropical night. A more romantic and seductive setting could not be envisaged.

Bruce, the houseboy, would serve dinner. Bruce was a 'muscle mary'. Hours spent in the gym, together with a little chemical enhancement, had honed his tight muscular body to perfection. He was invariably smiling and flirtatious with Ferdinand's male guests. All who saw him could hardly fail to admire his taut and alluring bum, and not a few were permitted to caress it. His one fault, if one were to be critical, was his short stature, but what he lacked in height he made up for in the sweet nature of his personality and his toned and buffed physique. He was undoubtedly the most admired of Ferdinand's extensive collection of

Author and new friend

possessions. Bruce enjoyed a formal relationship with his employer, always referring to him respectfully as 'Mr Coudert'. He was as adept at performing his role of butler as he was at raising the temperatures of the gay male guests. He saw no contradiction in his twin avocations.

Ferdinand had once been married and had only come out after his wife had died prematurely. When I first came to know him, he had a live-in boyfriend, a rather unsuitable younger man with a drug problem who quickly disappeared from view. Ferdinand was now of an age when he preferred the company of his books, antiques and fine wines to the rough and tumble of sexual exertion. He was rumoured to keep an extensive library of videos of a sensational nature devoted to the joys of flagellation. No doubt, his interest in old-fashioned pedagoguery was fuelled by his love of the cane. He admired the Greek ideal of a healthy well-disciplined body, coupled with a well-exercised mind.

On one occasion, as a thank-you for a memorable dinner party, some of us younger men stripped off and dived into the invitingly warm water of his pool and affected to spank one another – much to the delight of our spell-bound host.

What I loved about Ferdinand was his total lack of snobbery and his relaxed and natural charm. He was the perfect host and the pleasure that he derived from the dinners he gave was evident. To him, the dinner party was the perfect expression of the art of living; a sentiment I endorsed. There is surely no better way to spend time than in sharing a meal with friends in a tranquil and beautiful setting.

The highlight of the winter season in Key West was 'Fantasy Fest', a variation on the theme of Halloween or Carnival. The town was *en fête* for a long weekend, with a succession of parties and fancy dress competitions culminating in the annual parade down Duval Street. True to the spirit of Carnival, everything and anything was permitted. The gay boys who dominated the event paraded their sexuality and fetishes for all to admire; there were drag queens-a-plenty, leather boys on motorbikes, boys dressed as nuns (the Sisters of Perpetual Indulgence) and costumes of an intricate imagination of every conceivable type. Unfortunately, as is often the case, those with less to parade were often the most revealing, whilst the better looking were often more circumspect. People danced in the street and followed the parade, and then went on to the clubs and bars before going home after the dawn. The 'Lord of Misrule' went abroad for those few days to deliver sensuality and sodomy in a bacchanalian orgy of excess. Alcohol and other more fashionable and less legal substances fuelled the party.

Ferdinand owned a second property that attached to his back garden that fronted on to Duval, a perfect place to watch the parade. He gave a grand party every year for his friends on the island. Everyone came dressed in fancy dress appropriate to that year's carnival theme. Ferdinand handed out large strings of fake pearls to both boys and girls while Bruce served ice-cold champagne and vodka cocktails. Ferdinand presided over the occasion like a later day Nero or Caligula in flowing toga or Arab kaftan. He gave us all an evening to remember.

Ferdinand spent the summers in New England at his house in Old Lyme, Connecticut. In spite of numerous invitations, we never saw the house; for us, summers were invariably spent in the Mediterranean or at home in the glories of the English countryside.

Ferdinand's death in his late eighties left Key West diminished by his departure. Each time we cycle past, the Coudert mansion is now a sad reminder of happy times past.

Chapter Thirty-Four

DECIBELLE AND THE SCREAMERS

In the early 1970s, gay restaurants were all the rage. London had so few gay clubs back then. Those that did exist were small basement hangouts that apologised for their very existence by being hidden from view. Gay men were still a small, vilified minority, beaten down by years of legal and moral persecution. Homosexuality had only recently been decriminalised by the 1967 Sexual Offences Act, but only in private with adults over the age of 21 – never mind that the legal age of majority for everything else was 18. It was still illegal to 'proselytize', which was taken by the law to include the publication of the addresses of places where gay men consorted together, so it was by no means easy for an aspiring young man to locate gay haunts until he had acquired like-minded friends who knew their way around.

The gay world, especially its upper echelons, was small and cliquey, everyone either knew everyone else or at least had heard of them. There were a handful of unstylish gay pubs with hideously patterned carpets serving atrocious food and putting on tired drag acts; the patrons were usually just as dire. The gay world seemed divided between this sleazy low-life and 'Society Queens'. Society Queens (SQs) were mostly older men, invariably camp and intensely snobbish. They gave grand parties to which the young were invited; they all knew each other and could be fiercely competitive and bitchy. They had a regrettable tendency to call each other by girls' names. If they went out at all, other than to private houses, SQs held court in a handful of gay-run Chelsea restaurants. Sunday lunch was always a special occasion. Every SQ had his table reserved.

Christopher Hunter

There was a pub in Belgravia, The Pig and Whistle, where the young gay set would drink on a Sunday morning, showing off their conquests of the night before. The better off would then migrate to La Popote to take a late lunch and linger over coffee, well into the afternoon.

La Popote was every bit as camp as its clientele. The manager, Christopher Hunter, excelled at producing barely edible food but his salon had the scintillating and seductive atmosphere of a private club. Gossip and intrigue fed the appetite and cheap alcohol fuelled the revelry. The waiters were chosen for their looks rather than their knowledge of food and wine. The decoration was high camp, elaborately swagged curtains covered the windows and kept the inside dark and womb-like, even on the sunniest of days: purple was the dominant colour and pink the accent. Candles guttered on the tables to supplement the dim light from the cheap glass chandeliers. The pretty waiters minced from table to table in over-tight trousers, enjoying the badinage and appreciative stares of the patrons. The more sexually predatory of the punters surreptitiously fondled the waiters' pert bottoms as they served the soup. Gold chains and jewellery adorned the older diners, partly as a display of wealth and partly as an exercise in camp femininity. A new young face would become the immediate subject of gossip and speculation. Nothing earned a regular more kudos than to be seen lunching with a new piece of tasty 'chicken' – gay slang for a young man.

The gay world of those days appeared to be divided between butch 'tops' and feminine 'bottoms'. It was assumed that all young boys new to the scene were likely to be bottoms; there was a definite shortage of reliable tops. It was all a hangover from pre-war days when homosexuals were all effeminate and 'sisters' to each other. Sex was sought with rough trade or prostitutes, who represented desirable real males. Straight men were prized even if they had to be paid for. By some adroit self-delusion, working-class males, such as lorry drivers, were thought to be straight just because they were married men and eschewed any sentimental connection with their sex, even though they allowed themselves to be pleasured by the sisterhood in dark lay-bys.

Older gay men were either busy chasing younger boys or looking for rough trade in parks and bathhouses. There was a thriving but dangerous late-night scene in Holland Walk (beside Holland Park) and Hampstead Heath, where men cruised in the half-light and engaged in furtive couplings behind the bushes. Many gay men still frequented 'cottages' or public toilets – an activity fraught with danger as the police employed agent provocateurs, to engage men in illegal soliciting in order to gain convictions in the courts. Many a famous name had fallen foul of the law and had their careers damaged or ruined by the consequent adverse publicity. Both Sir Michael Redgrave and Sir John

Gielgud had endured such public exposure and censure. To some, the danger added to the excitement, but for many, public toilets remained the only available sexual outlet in their depleted sex lives.

Given what we now know to be the true percentage of gay men, estimated to be about 8% of the male population, there must have been a vast number of closeted gay men either in unhappy marriages or leading isolated, lonely lives of self-denial. All this unhappiness was bolstered by unfeeling churches, which preached the morality of sin punished by a mythical God, while not caring in the least about the damage done to young psyches driven either to suicide or into loveless marriages, causing unhappiness to all concerned.

A number of gay men chose to join the all-male professions such as the priesthood, teaching at boys' schools and the Army, thereby posing a danger to themselves and those placed in their trust. Only now have we learnt of the extent of such activity. The financial survival of some American dioceses is in question as they are battered by lawsuits from former abused children accusing their lecherous priests.

In the 1970s, a burgeoning leather scene in London consisted of middle-aged men in over-tight leather trousers with facial hair and beer bellies, sporting silver studs and chains on their cheap leather jackets. A few rode motor-cycles and appeared genuinely menacing, but for the most part these men were 'leather doughnuts' and about as scary as a pink blancmange. Their chosen watering holes were either cellar bars or dirty pubs devoid of style. Their 'butch' affectations were undermined by their invariably camp voices and 'queeny' conversational topics – 'Did you hear Callas in Traviata? Quite sublime, my dear.'

A new breed of gay men was emerging; straight-acting, normal men who, while acknowledging their feminine side, behaved and talked normally and sought sex with similarly disposed gay men. Such men were looking for specifically gay relationships that didn't ape straight society. They believed that it was possible for men to express their love for one another in a relationship of equality where sexual roles were not rigidly defined. They sought to break away from the confines of a self-deprecatory gay world that played up to all the worst prejudices of straights. The touch and feel of liberation was in the air. Year-by-year the number of men on the scene waxed inexorably larger, as more of us found the courage to participate and refused to remain hidden.

Society Queens on the other hand were often married and many had children. They deemed it essential to appear normal to the outside world and to participate fully in its structures and conventions. There were peers of the realm with grand stately homes, like the late Marquess of Hertford (Hugh), ex-Army officers a-plenty like Colonel David Laurie (a member of the Royal Household), captains of industry and successful entrepreneurs such as Sir Henry Marking (Chairman of British Airways). To these men correct form was all-important and their gay life had to be kept hidden, a guilty secret. Of course, there were also decorators like David Hicks (married to Lady Pamela, daughter of Earl Mountbatten of Burma – a grand alliance if ever there was one). Some decorators were 'out', but others believed that marriage would give them social respectability and advancement.

It seems that the grand and successful have always been able to indulge their predilections under cover of their marriages, whereas the more ordinary mortals were condemned by fear to live a 'straight' existence. They feared the loss of their jobs or being turned down for promotion, they feared that discovery and exposure would ruin their lives. The young urban working-class men, and the outcasts like Quentin Crisp had nothing to lose by being themselves. The world of the arts and entertainment provided a large contingent of queers, they seemed less inclined to shelter behind the cover of a false marriage, even though many were firmly in the closet. Michael Redgrave, despite his left-wing

views, was one who chose to marry and lead a secret gay life on the side, indulging in his predilection for masochism with his pick-ups. 'Sir Michael Redgrave, I'll be bound,' as the theatrical joke went.

For my part, I could never feel comfortable with the duplicity of married homosexuals and 'closet queens'. I disliked the way they hid the gay part of their lives like a guilty secret. Their attempts to pass for straight in the social world they inhabited were risible. Everyone knew they were 'buggers' and no one respected them for their futile attempts to hide it; they fooled none but themselves. Their 'county' friends would say as an aside, 'He's one of those, you know.' I heard my mother say

Barry Grigg

it often. Their wives were pitied and humiliated by the deception. In mitigation, I have to allow that, in their day, homosexuality was illegal and gay men persecuted, but that was in the past.

The saddest aspect of this duplicity was the way they kept the two sides of their lives so separate. They kept their young gay friends hidden like a guilty secret. I found this so insulting and demeaning – as if somehow they were grand and respectable enough to be seen in public and their young gay friends, like me, were not. I have always believed that other people take you at your own evaluation of yourself. If you live as though you have something to be ashamed of, most people will be happy to agree with you. If you treat your sexuality as a matter of no moment, others will have nothing to gossip about behind your back.

Two of the more prominent 'screamers' at La Popote were Tony Galliers-Pratt (known as 'Decibelle') and his friend, Barry Grigg. Decibelle was aptly named; his strident high-pitched banter and camp phraseology dominated the dining room. He affected that ultra-upper-class camp voice so beloved of certain queens, in a vain attempt to boost their aristocratic credentials, and popularised by the art critic, Brian Sewell. The only credentials such an affected accent boosts is a man's camp ones.

Decibelle was, like so many SQs of his day, married with three children, although his wife was never introduced to us younger gay boys. Always fond of dressing-up, his less kind friends quipped that he had married his wife for her wardrobe. Decibelle was tall and handsome; he dressed beautifully, usually in suits that were well-tailored. His wit was sharp and his repartee barbed. He entertained like an 18th-century grandee. His houses, in Belgrave Square and the grade-1 listed Mawley Hall in Shropshire, were decorated with flair and taste in the grand 18th-century manner. He had his own well-formed ideas on the subject of interior decoration and neither sort advice nor employed a professional decorator.

He poured much of his thwarted femininity into his curtains. His windows were dressed in enough fabric to fill a draper's shop; some of his curtains must have cost thousands of pounds, even in those days. The result was a stuffy formality that impressed but nauseated. His windows tended to look like an over-dressed grande dame of a former imperial age; yards of heavy patterned fabric; ornamented by huge swags and tails; golden fringes and tassels predominated. The extravagance of the tie-backs alone would have made the Lord Chamberlain of Ruritania blush. I think, like many a SQ, he could have had a successful career as a dress designer.

On one occasion at Mawley Hall, he had just hung some particularly feminine curtains made from shimmering candy-pink silk taffeta. They were reminiscent of an eighteenth-century lady's nightgown. 'Have I gone to far?' he enquired. 'But they simply are too beautiful.'

He didn't flower fully until his sons became teenagers in the 1960s. Seeing them spending money and leading liberated and sexually fulfilled lives, Decibelle decided to kick over the traces. He spent more time away from his wife and became increasingly extravagant and louche. He entered the world of boys, 'campery' and high-living. Up to that point, he had been a relatively sober married man with children, doing his duty and running the family business with a degree of business acumen. His extravagance was made possible thanks, in no small measure, to his wife's fortune. (She was a shipping heiress from the Cayzer family.)

Once he discovered how to discover young men, there was no stopping him. When not camping it up with boyfriends in La Popote, holding court in Belgrave Square or at his country-seat, he was chairman of the family engineering company, F. Pratt Engineering Plc. He used this quoted company as his private fiefdom. This was ultimately to lead to his downfall.

Tony took a shine to a young and attractive old Etonian with the highly improbable name of Tertius Murray-Threipland. This young man may have had many admirable qualities, but he lacked the experience and qualifications to assume the role of managing director of a publicly quoted company. Nothing daunted, Tony appointed him to the role. Unfortunately for Tony, Tertius took to his role rather too enthusiastically. As the recession started to bite, the company produced poor results and part of the blame fell on Tony's expenses as chairman, including the company headquarters, the house in Belgrave Square. Tertius sought to curb his chairman's extravagances. The result was a boardroom putsch in which, to his great chagrin, Tony was ousted.

For many years, Tony lived a gay life away from home. He travelled extensively and I encountered him again in Key West in Florida, where he shared a house with an American boyfriend. He had a number of boyfriends, none of whom lasted very long. Eventually, as he grew older and his personal finances dwindled, he moved back to Mawley and his wife. He always remained close to his mother, who lived to a great age on the island of Guernsey, and he would often visit her there.

Barry Grigg – 'Mother' – was genuinely kind, often funny and always considerate. On one occasion when I was a guest at his table and fell ill, he was sympathetic and genuinely concerned for my well-being in a most touching way. He was much given to wearing fur coats and jew-ellery, his hair was grey and bouffant, his gestures exaggerated. In fact, he could be both tough and determined, not one to cross when roused to anger. He had a deliciously witty turn of phrase and was an acute observer of his fellow man, as well as being delightfully self-deprecatory. When a new acquaintance affected surprise on learning that he had four children, Barry rejoined, 'Mother was very fecund, dear'; and when try-ing to master his tricycle in Key West, he referred to himself as, 'a rather wibbly-wobbly woman'.

I sensed that his camp act was at times tiring for him. Like many a comedian, he longed to relax and act normally. For many years and until he died he had a much younger boyfriend, Vincent, or 'Madame Vincente' as he called him. In his later years, Vincent became the main provider and even took Barry to Hong Kong as his spouse when his company posted him there.

Of Barry's children, one son in particular, David, is a close friend of all of us gay boys. He is handsome and charming and totally at ease in gay company. His father referred to himself as 'mother' and to David as 'my darling daughter, Daisy'. David was in fact more straight than gay, but he enjoyed the company of gay men, having been brought up with them and sharing many of their interests and pleasures. Barry was a director of the celebrated tailoring and cloth merchants, Kilgour, French & Stanbury.

The sight of these two public company directors, Mother and Decibelle, carrying on in a restaurant like a couple of stage queens was quite unbelievable. They were like a comedy turn at a burlesque. The display was undeniably entertaining in limited doses, but ultimately unedifying. With the passing of these two characters, the gay world has become grey and ordinary, but I am happy to be part of the normal world of gay men, behaving normally.

Chapter Thirty-Five

✖ A BISEXUAL MADE FOR THREE

Whenever a group of gay men discuss the subject of bisexuality, the debate is sure to become heated. Some will aver that such a state does not exist and that bisexuality is just a cover for a man still in the closet; as is often the case. The Press in particular, ever alive to the possibility of being sued, use bisexuality as a euphemism when they are at all unsure of their ground or the reliability of their informants. Some gay men will say that bisexuality is, of course, an observable reality; they do not want to destroy their cherished hopes of meeting and having sex with a real straight man. Such encounters are the holy grail of many a gay man's fantasy.

I have listened endlessly to many such debates and often the difference between the protagonists, as so often in argument, is actually one of definition. What do you mean by the word bisexual? The following facts are not in dispute:

1) There are men who have had sex with both men and women, either at roughly the same time or more often sequentially.
2) There are men who have been exclusively gay and then marry.
3) There are men who have been married and then come out as gay in later life.
4) There are men who have sex with men but are also sexually interested in women and vice versa.

Having sex with one sex or another or having no sex at all does not in my view determine sexuality. A large percentage of men have sex at least once with people of both sexes – this doesn't make them bisexual. Monks or priests who are celibate do not thereby prove themselves NOT to be heterosexual, just because they don't have sex with women. A man's sexual preference is a component of his personality and not determined by the person he actually has sex with; it is all in the mind or, if you will pardon the expression, in the groin. Nearly all men are capable of having sex with either sex, if the object is attractive and willing enough or the circumstances are right. I have already discussed adolescent homosexuality in an earlier chapter; boys often go through a homosexual phase. Men incarcerated in prison or in any all-male institution will turn to each other for relief and sometimes to fulfil an emotional need for physical affection.

A person's core orientation is so much harder to determine, the societal pressure to conform masks the truth. When the social and penal sanctions against homosexuality are draconian, few men are brave enough to appear openly gay. As a young Iranian poignantly expressed it, 'What for me is love is punishable by death'. Such has been the case in many cultures at different times, including our own. Gay men were made to wear a pink triangle in the Nazi death camps. The persecution of homosexuality derives entirely from the proscription found in Leviticus 18:22 which is used as a biblical justification. All three religions of the book; Christianity, Islam and Judaism, excuse their persecution in this way. They conveniently forget that Exodus 25:44 sanctions the ownership of slaves as long as they are not of your own tribe. In Exodus 35:2 it clearly states that those that work on the Sabbath shall be put to death. It seems that religions like to pick selectively which bits of the Bible they choose to obey.

I have mentioned that it is my belief that the percentage of those who are mainly or wholly gay does not change over time or between societies. It is merely the observable number of those that are out that changes. I base this belief on the certainty that a person's sexuality is not a choice but something innate.

There is hardly any gay scene in India where the subject is taboo and homosexuality is illegal, but there are many MSM (Men who have Sex with Men). Men marry because they are expected or even forced to do so, they then have furtive sex with other men or boys in parks and public toilets. Being married does not make them bisexual, they are as gay as a man dancing in Heaven.

I prefer to consider a person heterosexual if his romantic inclinations are towards the opposite sex. The test I would apply is 'Which sex do you dream about?' Who do you think about when you masturbate? In the flights of fantasy a man has when alone with his mind and his hand shall the truth be known. Proof is nearly impossible in this debate. But I have talked to and known intimately so many gay and 'bisexual' men, so I am more qualified than most to speak. To me a bisexual is someone who is equally attracted, sexually and emotionally, by both sexes at the same time. He can look round a room and find his gaze lingering romantically on first a girl and then a guy and fantasize about loving either.

A friend in my early years in London was or seemed to be wholly gay, and outrageously so. He hardly ever missed an opportunity to put on a frock and camp it up; he had sex almost nightly, either with a new friend met at dinner or in a bar or if unsuccessful there, he would go to Holland Walk or Hampstead Heath. When he reached thirty or so he suddenly announced that he was getting married and began to live a domestic life in conventional suburban married bliss. He now has four daughters and has been happily married for thirty years. Now I cannot know if on some dark moonless nights he does not steal away from home and, like a certain Labour MP, sneak out on to his local common for a breath of fresh air. I have never heard that he does nor has he been observed in a gay sauna. The word would travel fast along the gay gossip grapevine if he had. I believe he made a conscious decision to abandon gay life in order to enjoy a family and especially the joys of children. Like many gay men, he never had a gay relationship, only one-night stands.

Some gay men are only capable of anonymous sex; gay relationships kill the urge for them. Sex is so much about fantasy that a real person, especially another gay man, is a passion killer. The problem is always that the raunchy silent macho man of the first night transmutes into the queer boy who needs affection and who spends hours in the bathroom with his face creams. The image of rugged masculinity evaporates. The reasons that gay men marry are legion. It may be to become a father and have children or to find a life partner, even if the sex is not what they would ideally require. Society makes it so much easier for a man to have a lasting relationship with a women, and besides there are many other social and career benefits. This sort of married man is only sociologically bisexual.

Many gay men marry while they are still young – they dismiss the possibility of finding a male partner in a heterosexual world, maybe they live in the country or in a small town or maybe their religion pushed them into an arranged marriage. More likely, the mores of the time excluded any thought of an open gay life or gay relationship. Then, later in life they are widowed or divorced or their children grow up and then they fly out of the closet to claim what little happiness they can before age slams the door behind them again. Tony Galliers-Pratt and Ferdinand Coudert were both in this category. I had a sweet gay friend who died young of AIDS. His father was a dressmaker in a small town. The father came out in later life and now leads a gay life and has been able to catch the rays before the sunset fades. I think he could not contemplate the pain it would cause his ex-wife to have both a gay son and a gay husband.

Some gay men are fearful of coming out because they think they will not succeed as a gay man. It is hard enough to face the music with family and friends, only to become a lonely and miserable queer. The gay world of bars and casual sex can seem daunting and scary to a shy man who is not particularly attractive or confident. The magazines are full of buffed bodies and confident sexy male stereotypes. It's easier to give up the struggle and live with an undemanding woman in a sexless marriage.

Another variant is the older gay man who has a long-term relationship with a younger, often married or seemingly straight, man. One such relationship I have observed at close quarters is between a man of my age and a thirty-something blue-collar American who is married with children. His wife must know that their frequent sojourns together are more than business trips. The younger man is intensely sexual with my friend and claims to have had no other sex with a man. He is seeking a father figure, financial support and sex of a sort he feels he dare not seek openly; he is deeply ashamed of his needs and is openly homophobic in his views. He met my friend twelve years ago in a hooker bar in New York where such boys go to look for rich older men. A financial motive for sex in his eyes exonerates him from the charge of homosexuality; his conscience is clear.

There are a very small number of men who have sex with both sexes at about the same time. They like women a lot. Many gay men prefer the society of women, after all we have so much in common. Genuinely loving, but non-sexual relationships are often formed between gay men and their women friends ('fag-hags' is the slang term). Gay men can find straight men hard to talk to, they don't enjoy gossip or talking about decorating and opera and the gay man hates sport. Such gay men can easily be seduced by a determined girl. When you are young, casual sex is easy and pleasing, but a passing hunky male will soon divert his attention. Some gay men are more active than passive and find the mechanics of sex with a girl easier and more fulfilling. The reasons for apparent bisexuality are legion.

The only real question is: Are there people who can actually fall in love as easily with one sex as the other? I believe that the answer to this is a resounding *no*. Whatever we do in bed, our orientation is always firmly toward falling in love with one sex *or* the other – never both. People may change that orientation over time. Men can easily be gay in their youth and as they mature, they find women easier, less daunting and so develop the confidence and dominance of the true heterosexual in their relationships with women. It is also true that many gay men are only attracted to boys or young men and so find their range of possible partners diminish as they grow older. They then turn their attention to the opposite sex.

The issue is a complex one. It is an area where we need more research, a new Dr Kinsey. I will truly believe in bisexuality when I hear of a man who has loved and lived with a man then a woman and then a man again. I have yet to meet such a person.

Chapter Thirty-Six

❄ ROBERT MAXWELL – CAPTAIN BOB

The crashed tycoon – the monstrous 'Captain Bob', saw the emerging AIDS pandemic of the 1980s as yet another media platform for self-promotion. He publicly declared his willingness to contribute £500,000 to the cause and offered to place his Mirror Group of newspapers behind his fundraising campaign. The Government decided that he should head the fundraising arm of the nascent National AIDS Trust, of which Margaret Jay was chief executive. She happened to be the former wife of Peter Jay, supposedly 'the cleverest man in England' and Maxwell's recently appointed personal executive assistant. This cosy little cabal started to make a great deal of noise, but did absolutely nothing of substance.

As the founder chairman of Crusaid, the AIDS fundraising charity, I was asked to become a trustee of the National AIDS Trust and a member of its fundraising committee. By then, I had already decided to resign as chairman of Crusaid. I have always been a man of action and I found the endless discussion of minutiae such as the colour of the stationery to be a waste of time and effort. I believe that the board of an organisation has two prime functions: to set its goals and to hire and fire the chief executive. I hesitated to join yet another committee but I was curious to see what the notorious Captain Bob was really like. I decided to give him the benefit of the doubt, trusting his intentions were genuine; the cause certainly needed money and influence. He possessed both.

On being appointed to the fundraising committee, I received a telephone call from Peter Jay. 'Bob likes to know who he is dealing with, please submit a curriculum vitae.' I rejoined that I had already been appointed to the post therefore a CV was superfluous but, as I too liked to know who I was dealing with, I would be pleased to exchange CVs with Captain Maxwell. I also pointed out that my career details were available for all to see in *Debrett's People of Today*.

Committee meetings invariably took place in Maxwell's lavish executive suite in the Mirror building. My co-trustees were a mixed bunch of AIDS activists and Maxwell cronies. He chaired the meetings like a pro, managing and directing the agenda and the discussions with adroitness honed over the years of practice. He charmed, cajoled and bullied to get his own way. It would have been a brave man indeed who questioned him or crossed him.

To begin with there was not much controversy. We all appeared to share the same aims. As the months dragged out into more than a year, I became increasingly frustrated at the lack of action. Not a single fundraising project had been initiated and no money had been raised. It was not even clear if Mr Maxwell's £500,000 had actually been paid over. I don't believe it ever was.

During one meeting, a committee member, Sir Patrick Nairne, a former civil servant, by then comfortably installed as Master of St Catherine's College, Oxford, said he had to leave in order to catch the train to Oxford for an important function that night. In a flourish of power politics, Maxwell told him not to be concerned; his helicopter would ferry him back in good time. It was with such grand gestures, and through the force of his powerful personality, that Maxwell invariably cowed any opposition.

I was disheartened and embarrassed to see the supine way in which Peter Jay accepted Maxwell's condescension and bullying. Maxwell treated Jay abominably: he could have been the office boy. Jay, a former ambassador to Washington and son-in-law of a past prime minister (Jim Callaghan), must have been receiving a substantial salary to put up with such treatment. He could not have had much pride to remain more than a day in Maxwell's employ.

After about a year, I could stand it no longer. I stood up and said that while the committee were debating my friends were dying. I resigned in December 1989 and my resignation letter received considerable publicity. The Trust, formed in May 1987, had not initiated a single fundraising project in all that time.

I was interested to note that after Maxwell's suicide and disgrace, even though my judgement had been vindicated, I was not asked to rejoin the Trust. It seems there is seldom any recognition or rehabilitation for the whistle-blower who is proved right.

To this day, I remain unsure what real purpose the NAT serves that is not already well-catered for by other AIDS organisations and charities. I believe that its only significant source of funding, other than the Government, has been on the back of the death of Princess Diana and from activities associated with World AIDS day. The money raised could just as easily have been directed to other charities.

Chapter Thirty-Seven

❧ HENRY P MCILHENNY

When I was in my twenties, I was invited to stay with the American multi-millionaire, art connoisseur and collector, Henry P McIlhenny at his Glenveagh Castle estate in Co. Donegal. I first met Henry while he was on a visit to London, having been introduced by Julian Gibbs of the banking family. I found him amusing and intriguing and he took a shine to me. I was also an experienced rifle shot. Henry owned the only red-deer forest in Ireland. He liked entertaining young men; he needed to keep his ghillies occupied and his deer herd in check. I filled the bill on all counts – something of a rare commodity. I had been in my school shooting VIII for two years. My experience shooting game encompassed stalking in Scotland and Dorset with some months alone with a gun in Africa.

Glenveagh is a Highland-style sporting estate in the North-West of Eire, not far from the border with Northern Ireland. By the 1970s, IRA terrorist activity had become a serious problem, but even so, I had sur-

Glenveagh Castle

prisingly little difficulty in taking my rifle through Northern Ireland into the Irish Republic.

Henry was like a ringmaster in a circus. That weekend he had assembled a varied guest list: a former ambassador to Switzerland and his wife; Lady 'Baba' Metcalf, the widow of 'Fruity' Metcalf (King Edward VIII's best friend) and the daughter of Lord Curzon, Viceroy of India; John Galliher, the American socialite and 'duchess chaser'; Julian Gibbs; Sean Rafferty, the flamboyant broadcaster with the BBC plus two young American boys backpacking round Europe. One of them had a distant family connection with the castle.

The grandeur of Glenveagh and the magnificence of Henry's hospitality ensured that few refused his generous invitations. Having put together the cast list and set the scene, this great producer waited to see how the actors would perform and the scene play out. He took particular delight in observing the discomfiture of the grand when seated next to some pretty boy at dinner. He was amused to see how the one would cope with the other. In short, Henry created a civilised and seductive salon in a luxurious atmosphere of sexual and political intrigue.

The source of his inherited wealth was the subject of much speculation. Henry enjoyed keeping the mystery alive. Some said his grandfather had struck oil in Louisiana, others that he had patented the first gas meter and that Henry collected a royalty every time anyone put a coin in the slot. His name also gave rise to the myth that his family owned the McIlhenny Company, renowned for its Tabasco sauce. Henry mischievously encouraged such idle speculation by displaying a vulgarly large bottle of the eponymous condiment on the drinks-tray labelled, 'Specially bottled for Mr Henry P McIlhenny'. Of all his many qualities, I particularly liked his openness as a gay man, unlike so many of his generation. Of course, he had the benefit of cash and his distinguished status in the art world to shield him, but there were others with the same advantages who, none the less, felt it necessary to dissemble.

Henry was short and full of figure. He had a genial but enigmatic smile; flamboyant but not camp in the mincing, waspish way one associates with the term. He was not much given to deep or serious discourse. Like the dedicated socialite he was, he liked to keep the conversation light and uncontroversial. He began most conversations with his stock phrase, 'Well, my dears', delivered in his laid-back, slightly 'Deep South' drawl. He was at times capable of a ready wit. When asked by Lady Sarah Churchill to join her on a cruise in her chartered yacht, he chartered his own, declaring, 'My dear, I'm too old and too rich to share a cabin.'

The castle itself was not beautiful. A large and imposing late Victorian baronial pile built of granite and perched on the side of a lake, it was surrounded by magnificent gardens opening on to moorland as far as the eye could see. The peaty acid soil encouraged an overgrowth of rhododendrons and azaleas that invaded the deer forest, providing an excess of cover for the deer, and made stalking difficult. 'Them rosythendrons are a pest,' as the head stalker so quaintly put it.

The large estate was close to the village of Letterkenny and the telephone number was, as I recall, Churchill 7. One day I called to talk to Henry; calls were put through manually by the local operator. 'Could I have Churchill 7,' I asked? 'If it's Mr McIllhenny you'll be wanting, sure he's gone to Dublin today and won't be back until tomorrow,' came the operator's reply. I think she must have listened in to all the local calls and had known the daily movements of all her subscribers.

Henry himself was an enthusiastic horticulturalist; indeed his garden at Glenveagh was one of the great gardens of Ireland. He took pride in the variety of tender plants and trees that grew in a climate ameliorated by the Gulf Stream. There was a particularly tall and fine *Eucryphia nymansensis* covered in white autumnal blossom, while tree ferns flourished in the parts of the garden where shelter could be found from the driving winds of winter. Henry strolled proprietorially around his gardens and discoursed knowledgeably on plants with gardeners and guests alike. He had no need to be boastful, the opulence of his creation spoke for itself. I never saw him venture on to the moors; they were there merely to provide privacy, backdrop and status. Henry, whose principle residence was in Philadelphia, was foremost an urban creature.

I stayed for about a week, shooting nearly every day and sitting down to formal dinners every night. The guests were many and varied – neighbouring Guineses; Derek Hill, the artist who lived nearby in a pretty old rectory (but was mercilessly teased as 'the poor man at the rich man's gate'); and sundry Irish luminaries from both sides of the border. Henry seldom touched on the subject of politics, but it was never far from our minds with Glenveagh being surrounded by 'bandit country'. Henry did complain that the IRA sometimes used his deer as target practice; he could do little to stop them. Being of Catholic Irish stock and an American, he enjoyed immunity from the visceral hatred of the local Irish for rich absentee English landlords.

Patrick, the butler, ran the castle. His Republican sympathies were as evident as his toupee. Henry dressed his staff in a Tyrolean Jaeger-style livery with horn buttons and green trim to their felt loden jackets. The atmosphere of the place was theatrically Highland 'camp' in the

Brigadoon manner. The magnificent Landseer of a stag in the dining room completed the effect. The furnishings and table decorations were opulent with no expense spared on anything but the wine – a subject that didn't interest Henry – a spirit drinker – at all.

During my stay it seemed clear that Peter, one of the American boys, had taken a fancy to me and I to him. We ended up in bed together in his room across the courtyard. After making love, I tried to make my way back across the courtyard to my room in the main part of the castle, but the door was locked. I crept back into Peter's bed and awoke to the sound of Patrick with the breakfast tray. I had no escape. 'I take it will be breakfast in bed for two this morning?' he said, with a knowing grin. My mumbled apologies to Henry were met with a smile. 'My dear! Don't imagine it's the first time Patrick has seen two men in bed together. He is quite unshockable.'

Henry's house in Philadelphia was the last private home in Rittenhouse Square; he reputedly bought the house next door in order to enlarge his ballroom. The house contained his extensive collection of impressive paintings. As well as being an important art collector, he was a major benefactor and honorary director of the Philadelphia Museum, to which he bequeathed a large part of his collection. He was, in fact, a much-admired local luminary. To me, he was a rich and hospitable friend who enjoyed the company of the young.

I saw Henry for the last time, just before he died in 1986, in Key West

Henry P. McIlhenny and Derek

one Easter. He was staying at a stylish gay guesthouse of character and charm called La Terrazza di Marti ('La-te-da' for short). The proprietor, who went by the unlikely name of Lawrence (Larry) Formica, was a great party-giver. He had decided that the theme for that year would be *Alice in Wonderland*, Larry inevitably was the White Queen. The first course at dinner was half a gram of cocaine per person neatly piled on a small plate. The tropical garden was planted with mechanical playing cards that rotated from side-to-side, adding a surreal effect to an already surreal occasion.

I noticed Henry making a stately entry down a flight of stairs to join the party in full swing below. He was dressed in a flowing kaftan bedecked with a lay of frangipani flowers. At his side was a handsome young English boy whom I knew to be an expensive hooker. I asked Henry, 'How are things going?' with the implied question as to whether the sex was up to scratch. 'My dear, the libido is not what it used to be,' came the laconic reply as he descended the staircase to join the party.

Stalking party returns from the hill, Glenveagh, Derek (on left)

Chapter Thirty-Eight

❌ COLONEL NEWTY

The call to arms has always had considerable appeal to a certain type of gay man. The social cachet of a smart regiment is an irresistible draw, but so too are the tight masculine uniforms and rigid hierarchical discipline. Such men love the camaraderie and the archaic masculine atmosphere of the mess. When they join up, they may not consciously perceive the reasons behind their decision to seek out this male-only world of rugged masculinity. The subliminal appeal of rank, tight uniforms and male sweat is sensed but not fully understood. These types are by inclination misogynist. The Army life appeals to those who cannot quite face the cut-throat competition of Civvy Street. The Army provides an all encompassing security blanket as well as a world removed from the everyday complexities of modern life. It also is a world where male bonding comes naturally and intimate relationships between men living in close proximity are the accepted norm.

Newton Webb-Bowen

Second sons of landed families were traditionally encouraged to consider either the Army or the Church, both bastions of sheltered uptight masculinity. Their need to procreate went unrecognised and unencouraged as long as the eldest son had produced 'an heir and a spare'. Under the system of primogeniture in Britain the eldest son and heir alone inherits the father's property and landed estates. For younger sons of a more artistic or contemplative bent, the system held many advantages. The restrictions placed by these professions, and also the male-only universities, on contact with the female sex provided a ready-made excuse for a bachelor existence. Until recently, men choosing such a way of life did not open themselves to the automatic suspicion of homosexual inclinations.

I first met Colonel Newton Webb-Bowen ('Newty', as he was always known) at a gay dinner party in Battersea in the late 1970s. He was then a man in his late forties nearing the end of a distinguished military career, having commanded his regiment, the Welsh Guards. He was a jolly bachelor with a ruddy complexion and a good humour: an expansive, genial man with a girth to match. He appeared to me to be avuncular rather than martial, but it was clear that the Army thought well enough of him. I could hardly imagine him in a warlike guise leading his troops in a fierce assault of enemy positions. His army career was unlikely to advance further and he was about to leave for a cushy sinecure in the City of London, where his affability and contacts would stand him in good stead.

Perhaps Newty's recent decision to accept his homosexuality played a part in his decision to leave the army; he assured me, somewhat disingenuously I thought, that he had never experienced gay desires, let alone acted on them, during his time in the regiment. When Newty finally came out of his closet, he took the door off the hinges. His interest in males centred on adolescent boys, or at best young adults. Newty derived his pleasure from filming boys cavorting together. He realised and accepted that his age and looks precluded an equal relationship. He loved the company and friendship of the young and was a generous and

The Boys in Pink (from left) Jonathon Fisher, David Jeffers and Derek, 1980

kindly host. Indeed, it was not long before he had a following of pretty young friends who readily accepted his weekend invitations and became genuinely fond of him.

He shared a weekend retreat in Chichester with an old friend and they had a succession of handsome young males to stay. After a year or so, they decided to redecorate. They vacated the premises and called in the builders. One officious workman uncovered a cache of nude photographs of Newty's young guests and decided to do his civic duty and report the matter to the police. The house was raided and Newty was handcuffed and taken down to the police station, where he was subjected to a battering of intrusive and deeply personal questioning. He was later released without charge; the police were satisfied that nothing contained in his collection was illegal, however much they would have liked to have proven the contrary. The boys were consenting and all of age, so no crime had been committed.

Newty's reputation in the area was comprehensively destroyed by the consequent malicious gossip. The surrounding press publicity, so full of innuendo, was crushing. Newty was ostracised socially by all those in the locality he had thought of as friends, and felt he had no alternative but to leave the area.

Newty's exotic archive of nudes must have amused and diverted his gay friends after his premature death. The young and horny often enjoy exhibitionism and find being photographed a turn on. I was amazed by the quantity and beauty of the young friends he attracted who were happy to perform in front of an audience. Newty's photographs were not pornographic; he would have been far too embarrassed to take such photos to a chemist in a pre-digital age. The photos he took, had they been of young girls, would have provoked nothing more than mild amusement and perhaps a little jealousy at his ready access to such a tribe of gorgeous young beauties.

Yet in public life the Colonel was able to retain the high esteem in which he was held, as a result of his army rank and the prestige of his regiment. He joined the board of a City insurance brokerage and was elected to membership of numerous clubs, including the Royal Yacht Squadron. He was a keen amateur sailor and was often called upon to act as a starter for the yacht races in Cowes Week. His jolly, portly figure was well-suited to a blazer, club tie and a yachting cap – quite the rear admiral. I remember him best in his role as Starter for the juvenile sailing races at the Beaulieu River Sailing Club. Newton's jolly figure could be seen standing on the rickety starting platform at Needsore directing the fleet of scows through a loudhailer. Later I would see him unpacking a delicious looking picnic to share with a bevy of attractive young acolytes.

While Newty's proclivities remained a secret to his colleagues in the City and his fellow club members, locals near where he now lived in Hampshire became increasingly suspicious of his long line of attractive 'nephews'. In the nineties, society had become more accepting and sophisticated, but it did not take a genius to draw conclusions, given the absence of women in his life. Given his past experience, Newty understandably persisted in denial and subterfuge. He saw his boys as his innocent pleasure and never fully accepted the central role they played in his life. He would have been aghast to realise the extent to which his subterfuge was transparent.

His proclivities, once again, became the subject of behind the scenes gossip, but this time of a more affectionate and less hurtful nature. The purlieus of the New Forest are more sophisticated and less judgemental than the suburban curtain-twitching prevalent in Chichester.

He ended his days prematurely. He suffered a heart attack in the aisles of a supermarket while pursuing his second great passion, the purchasing of substantial quantities of good things to eat.

Chapter Thirty-Nine

✖ SIR EDWARD HEATH

At ten o'clock one Saturday evening the telephone rang at our country cottage in Hampshire: it was Sir Edward Heath. 'Those overpriced cushions you made for me are falling apart,' he said, with a twinkle in his voice, not quite joking but not altogether serious either. He didn't know quite how to call someone just as a friend, without making a business excuse. The call was to Derek, Sir Edward's interior designer.

Some half-a-dozen years previously, Derek had undertaken a major project to redesign and decorate Arundells, Sir Edward's magnificent Queen Anne house in The Close at Salisbury. The former prime minister had often demonstrated his wish to retain a friendship with us both, but always on unequal terms. He was invariably 'Sir Edward' – while we were 'Derek' and 'Jeremy'.

It was clear to us that he was lonely and looking for an excuse to meet, either at his house in Salisbury or as our guest at our cottage on the Solent. We sensed that, in his own highly inhibited way, he was reaching out to us as a gay couple. He undoubtedly felt comfortable in male company. With us he was relaxed and at ease.

Old Ted, as we couldn't call him, was a great raconteur and loved his own stories about important people and world leaders he had known. 'Chairman Mao gave me this hideous piece', he would declare with his characteristic unnatural laugh and heaving of his shoulders. The house was full of such memorabilia and photographs of world leaders and monarchs in silver frames on the piano. On one card President Nixon had added a hand-written note, 'In our line of business you need a second string', presumably a reference to his music and sailing interests.

While Derek was decorating Arundells, and for sometime after, we would often visit. Heath's delight in his new home was evident. He had never before worked with an interior designer to create a stylish personal home. He relished both the experience and the result. He was happy getting down on the floor to examine samples of fabric and to pour over Derek's plans, his comments were always thoughtful and considered. Through the experience of working closely with him on so personal a project, Derek was able to touch an intimate part of his make-up. The long-buried gay designer gene expressed itself in his enthusiasm. His keen intelligence and appreciation of another's skill made him an ideal client; he learnt a great deal and gave a great deal of thought and attention to the matter. He discovered a newfound delight in decoration and design. He listened and learnt fast from someone who had much to teach about how to make the best use of available space and to achieve a harmonious and stylish result. His pride in the result was evident to see, but he was niggardly in his praise and often took credit for Derek's ideas.

For some years after the job was finished, Derek would retreat to the study at Arundells with Sir Edward to discuss his long list of complaints and snags. It was as if he did not want to let go of either the experience or the relationship that it had engendered. I would recline in front of the fireplace in the drawing-room and admire the fine English 20th-century pictures and books. On one memorable occasion, Dame Moura Lympany was practising for a piano concert. She was a close friend and musical colleague of Sir Edward. I sat on the sofa and listened entranced to a private performance.

Derek found it difficult to say no to such a prestigious client. Sir Edward pushed the limits of what could be considered fair and reasonable in free after-care service. We suspected that these frequent requests for help were his way of keeping in contact and not loosing our friendship. He was an excellent client when it came to settling his account, but there were times when he stretched our patience with his niggling and petty requests.

Sir Edward revelled in the constant attention of staff and his ever-present police security. Whilst he retained the common touch in his ease of manner, he insisted on a level of formality appropriate to both his age

Derek and Edward Heath

and his former exalted position, in spite of our close friendship with his godson, Lincoln Seligman. I think this stiffness of manner kept Ted from enjoying the natural and close relationship with the young that he seemed to want. Although he could be quite entertaining, his conversation centred on himself; he never showed the slightest interest in our lives. His capacity for friendship rested solely on his entertainment and celebrity value; hence his loneliness. Our friend, Michael Wade, recalls a typical Heath reply to his question, 'What do you consider your greatest achievement?' Always ready with a sharp rejoinder and conversation stopper, Sir Edward retorted: 'Don't you think becoming prime minister is a sufficiently great achievement?'

We discussed gay matters in relation to politics and I asked him for his views on issues such as the age of consent for gay sex. I asked him why he had voted against equality; he claimed that he had always favoured an equal age, but that politically it was impossible until now. 'The rank and file of the party would never have stood for it', was his comment. Ever the politician, he put pragmatism before principle.

There was one occasion when I thought we might have finessed an honest emotional response. We were walking in his beautiful garden and chatting about the plants and flowers. He stopped to admire some white roses, Sir Edward paused and said, 'Roses make me rather sad. I associate them with Strauss's *Four Last Songs*.' I sensed he was about to reveal himself but he stopped, made a joke, and moved on. He knew we were a gay couple and we felt that he was trying to reach out to us but simply couldn't find the words or courage to do so.

As a gay man, I couldn't help but conclude that he was a deeply closeted gay man. He was clearly not rampantly heterosexual and, given that he was ambitious, it seems likely that he had decided early in life to sublimate his sexuality to his political ambitions. That he was right to do so was underlined by the tragic Jeremy Thorpe affair. At that period, at least, a political leader could not have risen to great heights and been a homosexual; he would have been discovered and exposed. His love of the organ (or so an organist told me), his exaggerated affection for his mother, his great artistic sensibilities and his bachelor, almost monastic, life lead me to the conclusion that if he had a sexuality, as nearly everyone must, he had to be inclined towards men. That impression was reinforced by his monosyllabic answers to questions about his love life and his one close women friend: he clearly had something to hide. Sir Edward was a master at monosyllabic equivocation and evasion. 'Yes, that's right,' was all he would reply to the question, 'Were you sad when she married someone else?'

How deplorable that society forced this man, like so many others, to make a choice between career and a love life. The right to be allowed to love whomsoever one chooses without fear is not much to ask; it is one of the most fundamental freedoms that most people take for granted, even in a totalitarian state.

Before his first visit to us on the Solent, Sir Edward's personal protection officers arrived to check out the location and to make sure he was safe. All ex-prime ministers are rightly afforded this protection and status for life. Much the same applied when we ate out in local restaurants; the security people would case the joint first and then they and the driver would sit on their own in the restaurant eating their meals while we enjoyed ours. Sir Edward often entertained us on our own, especially when we went out to eat. He did give the occasional lunch-party to which we were invited. The other guests included his private secretary who had previously worked for the Prince of Wales, as well as the publisher of his books on music, sailing and so forth.

On one never to be forgotten occasion, Sir Edward was our guest at dinner at home. The other guests included my eighty-year-old mother, and my business partner, Richard Taylor, with his boyfriend Rick Englert. During dinner, the telephone rang; it was for Richard. It became clear from the conversation that Richard was being told that his house was on fire. He didn't seem in the least perturbed and continued to tuck into his roast pheasant. Sir Edward, not knowing Richard's cool demeanour, simply could not understand how he could continue to eat when his house was burning to the ground. In fact, the house in question was a wreck and was about to be demolished to make way for Richard's amazing new Jacobean period castle. The fire had taken hold completely and there was nothing Richard could have done to save anything – the house was two hour's drive away in Sussex.

Sir Edward sat at the head of the table and my mother was at the other end. My mother was a

Richard Taylor – My close friend and business partner

life-long supporter of Mrs Thatcher and disapproved most strongly of Sir Edward, both personally and politically. He made no attempt to address a word to her either before or during dinner. My mother was of the old school and felt that as she was older and a woman it was his duty to address her first, so silence ensued. As he left the house after dinner, Sir Edward asked me, 'Who was that old lady at the end of the table?' I answered, 'My mother'. Sir Edward did not seem the least put out by his faux pas, or indeed by his frequent relapses into narcolepsy in the course of the evening.

Derek and I found it hard after a while to keep up the somewhat one-sided friendship. The last time we saw the old boy was before Christmas in 2004, when we called on him at Salisbury for a pre-Christmas drink. He was as hospitable as ever. His housekeeper provided some excellent cânapés and he opened a bottle of champagne. A curious and unexplained character greeted us at the front door; a young educated oriental man who seemed to be a close friend and confidant. He was clearly not an employee as he stayed with us during our chat as though he were a friend. No explanation was sought or proffered as to his place in the household. Sir Edward was his usual charming and entertaining self but he was now confined by his ample girth and swollen legs to the chair he sat in. We left somewhat saddened; it seemed he would not be long for this world. Sadly, he died in 2005 and we attended his memorial service at Westminster Abbey.

Talking to Lincoln Seligman, his godson, I found he had gained much the same impression as I: Ted was a deeply private man concerning his emotional life and not one to make friends in the usual sense. Lincoln said that he would respond very well to being asked for help, such as with contacts in China or Hong Kong, but that Ted never asked him about himself or showed much interest in his career as a well-considered fine artist.

I heard a story that seemed to encapsulate his character. A Chinese restaurateur in Peking was asked how he remembered Ted Heath: 'The appetite of an emperor and the face of a eunuch,' was his reply.

Chapter Forty

NOTHING BEATS THREE

Successful three-way relationships are rare. I have only known one that worked and it lasted nearly thirty years; the original couple were together for over sixty years. The relationship was between three men.

One day Derek and I received an invitation to a party at the Garrick Club to celebrate the 60th anniversary of the relationship, that of Eric Crabtree and Dr Rex Warren. They had been living together since they were twenty and twenty-one respectively. The party was also billed as Eric's 80th birthday celebration.

The Garrick Club is used to seeing gatherings of men only, but this party must have raised a few eyebrows, even in that urbane milieu. Not only was there a collection of smart elderly gentlemen – some of them like the outrageous old dandy Bunny Roger, wearing a touch too much rouge – but also many other men of all ages, including not a few strikingly handsome younger boys.

Don Heywood, the third person in the relationship, and a mere boy at fifty, stood up to make an announcement. With tears in his eyes, he said, 'I am sad to tell you all that Eric cannot be with us tonight; he suffered a stroke a few hours ago.' A somewhat subdued party crowd stayed for a short while before wending their way home. Eric never fully recovered; he survived for a few years but was never his old self again: Rex lived on for a couple more years after Eric.

Eric Crabtree

Eric, although the effeminate younger partner, was the businessman and money-maker in the relationship. He was elegant, petite and short with a boyish body and face; he hardly looked as if he needed to shave. His voice was high-pitched and his delivery theatrically camp. Rex was a bear of man with huge hands, an open friendly face and a gentle smile. This goes some way to explaining the excellent bedside manner that afforded him such success as a doctor in private practice. His patients felt they were in safe hands.

Eric enjoyed a stellar business career, building a chain of women's fashion stores called Cresta, which eventually merged with the Debenham Group of which he became deputy chairman. He told an amusing tale concerning his friend, the chairman, who received a telephone call from a fellow director who had just heard of Eric's impending appointment to the board. 'You can't possibly appoint that outrageous man to the board,' said the director. 'He's notorious and a flagrant homosexual.'

'Oh is that so?' replied the chairman. 'Perhaps you should speak to him yourself – he's sitting on my knee.'

At one time Derek and I saw a great deal of this threesome – Eric, Rex and Don -- in Key West, London and latterly in Cape Town where they bought a large house and settled down. The house was decorated in Eric's own camp style, that he termed, 'Caribbean Cresta'. The look he favoured was mostly white with a lot of pink, his favourite colour. Eric loved to entertain, but mostly in restaurants. He liked to play the host and he was always a generous one. He had one infuriating habit, if you were unfortunate enough to be placed next to him at dinner, of gripping your forearm to accentuate his every point. By the end of the evening, your arm was red and sore. He called every younger man 'baby'. Being clever himself, he admired cleverness in others, particularly business drive and acumen. His greatest admiration, though, was reserved for men in boots.

Eric's other passion was for leather; he loved military uniforms on handsome, masculine men. It was rumoured that he had personally designed uniforms for an unmentionable banana republic. He gave a squeal of delight when asked to review the troops in their smart new uniforms. His affection for leather gave rise to another amusing anecdote. While in New York, he was invited by a friend to meet outside a heavy, Greenwich Village leather bar. 'The dress-code is strictly leather,' he was instructed. Eric, with his usual disregard for convention, turned up dressed from head to toe in a pink Yves St Laurent leather suit.

After retiring from Debenham's, Eric became an investor and director of a medical laboratory run by Dr Margery Shanks. She undertook much of the pathology work for Harley Street. The company obtained a stock market listing and the share price soared. Once again, Eric had backed a winner. The only area where he consistently had bad luck, or perhaps bad timing, was in property. He invariably bought at the top and sold just before another property boom.

We still see Don, an accomplished fine artist, as he has a flat in Malta where we often visit friends. His identical twin brother, also an artist, is curiously, entirely heterosexual. This would appear to indicate that sexual orientation is not genetic, or at least not exclusively so. He plans to marry Joanna Briffa, an adorable and stylish Maltese friend of ours. We now see more of Peter Heywood than we do of Don. It is a curious experience to sit next to a person identical to one we have known for years, who has a different sexuality, but who is in so many other respects alike.

Eric, Rex and Don will surely go down in legend for the length and success of their curious domestic three-way arrangement. They were awkward guests to ask for dinner; they upset the usual arrangement of even numbers.

They seemed the embodiment of the lyrics of the song sung by Joel Gray with such relish in the musical, *Cabaret*. 'Twosees beats onesees but nothing beats three!'

Chapter Forty-One

✼ THE DESIGNER GENE

Before 1850, man simply did not know how to build an ugly building. From the simplest cowshed to the most massive temple complex, harmony and beauty came instinctively. Materials used were mostly natural or handmade, giving every edifice an individuality and honesty that is pleasing to the eye. The simplest structures of the nomad are expressive; the yurt of the Mongol, the tepee of the Plains Indian; and the Bedouin tent adorned with oriental rugs and beaten copper platters: all express an understanding of natural order and proportion, a feeling for what is inherently beautiful. It is usually the women in these cultures who take responsibility for the adornment of the interior spaces, such as they are.

Even the humblest dwelling is improved by the addition of a few wild flowers simply arranged or a rug and cushions carefully placed so as to be comfortable and pleasing. The earliest industrial mass housing, the Georgian terrace, was on a human scale and beautifully proportioned, better for having so little excess decoration. Harmony was achieved by means of perfect fenestration and a simple cornice. Except in the grandest of places, there was no need for designers and decorators.

After 1850 came the age of mass production and industrialisation, only then did ugliness begin to blight the scene; crowded tenements and towering factory chimneys, belching acrid smoke, blackened the landscape. Buildings were often built for speed and profit with little thought to their beauty; utilitarianism reigned supreme. Grander buildings were thought more grand the more intricate their adornment.

At some point men of a certain sensibility came to dominate design and the visual world, from the simple trade of flower arranger to the more exacting skills of interior decoration. Such men moved the arts of visual display to a higher plane. Women too played a part, but generally a lesser role. As the economic importance of these arts came to the fore, so the variety of the professions open to these talents increased; fashion, graphics, set design, window display, millinery, product and fabric design and interior design – in all of them gay men predominate.

Why are so many interior designers and decorators gay men? It would appear that they have a natural flair for ordering spaces, combined with a talent for choosing colour and pattern. In addition, they have an attention to detail and love of aesthetic harmony. Their vivid imagination allows them to see what can be achieved, not just what is.

Having lived with a skilled interior designer for nearly thirty years, I know that a designer is always arranging and harmonising; he is incapable of living in an ugly environment. It comes to him as naturally as breathing. Designers have an enhanced ability to visualise and imagine a finished and decorated space. What to the rest of us is a bewildering array of colour and fabric is to them a canvas on which they have painted a picture in their mind's eye. They love symmetry, balance and order, all of which are pleasing to the eye. Vistas and reflections are utilised to best advantage.

It is an observable fact that gay men seem to have a special talent for the creative visual arts particularly in the area of design in the broadest sense. I have long pondered why this should be. I have already largely discounted a direct genetic link, given that identical twins seem to be capable of being both gay and straight.

Gay men are natural nesters and possess an uncanny ability to imagine the correct use of space so that it will flow. The way a given space can be utilised to reflect the way people live, plays an important part in the whole. Interior design is a lot more than colour and fabric; it is about ergonomics and making the most of the space available. To the decorator, a room is a scene to be painted where every element plays a part and all things are considered.

The natural sociability of gay men, perhaps even their 'Duchess Chasing' social skills, combine to make them ideal decorators, milliners and dress designers, etc. They know how to decorate but they also know how to ingratiate themselves as social adjuncts to their rich patrons. A gay man, always the chameleon, learns quickly how to deport himself and how to behave in a social situation so as to impress. These things are also important to their professional success.

Naturally, Derek and I have known many interior designers and decorators, both men and women, traditional and modern. David Hicks, for whom Derek worked early in his career, was one of the most talented and innovative. He pioneered the design and use of brightly coloured geometric designs for carpets and fabrics. He designed modern furniture to complement his interiors; he worked with antiques in a fresh and contemporary way using classical shapes and objects such as obelisks and spheres and columns to decorate mantelpieces and his trademark tablescapes. His approach was fresh and original. He carefully cultivated the grandest contacts; in-laws (through his marriage to Lady Pamela Mountbatten) and clients who gave him access to a range of interesting work. Later in life, he dedicated his talent to garden and landscape design with equal flair and success. Although a gay man,

Author promoting his 'Gay-friendly Offices' in Covent Garden

Hicks chose to marry and raise a family, none of which inhibited his gay lifestyle. He had a succession of boyfriends who often went on to become successful designers in their own right.

It seems that gay men often have a distinctly feminine sensibility to their make-up. Some have even suggested we represent a sort of third sex. In tribal societies, such as the Plains Indians of North America, gay men became the shamans and were revered. It was believed that their inter-sex status gave them a direct line to the spirits. While I would not go that far, I do believe that this design and visual flair is innate in many gay men.

I have talked to a number of my gay friends who all report that they were aware of their different nature very early in life, in fact from their earliest childhood recollections. They did not know they were gay – they had no concept of sexuality – but they knew they were not like other boys. They tell of their fascination with bright colours, clothes and fabric and often women's clothes. Many friends report a life lived internally; a world where fantasy, theatre and the imagination predominated.

Gay boys create rooms or scenes of their own, either real or imaginary, where they feel safe and special. Because they sometimes feel excluded, they are likely to make such spaces grand or even outrageous in order to

Derek studying design plans at our Needsore cottage

compensate for a feeling of inadequacy. They are sub-consciously creating a world where they fit in and dominate. They may be soft and in ways effeminate, but most have determination and a will of iron. A Swedish friend, Hakan Tegelind, brought up in poverty, decorated the family's outdoor privy with curtains and framed pictures at the age of six. The result was shocking to his family, but his desire to do this was instinctive.

In this way, many gay boys learn to order space and colour and hone this talent over the years. They tend to appreciate fashion and art and are always learning from what they see, whether in real life or magazines. As they play the leading role in their own fantasies, gay boys are attracted to grandeur. They admire beautiful women and their clothes because part of them wants to be like those women; sophisticated, alluring and full of poise. It has been suggested that making a beautiful home is a substitute for having children. I think that the sense of security and serenity a beautiful home imparts maybe part of the explanation. Gay men are often obsessive in their need for order and tidiness; they are always arranging things.

Despite a number of prominent married male designers, I can hardly think of a single truly heterosexual male in the first league of interior design. Many of those that are married have parallel gay lives. There is no other profession so comprehensively dominated by gay men; even ballet dancing has produced great straight male dancers such as Baryshnikov and Russell Malliphant. Would you employ a straight man to decorate your home? As the American writer Fran Leibowitz so wittily put it: 'Honey, one man's trick is another man's design assistant'.

Chapter Forty-Two

❈ DRUGS AND THE LAW

The arrival of drugs as part of the culture of youth in the 1960s and 1970s liberated minds and taught many of my generation that other ways of looking at the world and other cultures were interesting and valid. Drugs, especially pot and LSD, formed an integral part of the cocktail that freed our minds from the stultifying conformity of the post-war period.

The truth is that most people of my generation have smoked dope and not a few have dropped acid or tried cocaine. Parents have to be honest and admit that it is hypocritical and counter-productive to tell children that this is so wrong, when they know that they too did the same thing. Their children probably guess as much. We all need to accept reality; they, like us, are going to experiment with drugs. I believe that it is right and normal for them so to do. We should be supportive and explain the dangers of both drug and alcohol abuse so that the young respect the addictive and damaging power of these substances. To place a blanket ban is to invite lies and disobedience that will estrange us from the young.

The Labour government appointment of Keith Hellawell, a former chief constable, as the Drugs Tsar was risible. His task was doomed to failure as surely as the fight against alcohol during prohibition in America. He was entirely the wrong person to deliver a message of abstinence to the young, being not only dull but deeply 'uncool': the very last type of person the young would be likely to listen to with respect. He dressed, spoke and acted like the policeman that he was. He presumably had no personal experience of taking drugs or their effects, which made it hard for him to convince others that the slender dangers of addiction, especially from marijuana and ecstasy, outweigh their undoubtedly pleasurable effects.

Drugs are popular for the simple reason that they provide insights and enhancement to pleasure, sex and life. They can expand the mind and the consciousness and sometimes produce a revelatory and seemingly enlightening experience. Their danger lies in their addictive qualities and the damage they can do to immature or unstable psyches. In a very few cases excessive use can trigger mental illness, but as little research has been undertaken, none of us know the truth. There are also many dangers associated with impurity and wrong usage of street-quality substances. A very large number of my acquaintance have taken drugs regularly without becoming addicted or having their lives depleted in any way, just as many friends use alcohol and are not alcoholics. Alcohol is a very dangerous drug that can cause extreme aggression and debilitating dependence, unlike marijuana where the user becomes calm,contemplative and rather childlike.

On the TV news, I see that another model has been caught using cocaine. The immediate impression given is that she is an addict in need of treatment. This gives the young the spurious impression that the consumption of drugs means that automatically a person is an addict. Experience teaches that this is normally not the case. This amounts to a dangerous lie and one that will be soon unmasked. Taking drugs does not make a person an addict any more than having a drink makes someone an alcoholic. That erroneous line undermines the rest of the prevention message, no matter how true it may be, and as such is deeply damaging. The blanket pejorative term 'drugs' brackets innocuous hashish with deadly heroin. The two could not be further apart in their chemical action and their addictive powers.

The police, in my experience, have little real knowledge of youth culture or the drug world. The very title of their special unit for policing nightclubs is confrontational, The Clubs and Vice Squad. How would the City of London take to a police unit called The Banks and Embezzlement Squad?

On one occasion, a member of staff at my club, Leopard Lounge, was caught dealing in small amounts of cocaine. An inspector from the police Club Squad came to my office to lecture me about my responsibility in this regard. I acknowledged that the law required me to take all reasonable steps to prevent dealing from happening on my premises but, I countered, 'How can I be expected to keep drugs out of my club when Her Majesty's Prison Service, with all the powers at their command, cannot keep heroin out of maximum security prisons?'

The legal fiction that makes criminals of us all is no different from that prevalent in America during (alcohol) prohibition. You can't tell people that their drug of choice is wrong but yours, alcohol, is OK; the reasoning is spurious and the moral argument specious. Taking moderate amounts of dope, and even ecstasy, is usually harmless and millions have done so with no ill effects. The fact that a number go on to become addicted is to be regretted, but it is no worse a problem that those who drink and go on to be alcoholics. The sad fact is that some people will become addicts anyway whether their drug of choice is legal or not.

All Society achieves by banning substances is the creation of dishonest politicians and public figures who are pressurised into 'saying no' to drugs; but who few believe sincere. If they really never took any drugs when they were young what sort of boring, dull 'nerdy' types were they and how can we respect them now? 'Did you experiment with drugs?' The question is one that invites a disingenuous response, like that of Bill Clinton who famously, 'did not inhale'. The question has again reared its head during David Cameron's candidature for leader of the Conservative Party. There is no 'right' answer that can be given. In my view, he is not correct in stating that it is a private matter. He, like other members of parliament, will legislate on drugs, so his experience is relevant. Politicians need to be honest enough to admit that trying drugs, even some Class A drugs, is the norm, so making it illegal makes criminals of a large proportion of the adult population.

On my first visit to New York in 1976, I was taken to a society party given by the renowned hostess, Bobo Rockefeller. To my naive amazement, I witnessed a US Senator snorting coke (presumably he denounced it in public?). The sad consequence of this hypocrisy is that the young feel lied to and cheated by both parents and the lawmakers; this breeds disrespect for law and authority in general.

From the Rave culture down to the local Saturday night disco, dance clubs are fuelled on drugs, particularly ecstasy. This is a reality. Nothing the law says is going to change this. This means that millions of teenagers are criminals in the eyes of the law. Is this a good thing? It brings the law into disrespect, as the law is patently unenforceable.

Street drugs are of variable quality and sometimes downright dangerous – is this really what we want for our young? Let us research the real dangers of ecstasy and give proper advice to those who are going to consume it. In Holland there is a service that offers to test your street drugs for impurities and so helps the young to avoid buying adulterated or sub-standard drugs. Little research has been done on the long-term effects of heavy and regular usage. It is no good pretending that drugs are not fun, that is why the young take them. Ecstasy produces a magical effect and enhances the pleasure of both dancing and sex: it makes your fellow dancers seem beautiful and desirable; it opens up the heart chakra and fills the soul with love. It may indeed damage brain cells and have other harmful effects, these need to be stated clearly and with authority, and then the individual can make up his or her own mind.

The only rational response to drugs is to make them legal. At one stroke, society would remove the financing from armed and dangerous gangs, such as the Mafia, the IRA and other terrorist groups. Drug money is the lifeblood of these dangerous organisations and they do far more harm than any drugs they might supply. The other benefit of legalisation would be to remove the motive for proselytizing and the marketing of drugs to the public. The government is hardly likely to hang around schools and university campuses pushing drugs to get the young hooked.

I am not saying that drugs are a good thing or that their use should be encouraged – quite the reverse; the dangers of addiction are all too real. We should evaluate where the balance of greatest evil lies. I don't believe that there would ultimately be more addicts if drugs were legalised, however the huge financial rewards of this pernicious trade would be interdicted. Instead, the profits from supply and sale would accrue to responsible government to be used for good, not evil. We would regain control of our streets from the drug gangs. For this strategy to work it is necessary for the government to control as a monopoly all links in the chain of supply. The Dutch halfway-house of partial legalisation of cannabis is doomed to failure; the criminals simply move up the chain of supply.

The arguments for keeping the illegal status quo centre round the fear that legalisation would lead to an explosion of use. I hardly think ecstasy could be more widely used than at present. Do we want downtown areas to remain no-go areas controlled by armed drug gangs on week-end nights? That is the current reality in some city centres.

In my view, we should not acquiesce in the abrogation of our power to make our own moral decisions about victimless activities. It is not the duty of government in a free society to legislate for how we should behave in areas such as homosexual sex, hunting with hounds, pornography, prostitution and drugs. These are victimless crimes and so should be matters of personal moral judgement.

The duty of government should be our protection and the smooth functioning of the economy and the body politic. Those duties include the elimination of armed crime from our streets. Can the government seriously maintain that this objective is best served by handing a monopoly of the drug trade to illegal gangs that terrorise our streets? Once we permit parliament to make moral decisions for us based on the majority wish, then we have a dictatorship of the many over the few; a perversion of democracy. It is important to remember that, as I have already stated, 'Liberty is about allowing others to do things of which you profoundly disapprove'. In a free society, it should not be for one group to make legally enforceable moral decisions for others, where no harm is done to third parties.

The drugs question should not be about whether drug use is right or wrong *per se*, but about the best way to reduce the damage to society that illegal drugs cause directly or, as I would contend, by virtue of their very illegality. Legalisation and control within a government monopoly is the sensible way forward and the only conceivable way to win the drugs war and bring peace to our streets.

Chapter Forty-Three

❧ THE NAME'S THE GAME

One of the first problems with starting a new business is what to call it. I have always enjoyed the creative process of choosing a name. A name should encapsulate the mood and spirit of the enterprise. Too many people opt, like the glossy magazines, for a pun. Puns are usually only funny for a nanosecond and then become a bore. A clever pun may mean a lot to the person who thought it up, but is often obscure and therefore lost on Mr Average. My friend, Caroline de Rothschild, told me that her mother had a home-decorating business in South Africa called Gloria Soames. The allusion to 'glorious homes' was lost on her many customers who would regularly ask to speak to the proprietor, Mrs Soames.

Another friend, Jeremy Rose, has enjoyed great success with his sushi business in London; he calls it Feng Sushi. I feel that the play on feng shui is a bit too clever. However, his strap-line, 'If our fish were any fresher you'd have to slap them' is inspired, witty and memorable. It succinctly conveys to the consumer the key point that the fish is super fresh.

My method of choosing a name is to sit round a table with all of those involved and give them a blank sheet of paper. I then bid them to write down all the possible names that come into their heads in a stream of consciousness – never mind how silly or odd. Then we read out the names and vote on the ten best in each list. We then repeat the process. The initial lists invariably spark off some new ideas and trains of thought. By this process, we arrive at a promising short list from which the clear winner emerges.

In the case of the Embassy Club, the process led us straight back to the club's historic name; it was so full of resonance and grandeur and was inextricably associated with that particular spot in Old Bond Street. We considered many weird and wonderful names including the anarchic send-up, The Buckingham Palais.

The naming process helps the entrepreneur crystallize his thoughts about the nature of the business, what and to whom he is marketing and what the essence is of the project's unique appeal. My wine business, started by my elder brother, Remington (how on earth did he come by that name; did my mother have a love affair with a typewriter or a liaison with a shaver?) was called La Reserve after the Michelin-starred restaurant and hotel in the South of France. The name is grand and is redolent of fine wine and food, as well as having that essential French connection: grand reserve is also a wine term. It is a name that reeks of patrician good taste.

In 1984, after the sale of Heaven, I opened my first gym. I took space in a warehouse building in the King's Road called the Furniture Cave owned by a friend, Richard Taylor, and four antique dealers. It was the start of a life-long business partnership with Richard. I called my small gym, Power Station, a bad pun for an ultimately unsuccessful venture. The gym was too small, ahead of its time and in the wrong location. But as a result I subsequently turned the space into a new style club, eMbargo. Eventually, Richard and I bought the whole building.

Our fresh pasta business, started in 1986, was called simply Pasta Pasta because it did exactly what it said on the label – produced the finest in fresh pasta and sauces. The strap-line was a new take on the New York slogan; 'So good they named it twice'. Sadly, the venture did not survive the intense competition it eventually faced from supermarkets.

The wrong name can give a bad impression from the outset and put customers off. It can be cheap or naff-sounding, too clever or simply cheesy. Ask yourself whom you are aiming at? Are you trying to be trendy, staid and reliable, grand, hip, quality or good value? It's no good calling a traditional tailor, Slick Willies, or a Carnaby Street boutique, Carlton & Cholmondeley, unless of course you are trying to be ironic. It is never a good idea to be too clever, especially if you are aiming to attract Americans.

Interior, eMbargo Club, King's Road, Chelsea (Design by Derek)

Pasta Pasta (Design by Derek)

The naming of a trendy restaurant or bar is the greatest challenge and the greatest fun. My private restaurant club and bar, one of the first of that breed, was named, eMbargo; now every high street bar that would like to consider itself hip has 'bar' in its name. It has become a cliché and therefore no longer cool.

An appropriate name is important only in the initial marketing phase; when a business is established the name becomes associated with the product and its success. For example, Ministry of Sound is clever because it is iconoclastic and therefore appeals to its core young club market. It says we are the top dog, yet we know how to mock the staid and boring establishment and, by the way, we do music.

Heaven, the name of my pioneering gay dance club, has become iconic, partly through its legendary and long-lived status but because the name is so appropriate. It represents the trance-like state of paradise the young, and especially gay men, can achieve through dancing and music. (There are echoes, too, of the famous song sung by Fred Astaire.) It literally transports people to another world of pleasure and sexuality – heaven on earth. It also mocks religion, the crutch of those who believe in fairy tales and elves. Gay men, whom religions reject, know they must find their heaven where it truly lies, on earth.

My most recent nightclub, in the early 1990s, was more difficult to name. It was aimed at a straight crowd of young Fulham and Chelsea boys and girls. My partner, Howard Spooner, and I sensed a trend away from large drug-fuelled dance clubs towards less noisy, more conversational clubs – more like bars with dancing. I appreciated the requirement for more seating and conversation, hence the incorporation of the word Lounge into the name. Leopards are dangerous felines and creatures of the night. So, Leopard Lounge it became. The name could be easily reflected in the logo and the decoration, leopard prints were everywhere and a clever graphic designer adapted a feline mask into a stylised logo that caught the imagination of the young, who tend to be graphically minded and use *emoticons* on their phones and computers.

The Furniture Cave, King's Road, Chelsea

The legendary Studio 54 Club in New York copied the name from the earlier successful gay club Studio 1, in LA. They both opted for the anonymity of a number, allowing the reader to imbue the name with the flavour of the product. A bit of a cop-out perhaps, but a safe answer to a problem – better no name than one that gives the wrong image.

Memorable and apposite names, as well as clever interior design, are both necessary qualities for a successful establishment. They are not sufficient to ensure success, but without them, a good business can easily fail to capture initial attention in a crowded market place.

The naming of a child or a pet gives rise to an entirely different set of dilemmas. Children are often named after relations or close friends, but first names go rapidly out of fashion as they become associated with an older generation. Who now calls a child Horace, Roland or Gertrude, all of which are redolent of Edwardian or even Victorian England? Religious names like Martha, Esau or Miriam are now the province of small Calvinistic religious sects or else devout Jews. Children today are more likely to be named after a current television or sporting celebrity, though this shows a lack of imagination, given that the particular star in question will be long forgotten by the time the child matures. Although Britain has gone some way to becoming a classless society, this is not the case with nomenclature. A child's name can immediately place him or her firmly in the lower orders; whoever heard of a Lady Sharon? Equally, someone named Peregrine or Algernon are unlikely to have an artisan as a father. Pop stars like to call their children hippy names like

Moon or River – hardly thoughtful for the child, who might well be teased at school. Many of us don't like our first names and adopt a nickname instead. We feel that our given name is simply not 'us'. A gentle boy may hate the name Fred or Tom and want to be a Rupert or Jeremy. The upper classes are fond of nursery nicknames – 'Podgy' or 'Poo'. Indians, aping their former colonial masters, are often 'Tiger' or 'Poppy'. In the end, we all become to be the name we are called and others like us may well be named after us – poor unfortunates.

The naming of pets says a lot about their owners. A friend wittily called his little furry lapdog Rimbaud (pronounced Rambo). Another neighbour, exasperated by the family disagreement over the dog's name, elected to call it simply Doggie. A tough-looking, but actually gentle, mutt belonging to the interior designer Jonathan Reed was named Bully. I named my golden retriever Debrett (Brett for short) as I considered his pedigree was not good enough to call him Burke.

The naming of countries and cities illustrates an interesting facet of post-colonial guilt and consequent political correctness. Newly independent countries usually change their names and that of their principal cities. With supine deference, the English tend to follow suit and change time-hallowed names for trendy foreign ones; Ceylon becomes Sri Lanka, Peking becomes Beijing, Bombay becomes Mumbai. A moment's thought indicates the illogicality involved. Mumbai is a Hindi word and Bombay its English translation. We would not consider

My business, Soho Gyms, Covent Garden Branch, with Jordi behind reception

calling Munich, München or Finland, Suomi, so why change the hallowed English name for Peking? It is racial discrimination, and patronising, only to adopt this policy for non-European countries. For me Livorno will always be Leghorn. It is amusing to recall the pitfalls of post-colonial name changes; the municipality of Johannesburg thought to change the name of their great city to the Bantu equivalent, E Goli – the city of gold – until someone pointed out that the citizens of that great metropolis would certainly become 'I Golliwogs'.

Finally, the title of this slim volume may grate with some readers, but it must have caught your attention. That was the intention.

The logos of some of my ventures

Chapter Forty-Four

✖ BADGERS AND BUGGERS

When the late Earl of Arran (known as 'Boofy') introduced his 'Badgers Bill' to the House of Lords, he was saddened by the sparse support it received, in marked contrast to the enthusiasm for his earlier bill, in 1967, to legalise homosexuality (colloquially referred to as the Buggers' Bill). A friendly peer was overheard to observe, 'Well Boofy, there aren't many badgers in the House of Lords.'

There are indeed, and I am sure always have been, a sizeable proportion of gay men amongst the ranks of the Peerage. Not so many proportionately as in the Commons, I would venture – just the national average. Peers for the most part enjoy the luxury of an independent means and so can indulge their proclivities with lordly disdain for convention; they are therefore more visible in proportion to their numbers.

Members of the House of Commons have, until now, had to be more circumspect. There are numerous examples of MPs and ministers who have been exposed as homosexuals or who have been caught soliciting, even on Clapham Common. The rise of the tabloid press and the intrusive coverage of journalists have ensured that little privacy remains to MPs who stray from the straight and narrow. The fiercest condemnation is always reserved for those guilty of hypocrisy. Marriage is of scant help and when exposed the married man who is a secret homosexual is rightly castigated.

The appointment of both the Tory, Alan Duncan and Labour's Chris Smith to the front bench has at last shown it is now possible to be an openly gay man and succeed in politics – not before time. Peter Mandelson had a hard time admitting publicly that he was gay, even after Mathew Parris 'outed' him on television. It was hardly a State secret and I can't help wondering why Mandelson found it difficult to admit the truth. It showed him in a poor light. Chris Smith was a brave early convert to truthfulness in this area, but was still reluctant to admit that he was HIV Positive until after he left Parliament. It was obvious to those of us familiar with anti-retroviral treatment and the side effect of lipodystrophy that Chris Smith was positive and on medication. Coming out afresh as HIV Positive is yet another hurdle, given the residual prejudice still found against those with HIV.

It is intriguing to speculate what attracts so many gay men to parliament and the pursuit of power. To my mind, there is no doubt that an above average number of MPs are actually gay men. I have known a few and I felt compelled to write to some of them when they were too cowardly to stand up and be counted in the lobbies when voting took place on gay issues – such as Clause 28 (Mrs Thatcher's attempt to ban the promotion of homosexuality as 'a pretend family relationship') and the equalisation of the age of consent. To have been voted into a position where you can change laws and then to refuse to stand up and be counted for what you know to be right is cowardly conduct. If you are ashamed of what you are then you have abrogated any moral authority to dictate to others.

One can speculate endlessly about why a significant proportion of gay men are high achievers and are often drawn to politics as a source of power and influence. I suspect that the male clubability of the House is also an attraction, as well as the desire to prove yourself after being put-down for so much of your young life.

I would calculate the number of gay males as follows: if the population of the United Kingdom is 63,000,000 and 50% are male then there are 31,500,000 males of which only half are between the ages of eighteen and fifty-five, giving a sexually active population of 16,000,000 males. The American sexologist, Dr. Kinsey, suggested that 10% of males are primarily or mainly homosexual; I believe a more conservative figure would be 8%, this gives us 1,280,000 sexually active gay males. If 50% of gay men are mainly 'in the closet', then it leaves an 'out' gay male population of 640,000 – a large number of voters. Now if there are 646 members of the House of Commons, I suspect that 10–12% are gay, giving a minimum of 65 gay members – who are they? I doubt if there are more than a dozen 'out' gay MPs. I wonder if the electorate would accept members voting on hunting without declaring their interest as a member of a hunt? I think not. Why then is it acceptable for gay members to remain silent on the subject of their homosexuality and yet vote on matters of sexual morality? As long as parliament believes that sexual morality is a fit and proper subject for legislation, we should insist that members are open about their personal life. The sad truth is that far from voting silently in favour of homosexual liberation, most closeted gay members vote against and with the moral majority.

I think that the issue of consenting gay sex and the age of consent has similarities with the hunting debate in that, in both cases, Parliament has tried to impose the morals of the majority over the liberty of a minority. I repeat – freedom is about allowing others to do things of which you profoundly disapprove. If not, democracy degenerates into the imposition of majority will on an unwilling minority – in effect, a dictatorship.

In the case of hunting, animals chasing and killing other animals is part of nature's law. What the anti-hunting lobby object to is people deriving pleasure from observing this process. That must surely be a personal moral decision. The argument cannot be about the cruelty to the animal that is being chased; otherwise, we would seek to protect rabbits from being torn to bits by foxes. Whether it is right or wrong to take pleasure in hunting is a personal moral choice, just as people can decide to take pleasure in observing a lion kill while on safari. A different criterion would apply where animals are artificially corralled and made to fight one another, as in bullfighting or cockfighting.

Let us rather agree to limit law-making in the field of morality to as few issues as possible and only prohibit where there is an overwhelming public interest at stake.

Following the Mark Oaten scandal, I had this letter published in *The Times*. The next day Simon Hughes admitted he had had homosexual relationships. Rather a limp response I thought; it reminded me of Portillo's equivocal statement at the time his love life was exposed.

The Editor, *The Times* Newspaper, January 25th 2006

Dear Sir,

Mark Oaten has resigned from his front bench position in the Liberal party over allegations concerning an affair with a rent boy. He has apologised for the 'embarrassment' caused to his family, friends and the Liberal Democrat party – well he might.

What about an apology to the Gay community? Yet again, an MP has shown that he still considers a gay sex life as something to be ashamed about, something to hide and something to be conducted with either rent boys or in public toilets. This image does a grave disservice to normal gay people who live normal lives that include partners of the same sex. It's time MPs grew up and understood that on this issue as on all others, the public expect honesty and decency from our leaders. We certainly do not expect, of all parties, a Liberal Democrat to have such an antiquated and deeply damaging view of gay sex.

Given that approximately 10% of people are now known to be wholly or mainly homosexual, where are the forty or so closeted MPs hiding? It's time they all came clean.

Yours faithfully, Jeremy Norman

I like to think that my letter might have influenced Simon Hughes's decision to come 'Out'?

Chapter Forty-Five

✖ FAUX GAYS

Faux gays are straight men that like to appear to be queer. They may also be simply eccentric and artistic, or they may be confused about their sexuality and have decided for other reasons to marry and lead a family life, but are not actively bisexual. They do not think of themselves as gay; not a few are simply well-adjusted straight men not afraid to express their more feminine and artistic side. Euphemistic adjectives often used to describe faux gays include 'extravagant', 'flamboyant', 'artistic', 'eccentric', 'camp' and 'epicene'. Most, but not all, affect an aristocratic style and a fruity voice. It takes confidence and élan, or in some cases a natural inclination, to aspire to the heights of camp while being sexually attracted to women. There is an interesting modern sub-set of the genre – straight personal trainers in gay-friendly gyms, but more of them later.

My friend Harry Lendrum is a charmer; he is always polite and fastidiously well-mannered, a veritable old-fashioned gentleman. He dresses in corduroy trousers and old brogue shoes. He earns his living execut-

Wendy and Harry Lendrum at Algy's christening

ing beautiful paint finishes to the walls of his rich clients; stippling, rag rolling and dragging. His artistry is such that he manages to support two sons at school through an essentially manual trade – (a nob doing a yob's job). All his clients know him well and treat him as a friend and honoured guest. It is because he is artistic, gentle and a bit fey that those who do not know him might well mistake him for a gay man. He married Wendy about thirty years ago and she has produced three sons, the boys are called appropriately Algy, Percy and Inigo, (the latter clearly destined to become an architect). Algy is our adored godson.

Harry, and all his family, are endearingly relaxed with gay men and always greet us with a kiss. Part of the reason may be that Harry was brought up by a gay father, Peter, but I think his urbanity and sympathy stems from a deeper psychological security in his heterosexuality. Like many of this type, he is a fogey as well as a faux gay.

Gerry Farrell is quite another case; he has no excuse. Gerry and his wife, Jo, met about the same time that I met Derek, about thirty years ago. Jo befriended Derek at Mary Fox Linton's interior designer firm where she worked and Derek was head designer under Mary. The young Farrells were a golden couple – good-looking, social and well connected, always in *Tatler* and *Harper's & Queen*, partying every night, often at the Embassy Club. Everyone knew and loved them; they were decidedly A-list.

Gerry showed early signs of eccentricity in his dress and eating habits. He developed a particular fondness for giant baked bean sandwiches made with white sliced bread, always consumed naked in the bath. A photograph appeared in a book, of Gerry naked wearing high heels; the only stitches to be seen were those brought on by the laughter of his friends. Gerry enjoys notoriety and is disarmingly unshockable.

As time progressed, he has become rotund and jolly, the art dealer par excellence. His girth is suited to the waistcoats he loves to wear. He ran Christies Contemporary Art and latterly has become a partner in the Sladmore Gallery. His home life revolves around their two children and the games they play together. He loves television and an oversize screen is the focal point of their living room. Food, especially of a nursery sort, is an obsession. He remains as lovable as ever, a veritable Mr Pickwick and a true faux gay.

Roger Bevan is the quintessential art master. His lecture tours of the London gallery and art scene are renowned and successful; they particularly appeal to young women. He affects the bow tie and elegant suits so typical of his profession. I suspect his faux gay persona disarms his young female protégées, so it comes as a complete surprise when his

Gerry Farrell

seductive intent becomes apparent. Women love to think their charms are capable of converting a gay man, Roger is happy to be a guinea pig.

The old Archbishop of Canterbury, Robert Runcie, affected such a camp canonical voice that even a gay man would have been suspected of 'camping it up' if he spoke in that way. The clergy, and especially the High Church, include a large element of both gay men and closet queens. ('Anyone for tea Vicar?') The Roman Catholic Church with its honorific titles, incense, lace frocks and beautiful choristers is surely a camp man's dream. Cardinals are often portrayed in art as rotund gourmands tucking into great platters of rich food; their other more private appetites were seldom alluded to until the recent scandals in America and Ireland brought them to light.

I once visited St Mary's Bourne Street, in Pimlico, a haunt of young fogeys and faux gays, the most 'High' of all Anglican churches, and the one favoured by Tom Driberg MP ('my passions are left-wing politics, High Church and low sex') – and was shocked to hear lascivious discussion of the sexual attractiveness of the altar boys. If Christ had a message, it was surely one of humility and simplicity, not idolatry and camp theatre. Incidentally, I have heard that Giovanni Montini's (Pope Paul V1, 1963–1978) love of lace gave him the nickname in Vatican circles of 'Margot Montini'.

Gym personal trainers are a modern phenomenon. The majority of trainers at my health clubs, Soho Gyms, are straight but spend much of their lives in the company of gay men. They train them in the gym and often choose to party with them after hours. The atmosphere and music is so much better in gay clubs and the few girls around are easy prey. Trainers by definition have good bodies and like to admire a toned male physique in others and themselves, often in the mirror, frequently when they should be concentrating on their clients.

One of our best-loved trainers at Soho Gyms is Dan Novelli. He is huge. He confessed that when he was younger he couldn't bear to remain in a room if there was someone larger and more muscular than him. He loves to hear all the gay gossip and often hugs his male friends or pinches then where he shouldn't. He is handsome and attractive, especially to men and women who like an extremely muscular body. Sexually, he is entirely heterosexual – or at least as far as I know. He keeps enormous pythons and boa constrictor snakes at home and recently brought in a 10-foot long sloughed skin for all to admire. I asked him what he would do if his girl asked him to choose between her and his snakes. 'She would have to go, of course,' he replied. I advised him to see a shrink. Freud would certainly have something to say about a man obsessed by both male muscles and large snakes. Dan sums himself up well, 'I'm just a gay guy who loves pussy!'

Chapter Forty-Six

❈ CONAL WALSH

Raised on a tobacco farm in Rhodesia, my friend Conal Walsh was the second of four sons of a pioneering farming family. He spent his childhood on the farm playing with his brothers and the children of the farm workers and, when older, tracking and hunting game in the bush.

Derek and I visited the farm with Conal in the mid-1980s and experienced something of the romance and isolation of his childhood. The farmhouse was a typical colonial bungalow with a corrugated green tin roof set among jacaranda and mimosa trees. The ugly protective wire-mesh fencing was still in place, a reminder of the counter-terrorist precautions of an earlier time. The family prospered in isolation with no television and little but their own company, save for the Saturday outings to the Kiroi country club for tennis and cricket and the occasional dance. They relied on books and the radio for their entertainment and the excitement of the farm and the open veldt beyond. The nearest white farm was miles away down roads that were often impassable in the wet season. The life must have drawn the family close together and bred a hugely self-reliant spirit.

Conal Walsh

Conal's father, Peter, was short like Conal and seemed overwhelmed by his baggy khaki shorts. His hair was cut short and his manner was brisk and to the point. He seemed part of another more distant era. The vastness of the farm reminded me of my earlier African experience in Kenya with the Delameres.

Conal took us for long hikes into the open country away from the cultivated farmland. We climbed isolated kopies, those rocky outcrops that seem to dot the plains of southern Africa and that serve as lookouts from which to spy out the land. I could visualise a Boer commando in the South African War holding out for days from just such a spot. We looked in vain for traces of the isolated bands of majestic Sable antelope that Conal assured us still roamed the farm. The plains were dotted with the characteristic termite chimneys from which swarms of flying insects issued after the rains. Our blood was chilled with tales of deadly snakes that threatened the tobacco pickers working under the tall lines of dark green fanlike leaves.

Our magical visit culminated in a couple of days spent on the family sailing boat on Lake Kariba, with its hippos and crocodiles and forests of dead trees, submerged and killed by the rising lake waters when the dam was constructed back in the early 1960s. The Kariba project had been the great co-operative hope of the ill-fated Central African Federation. It was meant to supply limitless electricity with which to unite Zambia and Rhodesia, but was a source of discord as soon as it was completed.

At the age of thirteen, Conal was sent to a mixed-race Catholic boarding school in Salisbury (as Harare was then called) run by strict monks. Here, no doubt, he was inculcated with feelings of shame for his burgeoning homosexuality. Like all young gay men, he was taught that the way he was made was sinful and the beautiful feelings of love and desire that he felt for other boys must be repressed and denied – as if the act of wishing to be another self could somehow make it a reality.

During the 1970s, the problems caused by Ian Smith's unilateral declaration of independence (UDI) from Britain began to multiply and terrorist activity started to pose a threat to the government of his country. The economy prospered, in spite of sanctions, as Rhodesia could still rely on the support of its neighbours South Africa and the Portuguese colony of Mozambique, but the security situation was deteriorating. The terrorists Zanu, led by the Communist thug, Robert Mugabe, and Zapu, led by Joshua Nkomo, gained in strength although the damage they inflicted was still relatively slight; such was their mutual hatred that they also fought one another. They intimidated and coerced their respective tribesmen into helping them. Zanu were drawn largely from the Shona, the largest tribe, while Zapu were Matabele, a Zulu tribe from the west. Their mistrust of one another was only exceeded by their desire to rid their country of white colonial rule and gain power for themselves. In truth, most black Rhodesians were happy with their government and prospered under white rule; the agitator's job was to sow the seeds of discontent and inflict retribution on those of their tribe who were adjudged to be collaborators.

Young Conal was increasingly aware of a conflict in his own heart. He experienced strange and unholy longings and desires that would not go away. He was soon called up to serve his country as an officer in the militarised British South Africa Police. He was aware of his strong attraction to another young officer, but was too inhibited to make his desires known. They were sent out on armed patrol in the bush to fight the insurgent terrorists. Only later, in England, did he discover that this same officer was gay and had longed to find the courage to approach Conal.

Conal appeared to be a tough and rugged farm boy but, in fact, he was an essentially gentle man. There was not a trace of camp or femininity to mar his masculine appeal. He struggled deeply with his conscience about the fighting that he was called upon to do. On one occasion, he was forced to kill a man in self-defence when his troupe was set upon by some 'terrs' in the bush.

Conal was short and wiry but made up for his lack of stature with an outgoing, sunny personality and a radiant beauty. He captivated all who knew him with his intelligence and charm. He could talk and write beautifully; his powers of description and use of language illuminated his words. He was clever, funny and endearing. The little boy in him was never far from the surface and added an underscore of vulnerability to his assertive charms.

His family were liberals and did not support Ian Smith, but loyally felt it their civic duty to meet the call to arms to defend their beloved country. His father had carved a successful tobacco farm out of the wild bush and provided employment, medical treatment and education to many hundreds of black workers and their families. Their employees liked, trusted and supported the family and the system they represented. His mother dispensed presents to the black farm children and scolded them in equal measure; she was loved and respected by all the workers and loved them in return. In addition to the tobacco cash crop, the farm produced maize and other foods by rotation to feed not only their workers but as a surplus to sell.

One wonders what greater good was served by a black independence that has visited famine, intimidation, loss of liberty and the breakdown of the rule of law on millions of people? The certification of that first election as 'free and fair' by Lord Soames and other, supposedly distinguished, Commonwealth observers was a patent fraud, as everyone now admits. Mugabe won by outright and massive vote rigging and intimidation. One of the most prosperous and free countries in Africa was thereby condemned to become a disaster area. Ian Smith predicted that 'one man one vote' would in reality mean 'one man, one vote, one time'. His government may have been guilty of old-fashioned paternalism and it's true that they did not do enough to promote black education and advancement, but those causes were hardly advanced by a headlong rush into anarchy.

When he was nineteen, Conal was sent to England to attend Exeter University; he then spent time in New York working for the Forbes family on their magazines. It was here that he had his first experiences of gay life, urban culture and sophistication. He soon realised that his future lay, not as a farmer, but in the wider urban world. Conal was intelligent and his good looks opened many doors. Through his close friendships with both Kit Forbes and his father Malcolm, Conal's career and social life prospered.

In New York, he found love for the first time with a beautiful young man, Donald Brown, who came from the Mid-West and, like Conal, was intelligent, ambitious and successful. They were both very much in love; no one who saw them together could possibly have doubted it. Their affair blossomed in New York where both could, for a time at least, work and live legally.

After his temporary American student work visa expired, Conal came back to England but to his dismay he found that he was unable to

Conal & Author

obtain British residency. Both his parents and his paternal grandfather had been born outside the United Kingdom. No matter that the family were entirely British and that the accidents of their births were just a matter of poor timing. His grandfather was born abroad, the son of colonial administrators and servants of the Crown. Under our mad, racially blind system of immigration his essential Englishness counted for nought. Conal was British by blood, education, language, culture and temperament but he only managed to get a passport after much agitation and thanks to the intervention of a sympathetic MP, Martin Stephens, who adopted his case.

Conal's problems were not over. Donald's student visa expired and so, in order for the lovers to stay together, Donald had to take menial jobs for cash. There were, at that time, no arrangements by which a foreign partner could get residence status. After about three years, Donald could stand the strain no longer and despite the strength of his love for Conal, his situation became unbearable. He reluctantly decided to return to America where he could get a proper job commensurate with his talents. After Donald left for home, Conal was inconsolable, but worse was to come.

In 1987, Conal learnt that Donald had contracted the deadly new virus that was spreading within the gay community, especially in America. We all came together the following spring for a holiday in Key West. By now Donald had the gaunt appearance we have come to associate with AIDS. Neither Conal nor Donald had fallen in love with anyone else and so they found it hard being together again; their longing for one another was palpable, but with resolution, knowing that their relationship was doomed by nationality, they resolved to find other partners. Their dilemma was exacerbated by Conal's desire to be near his sick lover. Donald would have none of Conal's pity and concern; he felt he had to fight his battle alone, leaving Conal to build his own life anew.

Back in London, Conal had started his own business in public relations, concentrating on food and restaurants. He acquired a loyal group of clients, including the Chez Gerard Group headed by the stout, cheerful and immensely competent Lawrence Isaacson. He helped Lawrence create the Carnivores dining club and a regular magazine for his customers that promoted good food in general, and the restaurants in the group. It was also Conal's idea to institute the National Food and Drink Awards sponsored by Glenfiddich, the whisky people; they are now the most prestigious in the industry. My own brother, Remington, received their Wine Writer of the Year award in 1992 for his book, *The Great Domaines of Burgundy*.

In 1991, soon after Donald's death from AIDS, Conal learnt that he too was HIV Positive. Conal choose to be deeply secretive about his status and instead of slowing down and taking good care of himself, he adopted the other approach of denial.

He did not want to discuss things even with me. In fact, this turn of events distanced us somewhat; I think I reminded Conal of his impending mortality. He worked even harder. He formed a series of unsatisfactory relationships with younger guys and took to clubbing, which involved the taking of recreational drugs; he was literally burning himself out in an orgy of life-affirming activity. I, as an older friend, represented a past life he was trying to forget. This separation saddened Derek and I. In those days, HIV and AIDS were dark secrets barely alluded to – such was the stigma – and so it was a battle fought in relative isolation.

By 1995, Conal was suffering from serious health reversals, including periods in hospital with serious opportunistic infections. Still he refused to slow down. He took on more clients and partied ever harder. His young boyfriends had neither the knowledge nor temperament to slow him down. I tried to reason with him, but he felt sure he would not live for long and having accepted his diagnosis as a death sentence, he partied on into the night.

In 1996, now weak and enfeebled by the disease, Conal decided to pay a last visit to his family in Zimbabwe. He flew home for two week's holiday. He became very sick and his loving parents could see that he was gravely ill. The expertise to treat him did not exist in his country and he was too debilitated to fly home on his own. Our mutual friend, Richard Taylor, flew out to accompany him back to London. When Conal arrived, he was immediately hospitalised. He had contracted a rare fungal infection and his whole body was covered in unsightly lesions that refused to respond to treatment. Derek and I spent much of his last day at his bedside, holding his hand and comforting him. We took him a home-cooked meal that he hardly touched and we arranged for a friend to give him a gentle massage; he found the touching soothing and comforting. That night he died and I experienced one of the blackest weeks of despair – when would the dying stop? Another dear friend was gone.

Conal's death in 1996 came less than a year before the life-saving triple combination drug therapy became generally available. Then the dying stopped and since then the lives of countless others have been saved. I miss Conal dearly and often think back to the happy times we spent together – weekends and meals shared, our workouts in the gym, and our many happy holidays. Sometimes I feel angry with him for not trying harder to stay alive; just a few months more and he would be alive today. Why did he have such a death wish? What made him so certain he would succumb?

Conal would be sad to learn that his family have been forcibly ejected from the farm and home they loved in Zimbabwe by Mugabe's murderous thugs. His mother died shortly before they were forced to leave. His father and brothers live on in New Zealand, having had to start all over again. I wish he could have the chance to start all over too.

Chapter Forty-Seven

❧ CIVIL PARTNERSHIP

Today, Derek and I have been hitched, married, espoused or civil part-nered, to use its formal and rather un-romantic name. It is the first day (21st December 2005) that in England such a contract is possible between two people of the same sex.

We registered, as required by law, about two weeks ago on 5th December. Since then, our minds have been somewhat concentrated on the matter and its implications.

Our neighbours, Mark and Anton, have decided to marry today too. They have been together, as we have, for over twenty-five years. We are, so I read in the newspaper, two of the twenty male couples in Westminster, who are getting married on this historic day.

I thought at first that this was just a legal formality of little signifi-cance to us personally. But such is not the case; in some indefinable way we feel more of a couple now that we are recognised in law. Perhaps it is the shower of e-mails, cards and flowers that we have received, not only from close friends here and abroad but also from work colleagues, that has made us think differently. With the predictable exception of the extremist fringe in Northern Ireland, we have neither seen nor heard a

Our civil partnership, witnesses, Marcus Harbord (far left) and Maurits Kalff (far right)

single unkind word or negative reaction either personally or in the press; such is the change of attitude in the last few years. I couldn't help noticing that the protesters in Northern Ireland were inveighing against the evils of sodomy, although the couple shown were lesbians, who do not as far as I know, include sodomy in their normal repertoire of sexual practices.

Everyone in England seems to believe genuinely that this change in the law is a right and moral action. Of course, there are a few religious extremists who object to what they perceive as a slight to the institution of marriage and a move contrary to God's ordained will – though goodness knows what gives them the right to be so certain that God, who presumably made us gay, would not want us to enter into a secure loving relationship. Being gay is not a choice. These people seem to conveniently forget that we are entering into a civil contract that has nothing to do with God or religion – thank goodness. What is it that frightens these people so much about two individuals wanting to live together in a union?

I would like to remind the religious right-wing that their position on marriage is inconsistent. According to the Bible, 'marriage is a holy estate ordained by God for the procreation of children'. Yet all Christian churches are happy to marry women who are past childbearing age. To do so is to flout the church's declared purpose for marriage, so one can only conclude that the church is in favour of recreational sex.

Derek and I made our commitment to each other privately in May 1978, over 27 years ago. We had known each other for about a year and had had pre-marital sex on a few occasions, but had not fallen in love. We went away together for a weekend in the south of France. I was in need of a break from the frenetic success of my new nightclub, the Embassy, and I thought Derek would be a fun companion – nothing more.

During that magical weekend, something happened between us. We fell in love. We reached inside and touched each other's souls. That is the only way I can describe what occurred. We both knew with a burning certainty that we wanted to be together forever – no if's or but's. We revealed our true interior beings to each other with total mutual honesty and trust. It was as if, according to the ancient Greek theory, we had found our missing other half and been reunited, never to be parted again until death. We needed no ceremony or magic formula of words to affect this transformation, we needed no legal contract to cement our union; it was a true union of hearts and souls; the sentiment is perhaps best expressed by my Elizabethan hero, Sir Philip Sidney, in his poem, *The Bargain*. I read this out at the reception following our union.

My true love hath my heart, and I have his,
By just exchange one for another given:
I hold his dear, and mine he cannot miss,
There never was a better bargain driven:
My true love hath my heart and I have his.
His heart in me keeps him and me in one,
My heart in him his thoughts and senses guides;
He loves my heart, for once it was his own,
I cherish his because in me it bides:
My true love hath my heart, and I have his.

I cannot know for sure what the secret of a happy lifelong union is, we have never had to strive too hard to stay together; it just came naturally to us both. I do know that you cannot love someone unless you respect them at all times and that means never lying over important matters. We don't hold sexual fidelity in too high esteem. Sex, particularly between gay men, is not that important in terms of love and relationships, the hot initial passion sadly does not last forever. But mutual respect does require each partner to be sensitive to the other's pride and feelings. I personally feel that it helps if the two partners are complementary, rather than too much alike; in a good working partnership, each should have a sense of where their respective talents lie. This is not to suggest that gay men should ape the sexual roles in heterosexual marriage, but a sense of difference helps promote harmony. Above all, you must cherish the happiness and fulfilment of your partner and that is the essence of true love.

My reflections on the significance of the new legislation are best expressed in my letter to *The Times*, published on Saturday, 24th December 2005 and reproduced below.

The Editor, *The Times* Newspaper,
22nd December 2005

Dear Sir,

Yesterday my partner and I signed the civil register and became legally joined. This small event was, along with the other 600 or so civil partnerships entered into yesterday, an event of historic significance.

The importance of yesterday's event was made painfully clear to me recently when my partner Derek's brother was rushed into intensive care and I was denied information on his condition on the grounds that I was not a family member. He is now my brother–in–law. Had it been

Derek and not his brother I would have not been the official next-of-kin to my lover of 27 years.

I grew to adulthood in a world where being gay was a criminal offence, indeed my friend Lord Montagu of Beaulieu served time in prison for something that is now officially recognised in law; such has been the social change in the last forty years.

I would also like to pay tribute to the very many friends who have died from AIDS and could not be with us to share this moment of joy, but whose deaths have in no small part helped to focus attention on such a manifest injustice.

It is sad that the church has yet again set its face against moral and social change. Reactionary forces within the church have always been against each major shift in thinking from the condemnation of slavery and the acceptance of the theory of evolution, to the ordination of women priests; always having to recant at a later date. To remain relevant, the church should be a moral leader not a laggard.

Finally, I would like to pay tribute not only to the campaigning work done on our behalf by Stonewall but also to our Prime Minister and the Government for having had the moral courage to promote this piece of legislation that is a milestone in the history of the grant of civil liberties to the people of this country.

Yours Faithfully, Jeremy Norman

For gay people marriage was, until now, not a possibility and so was of little concern to us. We attended many straight weddings but always felt that we did not need a piece of paper to hold our relationship together. I still feel that to be the case, but there is something extraordinary about declaring your love for one another publicly and in front of friends. One surprising revelation was that marriage means a lot to straight people and so it was our straight friends who most fully grasped the historic significance of this change in the law. They already knew what a big deal getting married is and how it changes one's perception of a relationship and the world's perception of you as a couple. Gay people must now reassess the nature of relationships and commitment. It will be interesting to see how all this will evolve in the years to come.

Chapter Forty-Eight

✠ Conclusion

I reflect that I have led a charmed and fortunate life; I have survived some near disasters on land and sea and I belong to the first generation for a hundred years not to be conscripted to fight and kill people. But I have fought a war of sorts against HIV and the devastating effect it has had on the gay community, of which I am a part, and I have witnessed many young friends lose their lives.

I share my life with Derek, my chosen partner of twenty-seven years with every prospect of a life together for years to come. I savour the pleasures of fine food, of art and music and travel. The old Harrow School song echoes in my brain: 'Forty years on when afar and asunder parted are those who are singing today… when you look back and forgetfully wonder what you were like at your work and your play.' The time has flown so quickly and so many friends are either dead or long forgotten. I have packed a great deal into the years between then and now. I am not 'feeble of foot and rheumatic of shoulder' as the song suggests, but am fit and in good shape; my regular visits to my various Soho Gyms – with my personal trainer, Stephen Hewson, keep me trim and well-toned.

The interior of the Soho Gym in Clapham

Author's seaside cottage at Beaulieu

Once you pass fifty, the male sex drive diminishes, not a bad thing as one becomes increasingly sexually invisible to younger men. I think it was George Melly who rejoiced in achieving the sanity of late middle age by saying that losing one's manic sex drive was 'like being unhitched from a team of wild horses'. He was right, but with the loss comes a sense of mourning for something that was so pivotal in one's life. I am not sure whether straight men experience quite the same intensity of drive as gay men, but I can say that my sex drive has been the engine that has driven my thoughts and my creativity until now. Without it, I doubt whether I would have achieved very much.

Gay men do not hold sexual fidelity in high regard and view the break-up of a loving relationship over something as inconsequential as a brief sexual affair or a one-night stand as the height of folly. We look at things differently; of course jealously exists in a relationship, but we don't throw the baby out with the bathwater. We view a loving relationship as one entered into freely by two people, not something enforced by a piece of paper or threat of divine retribution. (According to the Church, we are damned anyway.) A person will love you less or even come to revile you, if forced to remain with you against their will. You cannot trap and cage a free man; if you do so, it is at your peril.

I am delighted that gay men have played a part in breaking down prejudices of race, religion and class. Modern gay society is largely free of such barriers. We treat people just as we find them. While this is true of Southern England and London in particular, it may not be true of rural areas and the Celtic fringe. Indeed, I am amazed at the narrow-minded nationalism of some of our Celtic neighbours. Can they not see how petty, wrong and outdated their racial and religious nationalism is? Such attitudes exclude and stigmatise others, they perpetuate old hatreds and drive people to terrorism and war.

All religions are badges that people wear to exclude others or to rally behind, as though God is on their side and all others will burn in hell as heretics. I fear that I can find nothing good to be said in favour of religion; it alienates and breeds hatred of others of different or of no faith. It is as though the Greek philosophers had never lived and the Age of Enlightenment had never happened. Not to mention the required suspension of reason that is required to believe in Biblical fairy tales. The central problem lies in the monopoly of moral values which religion has stolen for its own; as though no morality can exist without belief in a God. I believe that we should teach a secular morality in schools, using as a text the excellent works of my new hero, AC Grayling, the philosopher. It has become evident in the light of recent terrorist attacks that the ancient texts on which the 'religions of the book' are based encourage extremism and intolerance. They are full of racial, sexual and other forms of discrimination and division; some of the sentiments expressed therein would be illegal if expressed in a contemporary publication.

Needsore cottage, Living Room

Without a moral code, it is easy, especially for gay men, to fall into the trap of seeking pleasure to the exclusion of all else. Sexual addiction can be as damaging as drugs or alcohol; I see the results in some of my friends. I am pleased too that there are still examples of young gay couples falling in love and staying together. For instance, my friends Richard Mason, the best-selling author, and his lover, the handsome Benjy Morse, met in the Bodleian Library at Oxford as undergraduates more than six years ago and are still very much together: like we have, they are planning to 'marry' soon.

Young London is an extraordinary society in which all are truly equal. My friend, Lord Edward Spencer-Churchill, grew up at Blenheim Palace in a world of conventional morality. He is decidedly straight and was until a few years ago, rather strait-laced. In Ibiza while dancing in a club, he spent time with a beautiful young girl who asked him innocently if he was gay. Although initially shocked, it soon dawned on Edward that her only reason for asking was that she didn't want to waste an evening with an attractive man who was not interested in her sexually. It was a revelation for Edward. Being gay is about whom you sleep with, not about whether you are a fit person to befriend. The attitude of Dan Novelli, the personal trainer mentioned earlier, shows that the gay world can now encompass even straight men. That surely holds great promise for a loving future.

I hope that the current wave of suicide bombings does not tear London apart socially and destroy the delicate flower of tolerance that it has nurtured to full bloom. Any race, colour, religion or sexuality is accepted as long as it is tolerant of others. Perhaps this unique polity should break free and become an independent state?

Sadly, few organised religious groups can lay claim to tolerance. I find it ironic that Christian churches are splitting themselves asunder over the issue of homosexuality. Their centuries-old persecution of homosexuals is coming home to roost.

Derek and I both have godchildren (without the religious overtones) of many different faiths – every child should have a fairy godmother. We love the fact that we have close contact with so many young people. We have ten godchildren between us: my first was Harriet Montgomery-Massingberd, acquired while I was still in my early twenties; Alice Allen, now twenty-four, is embarking on adult life; Hugo Taylor is a model and artist on his gap year; Robin Waterhouse is seventeen and still at Eton; Nick Beith has just left Stowe and wants to follow me into the nightclub world; Edward Wakefield is only five; Chloe de Rothschild is fifteen and at school; as is Sholto van den Bogaerde; little

Gareth & Cilla van den Bogaerde

Dolly Dunne who is only three and lastly our most recent addition, seventeen-year-old Algy Lendrum.

The last two named require some explanation. Dolly is the product of an unusual marriage: her mother is a Lady Rose Cecil, daughter of the late Marquess of Salisbury, and her father, Malachy Dunne, is Irish Catholic. They both honoured us by asking us to be their daughter's godparents because 'You represent the values we would like our daughter to grow up with.' By which we took them to mean values of tolerance and non-discrimination such as they, and we, all faced and overcame.

My godson, Nick Beith, aged sixteen

The last-named, Algy, did us the signal honour of asking us (when aged fourteen) to become the replacement for his godfather, Johnnie Gairdner, who had died of cancer. We have known Algy and his family since he was born, but this request was a wholly unexpected honour and privilege.

My sexually driven creative energy may have dissipated

somewhat, but I still have my business interests, especially in our five Soho Gyms. I am writing and reading a great deal. I have more time to appreciate the beauties of the natural world and particularly our beloved coastal retreat on the Solent, where we watch and enjoy the changing seasons, the bird life and natural history.

In 2000, I was asked to write a short piece for a local Beaulieu record to commemorate the Millennium. I wrote about the annual nesting of thousands of black-headed gulls on the marshes in front of our cottage, traditionally the harbingers of spring. I expressed the wish that they would be around to herald the new season for another thousand years. In only five years they have gone, the victims of a rising sea-level exacerbated by global warming. It has left us sad and with a sense of profound loss.

I have taken a break from writing this to stroll around our cottage garden. There are not many flowers out yet, just hyacinths and daffodils and of course the rosemary. Rosemary is a wonderful plant, aromatic and in leaf all year round; it flowers early with pretty blue flowers, providing an early source of pollen and nectar for the bees. 'Rosemary for remembrance', as Shakespeare said. I heard the hum of a solitary humble bee as it went about its busy business. I wish we saw many more of these delightful insects in our gardens and hedgerows.

We are fortunate enough to live down here thanks to the kindness and generosity of Lord Montagu of Beaulieu and his son Ralph. He has just

Dolly Dunne's christening in the private chapel
at Hatfield House, with her Mother, Rose

Edward Montagu at Needsore

called and asked us for drinks at the Beach House. It is the start of the season and he is opening up the house for the summer. He moves down to the Beach House and out of Palace House, to get some respite from the mass of tourists at Beaulieu. Derek and I have known Edward Montagu for nearly thirty years and he has become a much-loved friend as well as our landlord. Our little coastguard cottage at Needsore Point, although rented, is the place that is closest to our heart. We have shared with Edward the many vicissitudes in all our lives, as well as a huge amount of joyous fun. His health has not been good of late and it is sad to see his boundless energy and love of life temporarily curtailed.

Edward is an extraordinary person who has weathered the storms of the last sixty years, particularly his unjust imprisonment for an offence that is now not only no longer criminal but represents a relationship, namely a gay one, that is now the subject of legal recognition through civil partnerships – yet no pardon is forthcoming. Edward, with magnificent bravery and true patrician sang-froid, took his seat in the House of Lords upon his release and has fully rehabilitated himself through his public service as Chairman of English Heritage and his championship of the cause of historic homeowners.

He also is the Chairman of the National Motor Museum. Cars have always been a passion of his and he almost never misses a London to Brighton vintage rally. We see pictures of him in some early vintage car from the collection, wrapped up in an extravagant fur coat and goggles, sitting next

Michael Waterhouse

The view from Needsore cottage

to his chauffeur or often driving the car himself. His family were pioneers of early motoring and the museum was Edward's idea to provide a reference collection for early cars and as a boost to tourism in the area. He has succeeded in both aims.

Perhaps my closest old friend, Michael Waterhouse, the bird expert and author, lives across the Solent on the Isle of Wight. We talk often and meet when we can to share our love and delight in this special part of the world and its natural history. We are old friends from Cambridge days, so have been friends for thirty-seven years. I am glad to be close to many straight couples of all ages. Michael's mother, Lady Caroline Waterhouse (née Spencer-Churchill), died a few years back and The Queen, most exceptionally, attended her memorial service in person. During the mid-winter service, a butterfly flew upward with the anthem like a soul ascending. I hope this work will be my butterfly and live on after me, a testimony to a life of diversity and challenge.

I think I have said quite enough, and maybe even a little too much, so like Barnum the great American showman, I am posting a notice – as an encouragement to visitors to leave this collection of weird and wonderful trivia:

'THIS WAY TO THE EGRESS'

❧ LADY DELAMERE

1) Why did Diana want Joss so much?

He was the only man of her own age she had ever been attracted to and would be the only man for the rest of her life with whom she had a passionate relationship. He was a man with some feminine features, enormous charm and sex appeal that made him attractive to both sexes. I believe Diana despised men but wanted a conventional marriage because of the mores of the time and class she lived in. Up to then, she had had to make do with a *marriage blanche* which gave her luxury and social position and an element of sexual freedom. Here was a chance of a real love match and marriage to a man of her own age who excited her sexually.

2) Why did she react so violently to Joss's change of heart?

I think because she saw her only chance of married happiness evaporating and because she was spoiled and liked to get her own way. Never before had she been rejected. It is probable that Erroll confirmed her worst fears and beliefs about men; they were weak and shallow and unfaithful. She was livid with rage and filled with spite and anger at being thwarted. It is also possible that he accused her of having affairs with women, maybe even her closest girl friend, June Carberry. Diana could not risk such a reputation being spread abroad among her homophobic social circle.

Wilks, Diana's lady's maid, told James Fox, author of the book *White Mischief*, when he finally tracked her down to Durban many years later, that Diana and Joss were having a violent argument when they returned to the house on that fateful night. That row can be explained by the probability that Joss had called off the engagement that had been made so public by Jock's toast to the happy couple at dinner in the Muthaiga Club on the night of the murder.

3) What was the nature of Diana's marriage to Jock and her subsequent husbands?

She clearly had an arrangement of sorts with all of them. She did not share a bed with Jock; he wanted her both as a companion and as a trophy wife. He had fully accepted that the marriage was a business arrangement. He provided both money and social position and sexual freedom. I think he either knew or guessed that Diana preferred women to men. That is why he made the generous pact to set her free if she desired it: he thought the chance of her falling for another man remote. At that time, there was no question of someone of Diana's ambition and position in society setting up home with a woman. It was clear from the outset that Diana's marriage to Jock was a sham. Their pact makes this quite clear. Such a pact can only be explained in terms of her lack of interest in other men and her value to him as a trophy wife.

Her next husband, Gilbert Colvile, was a misogynist and a homosexual with a taste for black Africans, and the Masai in particular. He clearly admired Diana's masculinity and toughness. He was a loner, a man of few words, most of them terse and to the point. They formed a bond in adversity which grew into a loyal and enduring friendship. Diana remained close friends with Gilbert, even after their divorce.

Diana's third husband, Tom Delamere, was the prime catch in all of East Africa; rich, titled, landed and influential. Her marriage to Tom was also a sham; she loved him, but in a platonic way. She lived openly with Lady Patricia Fairweather at Soy Sambu for many years until Patricia's death from cancer. Tom was an affectionate, but somewhat patronised older friend, who paid the bills and gave status to her life. Both Gilbert and Tom provided her with the means of social rehabilitation within the colony after the scandal. They were also 'big game trophies'.

4) What really happened on that fateful night?

Jock may have told Joss about Diana's shortcomings in order to persuade him to drop his engagement plans. On the night of the murder, Diana was at home in their house at Karen as was Jock and Diana's friend, June Carberry. Joss had dropped Diana back at her marital home in the early hours of the morning, thus fulfilling his promise to Jock to bring her home that night.

I think all three of them, Diana, Jock and June, knew that she had committed the murder. Diana was heard talking in a loud and animated fashion, on her return to Karen, in her bedroom with June. June was too close a friend to expose Diana: she may even have been her lesbian lover: they are reported to have shared a bed on more than one occasion.

I believe that after the row on the way back to the house at Karen, Joss went inside to relieve himself and Diana dashed upstairs, changed out of her high heels into white gym shoes, grabbed the pistol and hid in the back of Joss's Buick. She probably confronted him as he slowed down at the road junction. She probably hoped to change his mind or just give him a scare, but harsh words were probably exchanged and Diana shot him in a fit of uncontrolled rage. Joss may even have accused her of being a lesbian.

5) Why was Jock prepared to be the fall guy?

Jock was happy to see the back of his rival Joss, but I believe that he felt deeply guilty that Diana had killed him as a direct result of what he had said to dissuade him from marrying her. Jock was getting old, and had lost much of his immense fortune – it has also been rumoured that he was impotent. He clearly did not care much for life as his subsequent suicide proves. He feared possible arrest and imprisonment for his two insurance frauds before the war, one concerning paintings stolen from his house in England, and the other, a matter of some valuable jewellery stolen from Diana in the South of France.

His aristocratic code would not have permitted him to expose his wife and see her face a capital charge; besides, he loved her in his own way and wanted to save their marriage. He never tried that hard to defend himself, he never accused or tried to implicate anyone else – hardly the actions of a man trying to save his own skin. He believed he had a very good chance of acquittal if all three stuck to their stories. Anyway, he knew he was innocent and had a belief in British justice. The evidence against him was thin, especially until Detective-Superintendent Poppy uncovered the firearms evidence from the farm belonging to Jock's friend Soames. Poppy cleverly retrieved some bullets fired from revolvers belonging to Jock at a shooting practice at the farm a few weeks before the murder. These bullets formed the basis of some equivocal ballistics evidence at the trial.

Jock was fundamentally a coward and unlikely to murder a man who stole a wife he was not 'in love' with. (He had conveniently developed sunstroke on the day his regiment embarked for France in the First World War and never subsequently saw action.) He was just piqued at his public humiliation.

6) Why did Diana go to such lengths to help and support her husband if she believed that he had killed her lover?

The only plausible explanation was that she knew that he was not the murderer. She could only have been certain of that if she herself had committed the crime. She flew to South Africa to engage a King's Counsel for his defence and she went on safari with him soon after the murder and before Broughton's arrest; neither actions are consistent with the natural behaviour of a vengeful lover toward the murderer of her beloved. Diana showed remarkable sang-froid after the murder. Her actions were not those of a distraught lover. She was shaken by what she had done but did not behave like a bereaved person. The safari with Jock so soon after the event is telling in this regard.

7) The most telling circumstance of all.

The key issue is that neither Diana nor Jock showed any real interest in discovering the murderer's identity. This means that they already knew the truth. Diana committed the actual murder, but Jock felt guilty for having instigated Joss to call off the engagement, thus precipitating events. I think, in desperation, he told Joss that Diana was a lesbian – the only sexual or moral issue that was unacceptable to her peers. If Jock told Joss to put him off the marriage, he must have felt that he had indirectly been the cause of Joss's death, hence his confession to young Juanita Carberry, June's stepdaughter, that he had killed Joss. He had done so as effectively as if he had pulled the trigger.

After the murder, the three principal players, Diana, Jock and June, closed ranks to preserve their honour and to save Diana from the gallows. They supported each other: the truth would have amounted to social suicide and humiliation. There was also a feeling of class solidarity; sneaking was not quite the done thing. Authority, and especially the police, was perceived as 'other ranks'. A similar situation pertained after the Lord Lucan murder, when his 'set' closed ranks and refused to talk, as if to do so would involve a loss of caste.

8) Juanita Carberry's evidence.

On the day after the murder, Jock personally lit a bonfire in the garden; an odd thing to do for a 'Bwana' who employed a 'Shamba boy' for this sort of work. Juanita recalls seeing a pair of gym shoes being burnt. This evidence is key. There were white scuffmarks on the back seat of the Buick, consistent with the white Blanco used on gym shoes in those days. If Broughton had committed the murder he would not have needed to change into gym shoes for the run home, but Diana would have needed to change out of her high heels. Broughton was helping to erase the evidence of Diana's guilt. Her gym shoes might have left tracks by the road near the abandoned car and the size would have told the police that they belonged to a woman. In the event, the police never looked properly.

Jock was a coward and a weak man. He must have suffered pangs of guilt and remorse at his part in the death of his friend Joss. He had used every piece of ammunition in his armoury to dissuade Joss from his plans, including revealing Diana's guilty sexual secret. He thought he was directly responsible for the crime because he had instigated the break-up leading to their furious row and Diana's impulsive decision to kill Joss.

9) What about the theft of Jock's two Colt revolvers a few days before the murder?

I believe that the theft was a co-incidence, and an unfortunate one for Joss as it provided Diana with the murder weapon. Jock had left the guns on a mantelpiece, a temptation to any thief. I think it highly probable that Diana saw them and thought it better to hide them to put them out of harm's way. She must have had a few highly unpleasant and angry rows with Jock about Joss and feared that he might be tempted to use a gun in anger. There was no evidence of a break-in at the house.

10) Diana's lesbian nature

After completing this piece on the murder, I was referred to a slim book, *Diana Lady Delamere and the Lord Erroll Murder*, by a Kenyan resident, Leda Farrant. The book was published – in Kenya only – in 1997. The work mentions her lesbian affairs and corroborates my assertion that Diana had a lesbian relationship with Lady Patricia Fairweather (page 79). It is apparent that Leda Farrant was no lover of homosexuals. She refers to the use of the word 'gay' in that context somewhat disparagingly. On page 78 she says, 'When the word (gay) did not hold the less attractive connotations that were to be attached to it... etc.' As a result, she is unable to see the full significance of her own revelation. To her, Diana's homosexuality was a mere peccadillo or perversion, and she fails to appreciate what a core force it must have been. I believe that, like most homosexuals, her sexuality motivated and inspired her actions and that her life can only be fully understood once this fact is grasped. Her actually or putative heterosexual affairs, suggested by Leda Farrant, could well be the product of social pressure to establish an alibi as a heterosexual or in other cases, as with her liaison with Hughie Dickinson, 'Hughsie Daisy', they are a figment of Leda's imagination. I am in no doubt that her lifelong friendship with 'Hughsie Daisy' was that of a good-looking gay man for a strong, glamorous, socially important woman. I have seen so many similar friendships, none of which were sexual. The nickname itself suggests a tease and a reference to 'whoopsy daisy', in other words 'limp wristed'. The fact that they remained such close companions over such a long period of time mitigates against their relationship being sexual, as does the fact that Diana treated him as her squire, someone to be ordered about.

Leda Farrant also mentions her belief that Diana had an affair with June Carberry, something I had already suspected. This strengthens my belief that all three of the protagonists who were at the house in Karen on that fateful night, knew the truth and covered up for each other. They all had good reasons for wishing Erroll dead. June was jealous of him, he was a threat to her love affair with Diana. Jock had the obvious motive of a jealous husband who had been publicly humiliated by Erroll. Diana's motivations were more complex; she had always had the upper hand with men, and here was a man making a fool of her and rejecting her. She was spoiled and used to getting her own way. She was not only thwarted in her ambition to marry Erroll, but risked exposure and ridicule by him into the bargain, particularly if she were to be seen to loose out to her rival as Erroll's lover, Phyllis Filmer, soon to return from South Africa.

One must understand the ethos of those times. Homosexuality was airbrushed out; gay people were invisible. As Leda Farrant clearly demonstrates, homosexuality was considered peripheral and not central to a person's existence. The fact that Diana married and appeared to have love affairs with men does not make her in the least bit straight, she was merely playing the social game and covering her tracks. She was ambitious to rise to the pinnacle of her chosen social group, white Kenyan society, and she succeeded with ruthless determination.

Diana's 'love' for Erroll was not real. She was flattered and enhanced by her success in capturing him, but that is all. Erroll was the top social prize.

I am sure Diana felt, like many homosexuals of her time, anger at the cruelty of society in denying the validity of her passions and she probably harboured a desire for revenge on those who denigrated her right to a love life; her revenge resulted in murder. – Anthony Blunt's revenge was to become a traitor to a society that mocked his sort. The removal of all references to gay life in their time has blinded commentators to view such feelings as irrelevant, transitory or even unreal. To Diana, as with all gay people, they were at the very centre of her being and a driving force in her life. Only with this in mind can Diana's motives and actions be fully understood.

Author with Diana in her swimming pool, Kilifi, Kenya

Brother Remington, Mummy and I

Picture Credits

All pictures other than those listed below are from the author's
collection and are the copyright of either the author,
Derek Frost or their companies.

First published in Great Britain by:

Elliott & Thompson Ltd
27 John Street
London WC1N 2BX

ISBN 1 904027 50 4 (10 digit)

ISBN 978 1 904027 50 8 (13 digit)

First edition

Book design by Brad Thompson

Printed and bound in Spain